FAITHFUL HANDMAID

To
Celia Westbrook
– with love –
and in memory of
Alison Wilson
her sister and my mother

FAITHFUL
HANDMAID

FANNY BURNEY
AT THE COURT OF
KING GEORGE III

HESTER DAVENPORT

SUTTON PUBLISHING

First published in 2000 by
Sutton Publishing Limited · Phoenix Mill
Thrupp · Stroud · Gloucestershire · GL5 2BU

British Library Cataloguing in Publication Data
A catalogue record for this book is available from the British Library

ISBN 0 7509 1881 0

Typeset in 10/13 pt Baskerville.
Typesetting and origination by
Sutton Publishing Limited.
Printed in Great Britain by
MPG, Bodmin, Cornwall.

Contents

List of Illustrations		vii
Illustration Acknowledgements		viii
Additional Notes on Illustrations		ix
Preface and Acknowledgements		xi
1	Entrance into the World	1
2	A Christmas Visit	15
3	Keeper of the Robes	29
4	Assassination Attempt	42
5	Royals, Rituals, and Retainers	51
6	Visits and Visitors	65
7	The Death of Mrs Delany	78
8	Taking the Waters	91
9	Two Prisoners	105
10	Summer by the Sea	121
11	Resignation	134
12	Royal Reporter	148
13	Marriage, a Son, and a Daughter	162
14	Cruelly Changed	177
	Appendix: Three Portraits	191
	Notes	194
	Select Bibliography	226
	Index	233

List of Illustrations

PLATES (*between pp. 112 and 113*)

1a. Fanny Burney by Edward Burney (1782)
1b. Fanny Burney by Edward Burney (1784–5)
1c. Watercolour with portrait of Dr Johnson
2a. Miniatures of King George III and Queen Charlotte by Richard Collins, based on portraits by Thomas Gainsborough (1781 and 1782)
2b. *The Three Eldest Daughters* by Thomas Gainsborough (1784)
3a. *A Milliner's Shop* by S.W. Fores (1787)
3b. *View of the Ball at St James's on the celebration of Her Majesty's Birth Night* (1786)
4a. *A View of the Garden Entrance of St James's Palace* (1786)
4b. *A View of Fauconberg Hall in Cheltenham with their Majesties taking an Airing* (1788)
5a. Mrs Schwellenberg and the Queen, from *The Prospect Before Us* by Thomas Rowlandson (1788)
5b. The Honourable Stephen Digby by Sir Joshua Reynolds (date unknown)
5c. *Restoration Dresses* (1789)
6a. *Royal Dipping* by John Nixon (1789)
6b. *View of Plymouth Fort and St Nicholas's Island* (1779)
7. *A View of the Court Sitting on the Trial of Warren Hastings* (1788)
8a. General Alexandre d'Arblay by Carle and Horace Verney (1817)
8b. *A View of the Queen's Levée in the Pump Room at Bath* (1817)

LINE DRAWINGS	*page*
1. *Writer's table*	14
2. *Henry VIII Gate at Windsor Castle*	28
3. *A pair of shoes*	41
4. *Badine, Queen Charlotte's favourite spaniel*	50
5. *Incident with a sedan chair*	64
6. *Herschel's telescope with background of Windsor Castle*	77
7. *Embroidered harebell by Mrs Delany*	90
8. *Tea equipage*	104
9. *Restoration fan*	120
10. *Sandsfoot Castle, Weymouth*	133
11. *Time to read*	147
12. *King George III's signature*	161
13. *Mickleham Church, Surrey*	176
14. *23 Great Stanhope Street, Bath*	190

Illustration Acknowledgements

PLATES

Fanny Burney (1782) and General Alexandre d'Arblay From the Collection at Parham Park, West Sussex, United Kingdom; Fanny Burney (1783–4) by courtesy of the National Portrait Gallery, London; portraits of King George III, Queen Charlotte, and *The Three Eldest Daughters*, The Royal Collection © 2000 Her Majesty The Queen; *A Milliner's Shop*, *The Prospect Before Us*, *Restoration Dresses*, © Copyright The British Museum; *View of the Ball at St James's* by permission of the British Library (1570/6173); *A View of the Garden Entrance of St James's Palace*, © The Trustees of the National Museums of Scotland 2000; *A View of Fauconberg Hall in Cheltenham with their Majesties taking an Airing*, Cheltenham Art Gallery and Museums; The Honourable Stephen Digby by kind permission of Mr John Wingfield Digby, photograph supplied by Photographic Survey, Courtauld Institute of Art; *Royal Dipping*, by kind permission of Portland Museum; *A View of the Court Sitting on the Trial of Warren Hastings*, The Trustees of the National Library of Scotland; *View of Plymouth Fort and St Nicholas's Island*, by courtesy of Plymouth Library Services; *A View of the Queen's Levée in the Pump Room at Bath*, Bath & North East Somerset Library and Archive Service (Bath Central Library).

LINE DRAWINGS

All except no. 12 have been drawn by Olivia Davenport.

Queen Charlotte's dog was copied from a portrait of the Queen by Thomas Gainsborough by kind permission of the Royal Collection; Mrs Delany's embroidery was drawn by kind permission of Ruth Hayden; the Restoration fan is drawn from an illustration © V&A Picture Library.

Additional Notes on Illustrations

1c. *Watercolour with portrait of Dr Johnson*

Not long before the book went to press I bought this small watercolour (17 cm × 14.5 cm) at an antiques fair, only later realising that the portrait of Dr Johnson is the one commissioned *c.* 1776 by Henry Thrale for his library. Are the figures therefore the Thrales, in a notional suggestion of Streatham Park (no house could be built quite like this)? Portraits of Hester suggest a strong resemblance to the woman, and the facial shape, heavy eyebrows and jowls make identification of the man with Henry Thrale possible. Copies of the Johnson portrait were made, but no other couple in the 1770s could have claimed the intimate relationship with Johnson implied by this grouping, the man and woman inclining their heads deferentially towards his image.

The artist is more problematic. The initials IC are inscribed on the carpet, and the painting was sold as being by John Collet (*c.* 1725–80), but comparison with Collet works shows no resemblance of style. If the initials (which like the labelling on the portrait could have been a later addition, perhaps indicating ownership) are ignored, then a suggestion made by an expert at the British Museum is Edward Burney. More research is needed, but such an attribution would make sense and not only because a connection can be made with the Thrales through Dr Burney. The picture is curious in that its central feature is not a person but a portrait; Edward Burney, a student of Reynolds who made a copy of the painting for his uncle, could be offering homage to the portraitist as much as to its subject.

3a. *A Milliner's Shop*

The cartoon displays the fashionable look of the day – achieved with huge bonnets and muffs, puffed out neckerchiefs and padded 'bum-rolls' – but its primary purpose is to satirise the King and Queen. They were laughed at for their homeliness in local shopping, and for their perceived parsimony. Underneath the picture is printed some verse by the satirist 'Peter Pindar' (the pseudonym of John Wolcot, which speaks of them 'doing wonders in the hagling [sic] art', and concludes sarcastically 'Reader: to make thine Eyes with wonder Stare/Farthings are not beneath the Royal Care!' 'Splitfarthing', the name of the millinery establishment, is seen over the entrance to the workroom (a farthing was the coin of smallest value).

5a. Mrs Schwellenberg and Queen Charlotte, from Rowlandson's *The Prospect Before Us*

The complex political cartoon from which the figures are taken targets the supposed desire of the Queen and Prime Minister, William Pitt, to seize power and prevent the Prince of Wales from becoming Regent (the Queen's list of items to be taxed relates to names of Whig Opposition leaders and their colours, blue and buff). Also satirised is what was thought to be the undue influence of Mrs Schwellenberg over Queen Charlotte. Flourishing a mace, she leads the Queen to an entrance labelled 'House of Lords'. In a speech bubble above her head she first tells the Queen to 'Take care to secure the Jewels', then declares 'I have hitherto been confin'd to the wardrobe but now mean to preside at the council and with Billy's [Pitt's] assistance the name of Schwellenbig shall be trumpeted to the remotest corner of *Rag Fair*'.

LINE DRAWINGS

Herschel's telescope against a background of Windsor Castle (page 77)

William Herschel's telescopes were built on the Newtonian principle. Light travelled down the tube to a mirror which reflected it back to a smaller one set at an angle; this in turn deflected the image to an eyepiece on the side of the tube. The telescope was mounted on an adjustable carriage.

Embroidered harebell by Mrs Delany (page 90)

Sometime in the mid-eighteenth century Mrs Delany created for herself a court dress which she embroidered with a mixture of richly decorative and simple flower designs. The delicately shaded harebell comes from the over-skirt which is scattered with a variety of little flowers; even when a particular type of flower is repeated it is always slightly different from the rest.

Restoration fan (page 120)

The fan, with pierced ivory sticks, is dark blue and gold. It bears the words 'Health is restored to ONE and happiness to Millions' along the top edge, and 'On the King's' and 'Happy Recovery' on the festoons. Queen Charlotte gave Miss Burney one of these fans.

Preface and Acknowledgements

On 31 July 1788 Fanny Burney, Keeper of the Robes to Queen Charlotte, watched while the Vice-Chamberlain, Colonel the Honourable Stephen Digby, carefully put a letter into the flame of a candle and let it burn. 'See, Miss Burney,' he said, 'when you send me any letters how safe they will be!'[1] It was his opinion that it was dangerous to keep letters. He asked:

> 'And what . . . is to become of yours, if anything happens? Think but how they will be seized; everybody will try to get some of them; what an outcry there will be! Have you seen Miss Burney's letters? Have you got any? I have a bit! and I have another! and I! and I! will be the cry all round.'[2]

'Oh,' thought Fanny at the time, 'could he see my hoards, what a conflagration he would make for me.' He would have been alarmed for himself had he known how little he was safe from *her*, for even these light words were not lost to the air but caught and preserved within the pages of her journals.

Fanny's Court Journals record the details of her day-to-day experiences during the five years of her service in the royal household. Her position was one she had neither sought nor wanted, but between 1786 and 1791 she fulfilled her duties conscientiously, at the same time describing in her journals, sometimes with ironic detachment, sometimes emotional engagement, a world in which she always felt an outsider. Historians of the period, and biographers of King George III and other personalities who feature in Fanny's journals, have long drawn from them. Some passages have many times been quoted by writers illustrating the life of the court, though isolated quotations inevitably fragment the writing and occasionally distort her meaning when taken out of context.

The journals mingle public events and private life, and one ambition in this book has been to look more closely at their interweaving of autobiography and social comment. For those five years Fanny's first-hand observation of the court world offers a continuous and intimate commentary on it, during a notably interesting period which includes the attempted assassination of the King, his time of 'madness', and the remarkable tour to the west country which followed it. In this aspect of the book I have wanted to allow Fanny to speak frequently in her own voice. At the same time, documentation of royal life from sources such as memoirs, letters, newspapers and archive material has been used to give greater understanding to the background of Fanny's own court experiences.

It was as a successful novelist that Fanny came to court and it is as a woman writer that she has been of particular interest to biographers and literary historians. For such authors the time Fanny spent at court away from the literary and artistic world, however fascinating, tends to be seen as an interlude in her life, not really central to it. But in terms of the traditional human life-span, those years between her thirty-fourth and thirty-ninth birthdays were at its core, determined by what went before and shaping what was to come. Another aim of this biographical study has therefore been to try to show their significance to Fanny's life as a whole. The first, introductory chapter concentrates on those events of her early life which led to the court appointment, and aspects of her character which determined the way she responded to it; in the final two chapters, which are devoted to the time after her resignation, the aim has been to show how her royal connections continued to be important to her. These chapters necessarily abridge events while trying to convey some idea of other major concerns of Fanny's later life.

The court years were not very happy ones for Fanny, a stranger in a strange land of alien rituals and social hierarchies. Yet she developed a close relationship with the courtier Stephen Digby who came from one of the foremost aristocratic families in England. Concentrating on this limited period of Fanny's life has allowed greater exploration of their intimacy than there is space for within a general biography, though objective narration is made difficult in that she is virtually the only source for it. Digby might have been less enthusiastic about burning all his correspondence had he realised the need for his own point of view to be represented.

Fanny did not follow his example and destroy everything. After the death of her husband in 1818 she began the laborious task of editing her journals and the mass of accumulated correspondence (family as well as her own), an occupation which lasted for much of the rest of her life. She listed, annotated, and organised what was to be kept, while cutting away, obliterating, or in some instances burning what she did not wish anyone ever to read. What remained was willed in the first place to her niece Charlotte Barrett, who prepared an edition for publication. The *Diary & Letters of Madame d'Arblay (1778–1840)* was published in seven volumes in

1842–6.[3] Only about half of the Court Journals were printed, what was left out being mainly but not exclusively about the Digby relationship.

As Stephen Digby had foreseen, Fanny's letters have become valuable commodities. The bulk of Burney manuscript material (which includes that of other members of the family) was purchased by the New York Public Library in 1941 and is part of the Berg Collection of manuscripts; this is where the Court Journals are to be found. Digby, astute enough to appreciate life's little ironies, would have been astounded to discover that a hastily written note of his sent to Fanny a couple of weeks after his conversation with her now lies protected in a fire-proof box in New York.[4] Other collections of Burney manuscripts are to be found in the British Library and in archives on both sides of the Atlantic.

The gathering together of so much material in institutions not only preserved it, but made it more accessible to scholars. The most notable of these has been Joyce Hemlow, who transformed understanding of Fanny's life and work by her 1958 biography, *The History of Fanny Burney*. She then embarked on meticulous editing of the *Journals and Letters of Fanny Burney (Madame d'Arblay) 1791–1840*, published in twelve volumes from 1972 to 1984. All Burney/d'Arblay biographical and literary studies since are indebted to her work. Hemlow's successor, Lars E. Troide, has with a team of scholars gone back to the beginning to edit *The Early Journals and Letters of Fanny Burney*. However, there is as yet no full, scholarly text for the years of Fanny's appointment at court. The interested reader, or the historian of the period, must still seek out either the mid-nineteenth-century volumes, their reissue nearly a hundred years ago, or an abridged modern version.

The principal source for this book is the 1904–5 reissue of Charlotte Barrett's edition, in substantially the same form, with preface and notes by Austin Dobson. The complete text of the Court Journals is held in transcript in the Burney Centre at McGill University in Montreal; through the kindness of Professor Lars E. Troide I have been privileged to read, refer to, and quote from the unpublished material. Other quotations from Fanny's letters and journals are drawn from the Troide or Hemlow published editions, or from unpublished texts in the British Library. There is consequently a discrepancy between those quotations which reproduce Fanny's writing exactly, with abbreviations, spelling variations, and the numerous capitals of eighteenth-century writing, and the 'tidied-up' language of the Barrett/Dobson version. This is unfortunate but not, I hope, obtrusive. For the sake of clarity I have restored Fanny's original text in quoting names, completing the name Port for what in the Dobson edition is 'P—', and changing back the pseudonyms used first by

Charlotte Barrett to mask identity and avoid offence. 'Fairly' for Digby is the obvious example ('Mr Fairly' has made an appearance as the name of a real person in more than one book about the period).

In the 1980s there was a movement to 'restore' Fanny to her formal name Frances, in the belief that 'Fanny' was somehow belittling. A counter movement among biographers has re-established Fanny, and that name is my choice too. To call her Fanny, the name by which she was known by those who loved her, seems more appropriate to the relationship, warm but not uncritical, which a biographer inevitably develops for her subject. Probably Fanny would find all accounts of her life offensive and, could she do so, would greet even the most sympathetic of her biographers with a 'cold curtsey'. Nevertheless she left, and chose not to burn, the autobiographical writing upon which all biography is based.

I am most grateful to Her Majesty The Queen for gracious permission to quote from papers in the Royal Archives. I should also like to thank the Registrar, Sheila de Bellaigue, for kindly organising my visits to the Archives and answering queries.

This book would have been shackled without the opportunity to visit McGill University and read the transcripts of unpublished sections of the Court Journals. I am hugely indebted to Professor Lars E. Troide for allowing me access, for his help with information about the Bogle miniature and facilitating its use on the cover, and for his general encouragement. His colleague, Dr Stewart J. Cooke, also kindly answered queries; the Burney discussion which I had with these scholars was both stimulating and pleasurable. I should also like to thank the New York Public Library for permission to quote from the original manuscripts of the journals.

An enjoyable aspect of research has been the visits to various libraries and record offices, where I have found staff consistently helpful. I should like to mention with gratitude the three of which I made most use: the public library in Windsor, the library of Royal Holloway University of London, and the magnificent new British Library. There I have been able to sit under the benign gaze of the bust of Fanny's brother Charles while reading his family's letters, and to speculate what His Majesty King George III would think about the great glass tower which now houses his huge collection of books.

I am immensely grateful to Ann Smith, Archivist at Sherborne Castle, for answering my questions and providing me with material which has helped my understanding of Stephen Digby and his background.

Cynthia Gaskell Brown, Museum Officer at Mount Edgcumbe House and Country Park, also provided me with useful information. I should like to record my thanks to her and the staff for making me so welcome on my visit to the house.

I feel myself to have been very fortunate in finding Catherine Dolman to guide me through the complexities of fashions of the period. She has also kindly checked portions of the manuscript. Any remaining mistakes are my own; without Catherine there would be more.

I spent a most enjoyable afternoon in Bath meeting Ruth Hayden, biographer of Mrs Delany. I should like to thank her warmly for her hospitality, and both for showing me the wonderful embroidery of Mrs Delany's court dress and for sharing her knowledge of her many-times great-aunt.

I should also like to thank Dr Geoff Roe for satisfying my curiosity about how eighteenth-century fountain pens worked; Dr Steven Blake of Cheltenham Museum for answering questions about Fauconberg Lodge; the Reverend Ronald Swan for information about St Katharine's Foundation; Penelope Hatfield, College Archivist, for responding to a query about Stephen Digby at Eton College; and Rachel Watson, County Archivist of Northamptonshire County Council, for photocopies of documents relating to Digby's marriage. I should like also to express my gratitude for their work on my behalf to Jaqueline Mitchell and Clare Bishop, my editors at Sutton's.

Many friends have helped and supported me as the book developed. I should like first of all to thank Alison Haymonds who has followed its progress from beginning to end, reading and offering professional commentary both on individual chapters and the complete manuscript. I have greatly valued her advice and her cheerful, dependable encouragement.

A number of Burney expeditions have been enjoyed in the company of friends. I am very grateful to Geraldine Lillicrap for two memorable days in Bath, for the chauffeuring through Bath traffic, and for her hospitality, especially the picnic with the Royal Crescent for backdrop. Thanks too to Stephen for his photography.

Lucy Norman explored Norbury Woods, Mickleham and the surrounding area with me; Audrey and Peter Paul took me to Kensington Palace; without Elaine Robson to urge me on I should probably not have gone beyond the gates at Nuneham Courtenay (I should like also to thank the Brahma Kumaris World Spiritual University for so kindly welcoming us and showing us over the house and grounds).

I am grateful to my daughter Imogen for hospitality in Dorset and to her and Matthew Low for coming with me to Sherborne Castle. Many thanks also to Matthew for his help with computing.

Antony Fanning provided me with information about William Herschel; Beryl Hedges, Fiona Reynoldson, Sheila Rooney and Jasmine Tarry all helped me with books. To Beryl I am also indebted for much sensible advice and encouragement. I should like to thank Ellen Dollery, Jane Langton, Judith Pascoe and Joyce Sampson for their practical help and support.

To all other friends who have taken an interest in the book's progress and wished it well I should like to express thanks and appreciation.

The idea of asking my daughter Olivia to provide some drawings of places and period objects to add to the illustrations in the book came from the example of Constance Hill, who at the beginning of the twentieth century wrote three books about places associated with Fanny which were illustrated by her sister Ellen. Olivia's drawings developed a distinctive character of their own, and I am both very grateful for the time and trouble she took with them and proud of the results.

Lastly but most of all I want to thank my husband Tony, who has been the sheet anchor of the writing. He has come with me on the Burney trail in Dorset, Oxford and Plymouth, has acted as volunteer research assistant, read and discussed the manuscript, and generally helped me over all stiles and hurdles encountered along the way. His support has been this book's most valued resource.

CHAPTER ONE

Entrance into the World

[Your journal] will one day be the delight of your old age – it will call back your youth, your spirits, your pleasures, your friends, whom you formerly loved, and who loved you . . . and lastly, when your own scene is closed, remain a valuable treasure to those that come after you.[1]

This Year was ushered in by a grand & most important Event, – for, at the latter end of January, the Literary World was favoured with the first publication of the ingenious, learned, & most profound Fanny Burney! – I doubt not but this memorable affair will, in future Times, mark the period whence chronologers will date the Zenith of the polite arts in this Island!

This admirable authoress has named her most elaborate Performance '*Evelina, or a Young Lady's Entrance into the World*'.[2]

With this fine flourish, in March 1778, Fanny Burney announced to her journal the book which would indeed make her famous, and without which she would never have spent five years of her life at court. The joke was that though increasingly curious, the literary world was in complete ignorance of the authorship of *Evelina*. Since even *reading* novels was then frowned upon in young women, the 25-year-old Fanny had written secretly, usually at dead of night. She had also assumed a feigned hand in copying out the manuscript, since she acted as amanuensis for her father, the music historian Dr Charles Burney, and her normal handwriting would be known to publishers. Only her three sisters were at first in her confidence, her elder sister Esther or Hetty, and the younger two, Susanna or Susan, as Fanny called her, and Charlotte. Then her brother Charles had been brought into the know to act as go-between with the publisher; his place in absence was later taken by their cousin, the artist Edward Burney.

So secretive was the affair that Fanny only learnt that her book had been published when her stepmother read out at the breakfast-table an advertisement in the daily paper. How extraordinary it was, Fanny wrote, that 'a Work which was so lately Lodged, in all privacy, in my Bureau, may now be seen by every Butcher & Baker, Cobler [sic] & Tinker, throughout the 3 kingdoms, for the small tribute of 3 pence' (at the circulating library).[3] But it was not tinkers and tailors whose opinions she worried about. Fortunately the critics approved, and the public bought her book eagerly. Evelina the heroine had made her entry into London society and charmed it; *Evelina* the novel took literary London by storm.

For some months Fanny listened straight-faced, but inwardly amused, as friends and relations all unknowingly sang its praises and speculated as to whether the author was a man or a woman. But, as she wrote, '*every body* longs to tell *one* body', and slowly the truth emerged. Dr Burney had known his daughter was trying to print *something* but had promised not to ask what; six months after publication, while Fanny was away from home, Susan told him the truth. He sent out for a copy, discovered the dedicatory poem to 'the author of my being', and, after reading and re-reading the novel, wrote to his daughter, 'thou hast made thy old Father Laugh & Cry at thy pleasure'. The proud father could not forbear telling his friend and patroness Mrs Hester Thrale (who, ironically, had recommended it to him); she told Dr Samuel Johnson, who told the blind poet Anna Williams . . . and so it went on. When Fanny heard that the great Johnson himself was reading and approving *Evelina* she was staying at Chessington, home of the man she called her second 'daddy', Samuel Crisp, and she astonished him by dancing round his mulberry tree in sheer delight. Fanny teased the old man about the novel, making him guess at the author; when he learnt the truth from her father she heard him exclaim 'Wonderful! – it's *wonderful!*' but he doubled his fist at her for her tricks.

If it can be summed up in a sentence, *Evelina* is a story told in letter form about a sixteen-year-old girl with the charm of youth who comes from the country to London and is introduced to its social delights, makes acquaintances both high and low, and writes artless accounts of her adventures to her clergyman guardian who, with the wisdom of experience, seeks to guide her conduct from afar. The writing is fresh, the characters drolly recognisable, the moral lessons impeccable. As her father had done, Fanny's readers laughed and cried in equal measure and were lost in admiration for the 'ingenious' author. Sir Joshua Reynolds offered £50 for the writer's identity; Edmund Burke stayed up all night to finish it; Dr Johnson said of the morality that 'there were passages in it which might do Honour to Richardson' and of the comic characters that 'Harry Fielding would have been afraid of her'.[4] The story of the secret publication would eventually reach the court and intrigue the King and Queen.

The success of *Evelina* was earned, but if she had been a crafty agent Fanny could not have managed matters better than by publishing anonymously and then accepting the slow seepage of her identity. Other things contributed to the spell: had the author been fat and forty it is (sadly) unlikely that *Evelina* would have been quite such a sensation, but Fanny was young and so diminutive of stature that she looked even younger. She was no beauty, but she had an expressive face which showed how embarrassed she felt when her book was praised to her face, a pleasing modesty which made her female authorship the more acceptable. Though she called herself a 'mere Worm of Literature' Miss Burney had become a celebrity, her life changed for ever.

Frances Burney was born on 13 June 1752 in King's Lynn (then Lynn Regis), where her father was organist at St Margaret's Church.[5] Her mother, the beautiful Esther Sleepe, was to bear nine children in all, but only six survived. The eldest was Esther, a virtuoso harpsichord player who by 1778 was married to her cousin Charles Rousseau Burney and had five children of her own. Next came James or Jem, who in Fanny's *annus mirabilis* was serving with Captain Cook's third expedition; he spent most of it in the north Pacific in a vain search for a north-west passage. Three years younger than Fanny was the sister who was dearest to her, Susanna Elizabeth. Then came Charles, who would become a noted classical scholar but who at the time of *Evelina* was in disgrace, banished from home after being sent down from Cambridge for stealing books. The youngest in the family was Charlotte Ann, a girl with a strong sense of humour and a talent for puns.

In 1760 the family moved to London where Dr Burney earned his income from teaching, and over the years built his reputation with the publication of *Musical Tours* through France, Italy and Germany, and a four-volume *General History of Music*. Tragically for the children their mother died in 1762. For the ten-year-old Fanny the blow was severe, and for many days she wept uncontrollably. She was always to feel the deaths of those she loved very acutely: her father's second wife, Elizabeth Allen, said of her, 'Here's a Girl will *never* be happy . . . for she possesses perhaps as feeling a Heart as ever Girl had'.[6] Mrs Allen, whom Dr Burney married in 1767, was a widow from King's Lynn with three children of her own, Maria who became a close friend of Fanny, Bessy, and Stephen. A half-brother, Richard, and a half-sister, Sarah Harriet (to become a novelist herself) completed the family. Unfortunately the second Mrs Burney was of a difficult, demanding temperament, and problems developed between her and the children of the earlier marriage.

Nevertheless, the household was a happy one, full of fun and laughter. Fanny was an excellent mimic who could 'take off' people, inventing speeches in their own styles, but this was for her family's amusement only: in company Fanny was so shy and silent, so gravely watchful, that Dr Burney's friends knew her as 'The Old Lady'.[7] When Fanny was fifteen her sister Susan summed up her characteristics as 'sense, sensibility, and bashfulness, and even a degree of prudery' and also commented that 'her diffidence gives her a bashfulness before company with whom she is not intimate, which is a disadvantage to her'.[8] Susan is said to have written this on her return from Paris in 1767, where she and Esther had been at school for two years. Fanny had been left at home and never received any formal education; her French and everything else was self-taught, using her father's library. But that was in her teenage years; until beyond her eighth year she could not read at all and was regarded as the family dunce.

But even before she could read Fanny had started to write; in old age she said that she would scribble 'little works of invention . . . in scrawling characters, illegible, save to herself'.[9] Once she could read and write properly, however, no less than 'Elegies, Odes, Plays, Songs, Stories, Farces, – nay, Tragedies and Epic Poems' flowed from her pen. But her stepmother did not approve, so writing was a clandestine activity tinged with guilt, and when Fanny was fifteen she made a bonfire of everything she had written, while Susan stood by weeping over the fate of a novel, *The History of Caroline Evelyn*, the tearful precursor of *Evelina*.[10] This destruction of her entire juvenile output reveals the steely will beneath Fanny's shy exterior.

The urge to write proved irresistible nevertheless, and Fanny began to keep a diary, making her first entry in March 1768, exactly ten years before the jubilant celebration of the publication of *Evelina*. She liked to write for an audience, so her earliest journals were addressed to 'a certain Miss Nobody', an imaginary friend in whom was to be confided 'every thought, every wish of my Heart'.[11] But by the time Fanny was twenty, the private diary had become journal letters exchanged with Susan, and also sent to Daddy Crisp. It was for Crisp that Fanny made what she called 'journalising' a craft. The confessional element remained with Susan, but for him Fanny developed the skills of a portrait painter in words; these were to enable her to create, after twenty years of practice, compelling pictures of the personalities of the court of King George III and Queen Charlotte.

Samuel Crisp was an elderly bachelor friend of Dr Burney; after the failure of his one and only play he had retreated to live with a small community of people in a rambling old house isolated on heathland at Chessington in Surrey. All the Burney girls loved him, but 'Fannikin' was his favourite and he was her 'flame' (it was a more innocent age than ours). Despite the failure of his own writing, Crisp was a discriminating critic, and after the sometimes affected gush encouraged by Miss Nobody, Fanny's journal writing became sharper and more natural when she was writing for him.[12] Through her he met a wider society and he told her that there was nothing he sucked in more greedily than her pictures of all the 'odd, unaccountable Characters' who flocked to the Burney home as if to a portrait painter's studio, for her to take their likenesses.[13]

From 1774 the Burneys lived in St Martin's Street near Leicester Fields (today's Leicester Square) in the heart of London, in a three-storey brick-built house which had belonged to Sir Isaac Newton. His observatory was on the roof and Fanny liked to take her writing there, recording her observations not on the stars above, but on the guests in the panelled drawing-room below: musicians, singers, actors, writers, foreigners, travellers in antique lands – all the celebrities, or 'Lyons' of the times. The year when the family moved into its new home brought one of the most exotic lions, young Omai of Otaheite (Tahiti), making his entrance into the old world from the new after begging a passage from Captain Cook. Jem Burney, who could speak fluent Otaheitian, brought him to dinner and afterwards Fanny presented him to Daddy Crisp. On introduction Omai had greeted her with tutored politeness, performing one of his '*remarkably* fine Bows'. He had earlier been to watch the King opening Parliament for which he had been fitted out with full court attire: 'a suit of Manchester velvet, Lined with white satten, a *Bag* [wig], lace Ruffles, & a very handsome sword the King had given to him'. But beneath the lace cuffs Fanny was aware of heavily tattooed hands.[14] It was this observation of appearance and behaviour that led Crisp to declare that 'there is not such a Painter in black and White' in the nation; in a comparison with Sir Joshua Reynolds he backed 'at least the Equality, if not the Triumph of your Pen, set against his Pencil'.[15]

Three years later, when Dr Johnson came to a morning party with Mrs Thrale, he presented as much of a strange figure as Omai, tall, stout, with a terrible stoop and his body 'see sawing up & down'. He was dressed in a snuff-coloured coat with gold buttons but, unlike the elegantly arrayed Omai, had 'no Ruffles to his Wrist, & Black Worsted Stockings' (white silk ones were expected wear for social occasions).[16] It was not just appearance, however, that Fanny wanted to capture; she waited eagerly for the great man to speak, but Johnson said little on this occasion, ignoring the company as he peered short-sightedly at the books in her father's library.

It was in what people said, more than what they did or looked like, that Fanny found personality most fully revealed, and what distinguishes her

journals is the direct, actual speech she records. Most of the guests
present with Omai would have remembered his proudly, but not quite
accurately, counting the number of women he was going to meet at his
next social engagement: '1.2.3.4.5.6.7.8.9.10. – *twelve* – *Woman!*' But few
people can hope to remember lengthy conversational exchanges with any
accuracy, as Fanny appears to do: her Court Journals are full of the
converse and chit-chat of the royal household. However, since Fanny was a
writer of fiction the question inevitably arises: could she really remember
what King or courtier said in such detail, or did she make it up?

It seems that, by and large, she is to be trusted. The Burney family were
distinguished for their remarkable memories. Jem's version was a talent
for languages, mastering Otaheitian simply from hearing it spoken.
Esther's and Susan's were musical; Susan could accurately repeat an
operatic aria after a single hearing.[17] Fanny's son Alex was to possess a
photographic memory and could 'spout' reams of poetry; she herself had
what might be called tape-recorder memory, developed probably as a
consequence of her slowness in learning to read. Instead of reading she
listened, absorbing passages of poetry just from hearing Hetty reciting
them. Her poor vision (she was short-sighted) would also have focused
her attention on what could be heard rather than seen, and her shyness
made her prefer to be a watcher rather than a participant; when only
fifteen one of Hetty's suitors called her '*The silent observant Miss Fanny*'.[18]
She consequently developed a journal-personality at odds with the self-
effacing one of social occasions: in her journals, reticent Miss Burney
becomes entertaining Mrs Voluble.

In the absence of a shorthand writer taking down the conversations at
the time it is impossible to test the accuracy of Fanny's memory, but she
herself was careful to indicate its loss, apologising when unwell and
therefore unable to attend closely to what was said, or admitting when her
memory failed her, writing, for example, 'And then he added some very
fine compliment, but I have forgot it', when she could easily have made
one up.[19] On another occasion she wrote of Dr Johnson that 'he added a
great deal *more*, – only I cannot recollect his exact words, & I do not chuse
to give him *mine*'.[20] Lars E. Troide in his editing of the *Early Journals* notes
this as an example of scrupulous reporting. He pays special attention to
occasions when Fanny's memory can be checked, and points to an
example where almost identical wording exists between an account Fanny
recorded in 1774 of the behaviour of women at bullfights in Spain, given
to her by the traveller Richard Twiss, and what he published the year
afterwards.[21] It may be guessed nevertheless that she selected and 'edited'
for greater literary effect, removing hesitations and repetitions; the King,

for example, peppered his speech with exclamations of 'What what!', but Fanny records them only at her first, disconcerting, meeting. Daddy Crisp once suggested that there was an element of fiction in her portrayal of a little girl called Selina Birch; Fanny responded proudly: 'I never mix truth and fiction: all that I relate in journalising is strictly, nay plainly, fact.'[22]

When Dr Johnson and Mrs Thrale paid their visit to the Burneys that morning in 1777 they took no notice of the small figure sitting in the corner, unaware of how closely they were being observed. *Evelina* changed that. As soon as Mrs Thrale learnt the identity of the author she asked Dr Burney to bring his daughter with him to her Surrey home, Streatham Park in Surrey, where Dr Johnson was also resident. Hester Lynch Thrale was then thirty-seven years old, the wife of a wealthy brewer and MP for Southwark. It was not an especially happy marriage, for Henry Thrale had a roving eye, and of the twelve children born to Hester only four survived past childhood (the eldest was the reserved, but formidably intelligent other Hester known as Queeney, whose music teacher was Dr Burney).

After Fanny's first day visit to Streatham Park in August 1778 she became almost a resident herself, known to Dr Johnson as 'dear little Burney' and pressed to stay by an ever more affectionate Mrs Thrale, who from time to time also carried her to fashionable resorts like Bath and Brighton. This new world provided Fanny with an 'immensity' to record in her journal of the converse and repartee of her literary idol and her witty hostess, though she found the constant praise of *Evelina* embarrassing.

The Streathamites quickly discovered that there was a contradiction between the assurance of the novelist and the diffidence of the woman; when Mrs Thrale proposed taking Fanny to meet some friends, Johnson joked:

'Ah! They will little think what a *Tartar* you carry to them!'
'No, that they won't!' cried Mrs. Thrale; 'Miss Burney looks so meek, & so quiet, – nobody would suspect what a comical Girl she is: – but I believe she has a great deal of *malice* at Heart.'
'Oh she's a Toad! –' cried the Doctor, Laughing, '– a sly Young Rogue! With her Smiths & her Branghtons!'[23]*

Mrs Thrale did not realise that the 'comical Girl' was recording as they spoke, to set it all down in her journals. This 'vanity' of Fanny's, in fixing

---

* Quotation marks have been regularised in accordance with modern conventions here and throughout.

in private writing what she did not like to listen to in public, did not emerge until the journals were published after her death. Her half-sister Sarah then found the volumes uncomfortable reading; she tried to explain the discrepancy as a consequence of extreme timidity:

> In her life, she bottled it all up, & looked and generally spoke with the most refined modesty, & seemed ready to drop if ever her works were alluded to. But what was kept back, and scarcely suspected in society, wanting a safety valve, found its way to her private journal.[24]

It was not truly a 'private' diary, however; Fanny records the praise for those who wanted to hear it, her small journal audience of Susan and Crisp, and with amazed exclamations of 'Good God! Susy' and some self-deprecating humour to offset the flattery, as when she pictures herself munching fast on a biscuit to cover her confusion.

During the next years the relationship between Fanny and Hester became very close; it is revealing of the characters of both, and was not without ambivalence on both sides. Fanny loved Hester for her wit, charm, and generous nature, but she also found her demands for affection overwhelming: Hester would have replaced Susan as first in her heart if she could. On social and material levels they were not equal, Fanny with nothing, Hester with everything, and Fanny found the gifts with which Hester loaded her oppressive; in 1781, for example, she sent Fanny a length of silk for a gown, a valuable present, but Fanny found it difficult to thank her and tried in a contorted sentence to show that her love, already given, could not be further bought:

> . . . I shall think you have the most rapacious of Hearts if you wish for still more Love and fondness than you now have from me, – for, seriously speaking, you *ought* not to gain an inch more, & *cannot* but by taking place of the very few who have a *right* to pre-eminence which I will fairly own to you I should blush to see them robbed of.[25]

Hester resented what to her was over-sensitivity. She was a diarist too, recording her thoughts in her *Thraliana*; there she complained of Fanny's being 'so restlessly & apparently anxious lest I should give myself Airs of Patronage, or load her with the Shackles of Dependance – I . . . dare not ask her to buy me a Ribbon, dare not desire her to touch the Bell, lest She should think herself injured'.[26] Fanny was to carry this sensitivity to patronage and her own social standing into her court life.

One of Fanny's greatest skills in her fiction was her ability to 'catch' a voice and convincingly suggest character through verbal mannerisms.

She was much admired for the understanding of human nature this seemed to reveal. Yet in real life she was caused problems by an inability to see beneath surface manner; this failing is also illustrated in her relationship with Hester Thrale who was a much more complex woman than she recognised. When Fanny was ill at Streatham in December 1779, for example, she wrote in her journal that 'I kept my Bed all Day, & my ever sweet Mrs. Thrale Nursed me most tenderly, letting me take nothing but from herself'.[27] Hester tells it to different effect:

> Fanny Burney has kept her Room here in my house seven Days with a Fever, or something that She called a Fever: I gave her every Medcine [sic], & every Slop with my own hand; took away her dirty Cups, Spoons &c. moved her Tables, in short was Doctor & Nurse, & Maid . . . & now – with the true Gratitude of a Wit, She tells me, that the *World thinks the better of me* for my Civilities to her.
>   It does! does it?[28]

Fanny did not suspect this waspishness in a woman who continually addressed her in phrases such as 'my sweet little friend', 'my beloved Tyo' (Otaheitian for *bosom friend*), and called her 'the sweetest girl in England'.[29]

These tensions did not, however, much impede the development of a strong bond of friendship, with admiration on both sides. At Hester's prompting in 1779 Fanny began to write a comedy, encouraged by Richard Brinsley Sheridan, playwright and theatre manager, who said that he would accept a play from her sight unseen. But when she sent the finished play for the approval of her two daddies, confident that they would like it, she received a 'Hissing, groaning, catcalling Epistle' against its production.[30] *The Witlings*, which has never been performed, makes fun of a group of women with pretensions to learning, who would have been taken for the Blue Stockings, women, and a few men, who met together for purposes of literary discussion.[31] Fanny had met the 'Queen of the Blues', Mrs Elizabeth Montagu, through Mrs Thrale (Mrs Montagu was one of the few who did not like *Evelina*). The decision was probably right: performance would have offended the female wits, and risked a lampooning attack in response. However, it affected Fanny's life further in that direct involvement in the theatre would have made her royal appointment very unlikely; the Queen was to say that she would not have liked Fanny to write 'for so public a thing as the Stage'.[32]

Fanny turned instead to the hard labour of writing another novel, made more difficult through consciousness of a heavy burden of expectation. But when *Cecilia, or Memoirs of an Heiress*, a longer, more sophisticated novel satirising society's worship of wealth and rank, was published in June 1782, applause was even louder than for *Evelina*.[33] The heroine, Cecilia Beverley, inherits a fortune on condition that in marriage she will retain her own surname; three guardians are appointed to watch over her affairs – a man of fashion, a man of business, and a man of rank – but all prove inadequate, and Cecilia loses her fortune and ultimately her wits in some melodramatic and, for its eighteenth-century audience, very affecting scenes. Hester Thrale was enraptured:

> . . . nothing was ever so entertaining – so seducing – so delightful, and Cecilia is beyond every Woman dead & alive . . . Adieu! charming Creature as you are you have killed me I believe: my Throat & Eyes are so *sore*. Adieu![34]

Cecilia brought Fanny new readers including, she heard with amazement, Queen Charlotte, though she found out only later that before the Princesses were allowed to read *Cecilia*, it had had to be given a bishop's seal of approval.

Fanny had never seen the King or Queen but royalty was then relatively accessible. The King held morning Levées twice a week during the London season, and the Queen had her afternoon Drawing-rooms on Sundays and Thursdays at St James's Palace, as Fanny would one day become all too aware. Tickets were available to those of rank or wealth, and women rivalled each other in the richness of their silks and extravagance of their dress trimmings. In 1781, at the Queen's Birthday Drawing-room, it would have been hard to outshine Mrs Thrale's 'Owhyhee' (Hawaii) dress; the silk was woven to a design copied from cloth brought back by Jem Burney, and the trimmings alone cost £65.[35] Fanny missed seeing Hester in her 'Glory', but Susan described the dress as 'Magnificent & not heavy – part of the trimming is composed of Greb[e] feathers made up in bells for tassels' (it is difficult to visualise).[36] Fanny would probably not have been impressed, as secretly she thought Mrs Thrale spent too much money on dress and had no taste. To Hester's chagrin it was 'too dark for the King to see when he passed our place in the Circle, & the Queen only said how warm it was', so she got no royal praise.[37]

Dr Burney was also present at the Drawing-room (and admired the dress appropriately). A strong royalist, he attended such functions in hopes of royal favour, which he further cultivated by dedicating his *History of Music* to the Queen, and his account of the Handel Commemoration of 1784 to the King, who had a passion for the composer.[38] He was granted an audience to present this work personally, and Fanny's 1832 *Memoirs of Dr Burney* records that when the King noticed that her cousin Edward Burney had contributed illustrations, he commented:

'All your family are geniuses, Dr Burney. Your daughter —'
   'O! your daughter,' cried the Queen, lifting up one of her hands, 'is a very extraordinary genius indeed!'
   'And is it true,' said the King, eagerly, 'that you never saw Evelina before it was printed?'[39]

Since Fanny was not present at this meeting this must be a fictionalised account of what her father told her had happened, though the gesture is no doubt one she had often observed in the Queen. Whether the Queen did use the exact phrase 'very extraordinary genius indeed' is open to question, but it is certain that by this date she had read *Evelina* and *Cecilia* and thought well of the modest little woman who wrote them.

The year 1782 saw not only the success of *Cecilia*, but also Fanny's thirtieth birthday and the end of youth. Despite the triumph of the novel, the years following, which lead into and form the background to Fanny's period of court service, brought much heartache: in one sense or another she lost a sister, a friend, a potential husband, and her dearest daddy. First came the marriage of Susan to Molesworth Phillips, an Irish marine Captain, who had been with Jem on Cook's last expedition. Fanny's pipe-dream, half a joke but a hope as well, was that she and Susan would grow old together as two 'loving Maiden Cats'. Susan was not only the person dearest to her heart, but had been her bed-fellow at home, so there was a real sense of widowhood when she left home.

Fanny's attitude to marriage and men reflected her social uncertainty. Despite her lack of beauty men seem to have found her company attractive; in her twenty-third year she received a proposal of marriage from a Thomas Barlow after a single encounter.[40] He commended her 'Affability, Sweetness, & Sensibility', and other men seem to have found her combination of shyness and wit attractive, or as Hester Thrale put it in 1780:

Miss Burney was much admired at Bath, the puppy Men said She had such a drooping Air, & such a timid Intelligence; or a timid Air I think it was, and a drooping Intelligence . . .[41]

But after the eager Mr Barlow no relationship progressed beyond its early stages, in fact a pattern developed of a promising beginning, then an incomprehensible falling away. An example was Jeremiah Crutchley, rumoured to be Henry Thrale's natural son and an executor of his will following his death in 1781. Mrs Thrale believed that Crutchley's 'close Attendance' at Streatham that summer was for Fanny, and Fanny's journals are full of her dialogues with him, but nothing came of it. By September Mrs Thrale noted that while Fanny 'honestly loves the Man', he seemed to have turned his attention to Queeney.[42]

More important and much more painful to Fanny was the relationship which began at the end of 1782 with a clergyman four years younger than herself, George Owen Cambridge.[43] Mr G.C., as he became in her journals, was the son of a minor writer and wit, Richard Owen Cambridge, who lived at Twickenham; Fanny was also to become a friend of George's sister Charlotte. Fanny met George frequently at assemblies and dinner parties and liked him immediately because unlike everyone else he avoided talk of *Evelina* and *Cecilia*, and paid her no compliments at all. They shared a sense of humour and she thought him 'both elegant and sensible', a rare combination.[44] The relationship flourished; Hester wrote in April 1783 'My dearest Miss Burney has apparently got an Admirer in Mr. George Cambridge', and speculated about their future marriage.[45] But something went wrong and Mr G.C. did not propose. Yet they continued to meet at social gatherings and for months and years Fanny's self-conscious scrutiny of his every word, look and gesture gave the lie to her declarations to Susan that her heart was unaffected. Even when she was at court and had not seen him for a considerable while, she would not visit his sister at Twickenham for fear of encountering George.

Neither of these men, nor later Stephen Digby, wrote their sides of the story, and it is difficult to know what went wrong from Fanny's words alone. Probably one problem was a fear of physical intimacy, and instinctive retreat from any male advance: why else did Thomas Barlow's proposal throw her into such a panic? Her journals reveal that Fanny responded to verbal flirtations, but even with the man she was to marry they also make clear how she would turn the conversation if it threatened to become too intimate. Fanny was no Victorian miss, in total ignorance of the mechanics of sex until her wedding night, but she may well have found them alarming. There is a startling letter to her when she was sixteen from her stepsister Maria Allen, proposing a radical solution to the problem of 'that vile race of beings call^d man . . . suppose we were to Cut of [sic] their *prominent members* and by that means render them Harmless innofencive Little Creatures'.[46] Despite Maria's scorn of the vile race, she eloped with and married one of them a year later, but Fanny was embarrassed even to see Maria sitting on her husband's lap. Marriage also had disturbing consequences: Esther with her succession of babies making her ill and taking her from her music, Susan with a child scarcely more than nine months after her wedding day, and Hester Thrale with twelve children in fourteen years to a man she did not love. It was much safer to give one's heart to elderly men like Daddy Crisp. But he died in April 1783, a loss Fanny felt keenly; the death of Dr Johnson, another father figure, followed the year after.

A disquieting backcloth to Fanny's feelings for George Cambridge was provided when, after her husband's death, Mrs Thrale fell desperately in love with the Italian singer Gabriel Piozzi.[47] Society was appalled by this mutiny in a matron's bones. She was a wealthy widow with four daughters to bring out, while he was a foreigner, a Catholic, and most deplorable of all, he earned his living as a teacher and was indeed Queeney's singing tutor. Hester turned to Fanny for sympathy, which Fanny willingly gave her, while consistently advising against the match. Queeney also was implacably opposed to Piozzi, and in early 1783 he was sent back to Italy; but when her mother's health threatened collapse a year later she reluctantly gave consent to his recall. In May 1784 Fanny and Hester had what neither realised would be their final meetings as friends. Fanny told Susan:

> I parted most reluctantly with my dear Mrs. Thrale, whom, when or how, I shall see again, Heaven only knows! But in sorrow we parted – on *my* side in real affliction.[48]

Next month Hester was still writing to Fanny as 'Dear, irrestistible, *perfect* Burney!'[49] But Fanny could not be a hypocrite and wish her well in a marriage she believed would be a disaster. An exchange of reproachful and defensive notes ended with the new Mrs Piozzi reassuring Fanny that 'All is well, and I am too happy myself to make a friend otherwise', yet it was the last Fanny was ever to hear from her, and thereafter the former sweet girl was dubbed 'l'aimable traitresse'.[50] Today Fanny's attitude seems narrow-minded and snobbish, but she echoed the opinion of the time: 'insanity' and 'madness' were the words most commonly used of the marriage. Hester's abandonment of her became an enduring grief to Fanny; while at court she wrote that she could never hear her name without a 'secret pang'.[51]

It was as well that Fanny made two new friends during this period, both intelligent, sensitive and artistic women, but with none of Mrs Thrale's sharp edges. The first was Mrs Frederica Lock, Swiss by birth; she was closer in age to Fanny than Hester had been and they were on first name terms: Fanny knew her as Fredy. William Lock, her husband, was a man of the

Enlightenment, cultured, learned, and liberal-minded, honoured by all who knew him.[52] They had five children and had their principal residence at Norbury Park between Leatherhead and Dorking in Surrey; this house, designed by Thomas Sandby and built high on the wooded slopes above the river Mole, commands a magnificent prospect towards the chalk hills on the other side of the valley. Fanny paid long visits to Norbury, becoming strongly attached to her friend and to the beautiful woodlands around. The place became even more dear when Susan moved to a rented house in the village of Mickleham in the valley below. A gate in a wall still shows where the Phillips' property was; it had a pretty garden tended by Susan, an orchard and a meadow. Susan became intimate with the Locks too and while Fanny was at court her journals were addressed to Fredy as well as her sister. For Fanny, Norbury Park with its loved inhabitants and wooded walks was an earthly Paradise; the worst deprivation of her court years was that she found herself shut out of this Eden.

Fanny's second new and dear friend was an elderly lady: Mrs Mary Delany. The hidden flaw in this friendship was that Mrs Delany was also much loved by the King and Queen, who had given her a grace-and-favour house in Windsor. A Christmas visit there in 1785 was to lead directly to Fanny's court appointment.

CHAPTER TWO

A Christmas Visit

Upon the whole, and for me, don't you think, my dear father and Susan, I comported myself mighty well in my grand interview? Indeed, except quite at first, I was infinitely more easy than I usually am with strangers . . .[1]

Old Mrs Delany was as old as the century. Born Mary Granville, she was a descendant of the Elizabethan sea-dog Sir Richard Grenville, while her great-grandfather, Sir Bevil, died fighting for the King in the Civil War. But Mary's father was an impecunious younger son, so a 'good' marriage was looked for. When she was seventeen Mary went to stay with her uncle, George Granville, Lord Lansdowne, at Longleat in Wiltshire, and while she was there Alexander Pendarves, MP for Launceston, arrived. Mary discovered to her horror that she was expected to marry this 'large unwieldy person' of 'crimson countenance' and more than three times her age.[2] When Fanny visited Longleat with the King and Queen in 1789 on their return from Weymouth, its grandeur was tainted in her eyes by the indignation she felt at the way the young girl had been treated:

> With how sad an awe, in recollecting her submissive unhappiness, did I enter these doors! and with what indignant hatred did I look at the portrait of the unfeeling Earl, to whom her gentle repugnance, shown by almost incessant tears, was thrown away, as if she, her person, and her existence were nothing in the scale, where the disposition of a few boroughs opposed them! Yet was this the famous Granville – the poet, the fine gentleman, the statesman, the friend and patron of Pope, of whom he wrote –
> *What Muse for Granville can refuse to sing?*
> *Mine*, I am sure, for one.[3]

The marriage lasted only seven years before Pendarves drank himself to death.

Mary's second marriage was as happy as her first was miserable. Through their mutual friend, Dean Swift, Mary met the Irish divine Dr Patrick Delany; he was then married, but when he became a widower he remembered Mary Pendarves, sought her out and married her. Twenty-five

years of agreeable companionship, mainly spent in Ireland, allowed Mrs
Delany to develop her love of nature and her artistic talents. She could
both draw and paint, but it was as a designer and craftswoman that she
excelled, creating delicate embroideries of leaf and flower, extravaganzas
of shells in grottos, and elaborately worked quilts, carpets and chair-covers.

After Dr Delany's death in 1768 Mrs Delany returned to London and
entered its social scene. Though no pedant, she associated with the Blue
Stockings and formed a friendship with another intelligent woman with a
zest for knowledge, the Dowager Duchess of Portland.[4] She set
Mrs Delany up in a town house in St James's Place, and invited her to
spend her summers at Bulstrode, her country estate near Beaconsfield.
The two women shared a fascination with natural history, especially
botany, then a new field of study. It was at this time that Mrs Delany
developed the art for which she is admired today, what she modestly
called her 'paper mosaicks'. She had always been skilled in paper-cutting
and now used that talent to create, by eye, exact and lifelike images of
individual plants; every feathery petal, every tiny stamen or spiny thorn,
was cut out individually and stuck onto a black background. Fanny, shown
examples in 1783, explained the craft to Susan:

> It is staining paper of all possible colours, and then cutting it out, so
> finely and delicately, that when it is pasted on paper or vellum, it has
> all the appearance of being pencilled, except that, by being raised, it
> has still a richer and more natural look. The effect is extremely
> beautiful. She invented it at seventy-five![5]

In 1776 King George and Queen Charlotte, herself an enthusiast for
botany, visited Bulstrode, and asked to meet Mrs Delany and to see her
'*hortus siccus*' [dried garden]. They soon prized her not only for her art
but for herself. The Queen encouraged the botanist Joseph Banks to
send plants from Kew, and other specimens both exotic and humble
arrived at Bulstrode. Before her eyesight failed, Mrs Delany completed
nearly a thousand of her pictures, signing each one with her cut-out
initials, colour-coded for the years. She poignantly told Fanny that 'the
last year, as I found my eyes grew very dim, and threatened to fail before
my work was complete, I put my initials in white, for I seemed to myself
already working in my winding-sheet'.[6]

Fanny had first been introduced to Mrs Delany by Mrs Hester Chapone,
one of the Blue Stockings and author of *Letters on the Improvement of the
Mind Addressed to a Young Lady* (1773), a conduct-book cited as influencing

Evelina. Fanny had already heard that though they had not at first wanted to read *Cecilia*, when they had done so the Duchess and Mrs Delany could talk of nothing else; she was equally interested to meet 'Swift's Mrs Delany', so a visit was arranged to St James's Place:

> Mrs. Delany was alone in her drawing-room, which is entirely hung round with pictures of her own painting, and ornaments of her own designing. She came to the door to receive us. She is still tall, though some of her height may be lost: not much, however, for she is remarkably upright. She has no remains of beauty in feature, but in countenance I never but once saw more, and that was in my sweet maternal grandmother.[7]

Fanny was to repeat her sense of the resemblance between Mrs Delany and her beloved grandmother after other meetings, and it contributed to the devotion she came to feel for the old lady. Mrs Delany likewise developed an affectionate regard for the novelist, trusting her enough to allow her to 'rummage' through her correspondence and read letters from the great Dean Swift himself. Two years after first meeting her, Mrs Delany wrote of Fanny that her 'admirable understanding, tender affection, and sweetness of manners, make her valuable to all those who have the happiness to know her'.[8] This was in the summer of 1785 when Fanny was staying with her following the sudden death of the Duchess. Fanny's ready sympathy, and her quiet, tactful manner, would have made her an ideal companion at such a time.

The Duchess's death was more than an emotional blow to Mrs Delany. All assumed that she would have provided for her friend in her will, but she had not done so, apparently at Mrs Delany's insistence.[9] Anxious for their favourite, the King and Queen offered her a residence in St Albans Street in Windsor, near the Castle, with a pension of £300 to cover her living costs, and the Queen urged her to accept in a warm and imaginative letter:

> You may not possibly be aware that I am among the heirs of the Duchess. She has left her well-beloved Delany to my charge and friendship; and I hope you will grant me the privilege of fulfilling this last part of her last will, and settle in the house which I have ordered and where I shall often be able to see you – Charlotte.[10]

Fanny recorded Mrs Delany's hesitation in 'accepting what she feared would involve her in a new course of life', but the offer was taken up, and on 20 September she moved in, accompanied by her servant Anne Astley, and her fourteen-year-old great-niece, Georgina Mary Ann Port, known to Fanny as Marianne, who had spent much of her life with her great-aunt. With the Queen's permission Mrs Delany was also anxious to have Fanny as an invited guest, and in late November Fanny joined her in her new home in Windsor.

Though St Albans Street still exists, Mrs Delany's house has long since disappeared. But it has been identified as forming one wing of a building near the corner of the street, opposite the massive Henry VIII Gate into the Castle.[11] The King, who had personally welcomed Mrs Delany into her new home, had seen to it that the premises had been thoroughly scoured, the chimneys swept, a load of fine gravel laid in the garden, the well new-furbished, new iron bath stoves installed and 'a large New Windsor Arm'd Chair' provided.[12] Mrs Delany was instructed by the Queen to bring nothing with her but '*herself and clothes*', as they would provide everything down to 'wine, sweetmeats, pickles, etc, etc'.[13] Fanny commented that 'They seem to know and feel her worth as if they had never worn crowns, or, wearing, annexed no value to them', though it was probably their crowns which blinded them to the way they were taking control of her life. The King also provided Mrs Delany with a new sedan chair and the liveries for servants to carry it, so that she might attend services in the private Chapel of Windsor Castle, or visit them in their own residence nearby, Queen's Lodge.

The royal family did not live in one place, but spent their year moving between London, Kew and Windsor. Court functions took place at St James's Palace, but the King and Queen's London residence was the small Queen's House, enlarged by George IV into today's Buckingham Palace. At Kew there was the White House, built in the Palladian style by William Kent that century, but already rather run-down, dingy, and dirty.[14] The nearby Dutch House, today known as Kew Palace, was also used by the family. Windsor was the favourite place of residence, though the King and Queen did not then live in the Castle, but had rebuilt a little house which had belonged to Queen Anne, on the south side of the Castle. It was again in classical style, with a long barrack-like extension, and was known as Queen's or Upper Lodge. Even so there was not room for all the six Princesses and their households so another house, once the property of the Duke of St Albans, son of Charles II and Nell Gwyn, had been bought to house the three younger girls. It was known as the Lower Lodge. This house had given its name to St Albans Street and was just down the road from Mrs Delany's new home.

The Victorian publisher Charles Knight, who was brought up in Windsor and whose father kept a bookshop patronised by the King, remembered from his childhood that Windsor was a 'continual din of Royalty going to and fro – of bell-ringing for birthdays – of gun-firing for victories', while royalty itself lived 'in a glass-house', the Castle grounds open to all and a public road running right under the windows of Queen's Lodge.[15] However, the King loved Windsor and its environs for the chance it gave him to live like a country squire and enjoy farming and other country pursuits, thereby earning himself the mocking title of 'Farmer George'. But he was held in affection in the town where he was a familiar figure, 'the gossiping and inquiring gentleman who dwelt up the hill' as Knight put it. He recalled how as a boy he would bow to the King 'as he walked to his dairy at Frogmore, and passed me as I was hunting for mushrooms in the short grass on some dewy morning'.[16]

It was a different kind of hunting which the King enjoyed. He was a tireless rider and when he was at Windsor he rode out every day. Stag-hunting was his passion, though the horses were more in danger of death from being over-ridden than the stags were from the hounds; they had names like Starlight, Moonshine and Highflyer, and epic tales were told of chases over thirty miles and more before the stag was cornered and preserved from the hounds for another day.[17] When Fanny and Mrs Thrale were on their way back from Bath in 1780 they were warned away from Windsor on a hunting day and found it a necessary caution, 'as we were with difficulty accommodated even the day after the hunt; several stragglers yet remaining at all the inns, and we heard of nothing but the king and royal huntsmen and huntswomen'.[18] The Queen did not hunt, though she had a phaeton with four white ponies in which she would drive around the Little Park. When Dorothy Wordsworth visited the Castle in 1792, she looked down from the Terrace and was charmed by the 'very pretty Effect seen from above' as the Queen wove in and out of the trees.[19]

The Queen enjoyed the domestic aspects of life at Windsor, choosing the wallpapers and furniture for Queen's Lodge. She herself created many of the furnishings with her needle, including chair seats to designs supplied by Mrs Delany of leaves appliquéd in different shades of brown satin onto a dark blue background. Mrs Delany herself described the principal room as 'all furnished with beautiful Indian paper, chairs covered with different embroideries of ye liveliest colours, glasses, tables, sconces, in the best taste, the whole calculated to give the greatest cheerfulness to the place'; but for one woman who worked there it was not an entirely comfortable building, 'and it always had the appearance of a scramble'.[20]

Fanny was to observe the affection between the King and the Queen when one day she was alone with the Queen and the King came in and, not aware of Fanny, kissed his wife on the cheek.[21] Yet it had been an arranged marriage. Queen Charlotte came from the small principality of Mecklenburg-Strelitz in northern Germany, chosen to be the bride of George III when only seventeen, six years younger than he was. She had then known no English and had to be tutored on arrival, but Fanny noted that 'She speaks English almost perfectly well, with great choice and copiousness of language, though now and then with foreign idiom, and frequently with a foreign accent'.[22] She was an earnest girl, of deep religious faith – she told Fanny that she had held the Cross and Order of a Protestant nunnery for aristocrats before she came to England – and she did her conscientious best to carry out her duties as Queen. Part of that function was of course to provide an heir to the throne and in this she performed splendidly, producing three princes one after another before the first princess arrived. In all Queen Charlotte bore, without complaint, fifteen children, nine sons and six daughters, of whom all except the two youngest sons grew to adult life. Extraordinarily, though neither King nor Queen could be called handsome, the King with his bulbous eyes, thick lips and prominent nose, and the Queen with her large mouth and 'mulatto' look, the children were all very good-looking, at least in youth. Fanny was to write of the girls that 'Never, in tale or fable, were there six sister Princesses more lovely'.[23]

The six divided into two groups, perhaps to their disadvantage as individual personalities; the elder three were Charlotte, the Princess Royal, who at Christmas 1785 was aged nineteen, seventeen-year-old Augusta, and fifteen-year-old Elizabeth. Princess Elizabeth's health that Christmas was causing concern, as she was suffering from some 'complaint on the chest' for which she had been 'blooded' twelve times in a fortnight.[24] She was the most artistic of the girls and the wittiest, an enthusiastic letter-writer who once sent 143 letters in six weeks to Lady Harcourt, a Lady of the Bedchamber, when she was ill, hoping they would 'break the tediousness of a sick room'.[25] Princess Augusta was a talented musician; as a girl she also enjoyed playing boys' games such as cricket, and she was forthright in expression. The Princess Royal was a shy girl and descriptions of her tend to be negative; she did not like music, was not interested in dress, and was rather clumsy; when she lost a shoe while dancing with the Prince of Wales at her first ball, it was her brother who deftly managed to cover over the situation.[26] But like all the sisters, 'Royal' was kind, unaffected and unassuming.

The next two Princesses were close in age, nine-year-old Mary, and eight-year-old Sophia. They were described by Marianne Port as looking like 'little angels' with their blue eyes and very fair hair curling down their backs.[27] The youngest of the family was two-year-old Amelia, the darling of her father. The Queen called her daughters 'La Bande Joyeuse' and they formed then a happy family, pictured by Mrs Delany at Queen's Lodge on a November evening in 1785:

> They sit round a large table, on which are books, work, pencils, and paper. The Queen has the goodness to make me sit down next to her and delights me with her conversation . . . whilst the younger part of the family are drawing and working, etc, etc, the beautiful babe, Princess Amelia, bearing her part in the entertainment; sometimes in one of her sister's laps; sometimes playing with the King on the carpet; which, altogether, exhibits such a delightful scene, as would require an Addison's pen, or a Vandyke's pencil, to do justice to it.[28]

Absent from this scene of domestic bliss are any of the sons.

It was only the three elder Princes whom Fanny saw during her years of service, since all the younger ones were out of the country throughout the period. Apart from the third son, Prince William, who had been sent to sea at the age of thirteen, they were being educated in Hanover, under the eye of Frederick, Duke of York, the second son and the King's favourite among them. The decision to send the boys abroad had been taken to keep them away from what was seen as the baneful influence of the heir to the throne, George, Prince of Wales. The antipathy between the King and his eldest son, twenty-three years old at this time, is well known. The King, frugal, abstemious, faithful to his wife, was infuriated by the Prince of Wales' spendthrift ways, his addiction to gambling, his drunkenness, gourmandising and womanising. Yet the Prince was adored by his sisters, and Fanny was to recognise his charm. Once he came to his mother's room in Queen's Lodge to fetch her to see a fine display of northern lights; another time he spent half an hour talking entertainingly to Mrs Delany. What no one knew at the time of Fanny's visit to Windsor in December 1785 was that the Prince was about to engage in a secret and unauthorised marriage with a Roman Catholic widow, Mrs Maria Fitzherbert.[29]

Fanny's Windsor visit began inauspiciously as the old lady was unwell, and Fanny feared for the consequences when, a day or two after her arrival, she came down to breakfast to find Mrs Delany's African weaver bird lying dead in its cage. This bird had belonged to the Duchess of Portland and was of great sentimental value as a keepsake of her friend. While Fanny stood irresolutely with the lifeless form in her hand, Miss Margaret Planta, English teacher to the Princesses, came to enquire after Mrs Delany for the Queen. She carried the news back and the Queen at once sent down her own weaver bird in a handsome cage, either to be a substitution or a gift. Fanny saw that despite her failing eyesight Mrs Delany was not going to be deceived into confusing the royal bird with her own, but news of the gift helped to soften the blow of the death, and the incident impressed Fanny with the Queen's thoughtfulness.

Fanny was well aware that the King and Queen had expressed the wish to be introduced to her, though it was an encounter which she herself was nervously anxious to avoid. The death of the Queen's brother which plunged the court into mourning, and Princess Elizabeth's illness, made her hopeful that she would escape it; Mrs Delany nevertheless instructed her lengthily on the etiquette of private meetings with royalty and the expectations of royal conversation:

'I do beg of you,' said dear Mrs. Delany, 'when the Queen or the King speaks to you, not to answer with mere monosyllables. The Queen often complains to me of the difficulty with which she can get any conversation, as she not only always has to start the subjects, but commonly, entirely to support them: and she says there is nothing she so much loves as conversation, and nothing she finds so hard to get. She is always best pleased to have the answers that are made her lead on to further discourse. Now, as I know she wishes to be acquainted with you, and converse with you, I do really entreat you not to draw back from her, nor to stop conversation with only answering Yes, or No.'[30]

Fanny promised to do her best, but when a thundering at the door signalled the Queen's arrival 'away flew all my resolutions and agreements, and away after them flew I!' However, she was not to evade an introduction much longer.

The first encounter between Fanny Burney and King George III shortly before Christmas 1785 is one of the best-known and most frequently quoted passages in her journals. She wrote her account jointly to Susan and her father immediately afterwards, and when she was feeling jubilant at having survived it successfully; needless to say, she had no idea that this was to be the first of many meetings. New visitors had arrived, Mrs Delany's nephew Bernard Dewes and his small daughter Anne, and one evening they were all gathered in the drawing-room; Mrs Delany had just come in, and Fanny was teaching the little girl some noisy Christmas games:

We were all in the middle of the room, and in some confusion . . . and I was disentangling myself from Miss Dewes, to be ready to fly off if any one knocked at the street door, when the door of the drawing-room was again opened, and a large man, in deep mourning, appeared at it, entering and shutting it himself without speaking.

A ghost could not more have scared me, when I discovered, by its glitter on the black, a star! The general disorder had prevented his being seen, except by myself, who was always on the watch, till Miss Port, turning round, exclaimed, 'The King! – Aunt, the King!'

Oh, mercy! thought I, that I were but out of the room! which way shall I escape? and how pass him unnoticed? There is but the single door at which he entered in the room! Every one scampered out of the way: Miss Port, to stand next the door; Mr. Bernard Dewes to a corner opposite it; his little girl clung to me; and Mrs. Delany advanced to meet His Majesty, who, after quietly looking on till she saw him, approached, and inquired how she did.[31]

What Fanny emphasises in this account is the abnormality of monarchy, the contrast between the ordinariness of the situation – a large man in a black coat comes in through the door – and the extraordinary response which recognition of the glittering Garter star produces. Had the King been a normal guest the movement in the room would have been towards him and with words of greeting; instead, everyone hurries away in silence or in Fanny's case, panic. The word 'scampered', used of children or animals, next led her to present the King's entrance as an extension of the games they were playing, imagining that at any second someone might cry 'puss! puss! puss!' and expect her to dash for the opposite corner. Even when the King began to converse with Mrs Delany, she noted the oddity of everyone standing in a room full of chairs. This unnaturalness suggested another artificial situation, a stage set, and she fancied them all characters in a drama – the King as King, Mrs Delany as a 'venerable confidante', Marianne as a 'suppliant virgin' and herself as 'a very solemn, sober, and decent mute'. A further bizarre moment came later when the Queen arrived. No one could turn their back on the monarch so in order to light the Queen into the room Marianne backed to the door, reaching behind her for the handle.

Fanny was not allowed to adopt her role of silent observer for long. After a first attempt to speak with her resulted in mumbled inaudible answers, the King gave her time to compose herself then, while examining a book of prints belonging to Mrs Delany, began a determined assault. Fanny had been warned of his idiosyncracies of speech, yet found herself not just nervous but confused:

'Pray, does Miss Burney draw, too?'

The *too* was pronounced very civilly.

'I believe not, sir,' answered Mrs. Delany; 'at least, she does not tell.'

'Oh!' cried he, laughing, 'that's nothing! she is not apt to tell; she never does tell, you know! – Her father told me that himself. He told me the whole history of her *Evelina*. And I shall never forget his face when he spoke of his feelings at first taking up the book! – he looked quite frightened, just as if he was doing it that moment! I never can forget his face while I live!'

Then coming up close to me, he said,

'But what? – what? – how was it?'

'Sir?' – cried I, not well understanding him.

'How came you – how happened it – what? – what?'

'I – I only wrote, sir, for my own amusement, – only in some odd, idle hours.'

'But your publishing – your printing – how was that?'

'That was only, sir, – only because . . . I thought – sir – it would look very well in print!'

I do really flatter myself this is the silliest speech I ever made! I am quite provoked with myself for it; but a fear of laughing made me eager to utter anything, and by no means conscious, till I had spoken, of what I was saying.

He laughed very heartily himself, – well he might – and walked away to enjoy it, crying out, 'Very fair indeed! that's being very fair and honest!'[32]

He was soon back with a string of further questions about the secret publication of *Evelina*, amused to learn that Giuseppe Baretti, a friend of Fanny's father, had wagered that it must be by a man, 'for no woman, he said, could have kept her own counsel'.[33]

When the Queen arrived the King immediately embarked on a word for word account of all that he had managed to extract from her; when told of Baretti's wager the Queen turned to Fanny and laughingly responded, 'Oh, that is quite too bad an affront to us! – Don't you think so?' She seated herself, with a little table at her side, and called Fanny to her. Despite her promises, Fanny could only manage one-word replies, and when Queen Charlotte took up the subject of her writing she became completely tongue-tied:

'Miss Burney! . . . shall we have no more – nothing more?'

I could not but understand her, and only shook my head.

The Queen then, as if she thought she had said too much, with great sweetness and condescension, drew back herself, and, very delicately, said, 'To be sure it is, I own, a very home question, for one who has not the pleasure to know you'.

I was quite ashamed of this apology, but did not know what to say to it . . .

'But, indeed,' continued she presently, 'I would not say it, only that I think from what has been done, there is a power to do so much good – and good to young people – which is so very good a thing – that I cannot help wishing it could be.'[34]

Into the silence the King interjected 'Oh, but she will write! – she only waits for inclination – she told me so'; both would have been pleased with Fanny's modesty.

This flattering interest in her writing was only one topic of conversation; the company learned of the touch of rheumatism in the King's shoulder, the tendency of his constitution to fat, of the younger children's whooping cough, and of the fog which penetrated the previous week's Drawing-room; the King knew of Susan's being brought to bed unexpectedly at Norbury Park and wanted to know the details. Eventually he looked at his watch and announced to the Queen that it was nearly eight o'clock 'and if we don't go now, the children will be sent to the other house'. It was all cosily domestic, perhaps to help Fanny overcome her reserve; she certainly became more relaxed and communicative as the evening progressed and less conscious of the contrast between the everyday nature of the royal chit-chat and the ceremony attendant on majesty.

In a further royal encounter the talk did turn to more intellectual subjects, the Queen speaking of books and writers, and the King of plays and players. This was when he made his often-quoted comment on the 'sad stuff' of Shakespeare:

> 'Was there ever,' cried he, 'such stuff as great part of Shakespeare? only one must not say so! But what think you? – What? – Is there not sad stuff? What? – what?'
>
> 'Yes, indeed, I think so, sir, though mixed with such excellences, that –'
>
> 'Oh!' cried he, laughing good-humouredly, 'I know it is not to be said! but it's true. Only it's Shakespeare, and nobody dare abuse him.'[35]

The King's remarks have been used as evidence of poor literary judgement. But the man who after his illness of 1788–9 said of his three elder daughters that he was lucky to have had no Goneril or Regan only Cordelias, was not unappreciative of Shakespeare's finest writing, and the context shows that what he was objecting to was indecency. He had been talking with Fanny about the 'great want of good modern comedies, and of the extreme immorality of most of the old ones'. He named several, all unknown to Fanny, 'till, at last, he came to Shakespeare' and after the comments quoted above 'enumerated many of the characters and parts of plays he objected to'. What the King disliked was Shakespeare's bawdy, so if he is guilty of anything it is prudery, not philistinism.

After the success of her novels Fanny had grown used, if not accustomed, to men and women of rank and distinction wanting to be introduced to her but she could never have dreamt that the King and Queen would seek her acquaintance and take such trouble to put her at her ease. No wonder that Fanny wrote enthusiastically of the 'unaffected conversation and unassuming port and manner' of the King, and of the Queen's 'sense and graciousness, mingled with delicacy of mind and liveliness of temper'. Yet a more rebellious side remained and found expression in a letter to Hetty. Fanny's letters to her older sister differed from those to Susan; there is frequently a sense of bravura performance in them, of showing off her verbal skills, perhaps as an equivalent to Hetty's flying fingers on the harpsichord. Once while at court she sent her a letter which looks normal, but which reading proves to be written throughout in verse.[36] Another time her letter took the form of a pastiche of Lancelot Gobbo in *The Merchant of Venice*. On this occasion her literary model seems to have been Swift; under pretence of advising her on the proper etiquette of appearing before 'crowned heads', Fanny offered Hetty a satiric parody of her own tutoring in behaviour, sending her some '*Directions for coughing, sneezing, or moving, before the King and Queen*':

In the first place, you must not cough. If you find a cough tickling in your throat, you must arrest it from making any sound; if you find yourself choking with the forbearance, you must choke – but not cough.

In the second place, you must not sneeze. If you have a vehement cold, you must take no notice of it; if your nose-membranes feel a great irritation, you must hold your breath; if a sneeze still insists upon making its way, you must oppose it, by keeping your teeth grinding together; if the violence of the repulse breaks a blood-vessel, you must break the blood-vessel – but not sneeze.

In the third place, you must not, upon any account, stir either hand or foot. If, by chance, a black pin runs into your head, you must not take it out. If the pain is very great, you must be sure to bear it without wincing; if it brings the tears into your eyes, you must not wipe them off . . . If, however, the agony is very great, you may, privately, bite the inside of your cheek, or of your lips, for a little relief . . . if you even gnaw a piece out, it will not be minded, only be sure either to swallow it, or commit it to a corner of the inside of your mouth till they are gone – for you must not spit.[37]

This passage too is frequently quoted in histories of the period, often wrongly attributed to Fanny's actual period of service when she would never have written so disrespectfully. It has even been taken as a serious list of rules.

In the company of his former friend, Mary Delany, Fanny would easily have brought Swift to mind, and would have remembered also that the court of Lilliput in *Gulliver's Travels* was a satirical picture of that of George I, George III's great-grandfather. In turn this stirred an old memory. Eleven years before, while staying at Chessington, Fanny entertained the company with flights of fantasy about a nine-volume *Treatise upon politeness* she claimed to be writing on the subject of refined conversation, which would offer all the '*newest fashioned* regulations':

'In the first place, you are never again to Cough.'

'Not to *Cough*?' exclaimed every one at once, 'but how are you to help it?'

'As to *that*,' answered I, 'I am not very clear about it myself, as I own I am guilty sometimes of doing it. But it is as much a mark of ill breeding as it is to *Laugh*, which is a thing that Lord Chesterfield has stigmatized.'. . .

'And pray,' said Mr Crisp, making a fine affected Face, 'may you *simper*?'

'You may smile, Sir,' answered I. 'But to *laugh* is quite abominable. Though not quite so bad as *sneezing*, or *blowing the Nose*.'[38]

The intention of the new system was to banish 'whatever is Natural, plain or easy . . . from polite circles'. Crisp recognised the link with Swift's *Polite Conversation*, which attacked hackneyed speech while purporting to instruct in the best language 'now used at Court, and in the Best Companies of England'.[39] Now in her 'directions' for Esther, Fanny poked fun at the unnaturalness of royal etiquette, and showed awareness that had such a one as Swift been listening he would have judged the converse of that evening banal.

Fanny's attitude to royalty after her first direct experience of it was ambivalent. On the one hand she was flattered by the attention, the kindness, the patience and the good humour, summed up in the word 'condescension', which carried no pejorative sense of offensive patronage but meant the showing of respect and consideration to an inferior. Yet on the other hand the rituals Fanny had observed, the standing, the scattering to corners, the walking backwards, the not speaking unless spoken to, appeared to her as outlandish as any of the customs of Otaheite might. She had no expectation that she was about to join the natives.

CHAPTER THREE

Keeper of the Robes

I am married, my dearest Susan – I look upon it in that light . . . What then now remains but to make the best wife in my power?[1]

On 21 May 1786 Fanny and her father travelled to Windsor to attend one of the King's summer evening promenades on the South Terrace of the Castle. The Master of the King's Band had just died and Dr Burney was hoping to be offered the post. He was advised to go to the Terrace by Leonard Smelt, a man who was to play an important part in Fanny's future life. A former Captain in the Royal Engineers, he lived in a grace-and-favour house in Kew; he had been sub-governor to the two eldest Princes, but had resigned from that position in 1781 and had refused another post, preferring simply to be known as the King's 'Friend'. He now told Dr Burney, 'Take your daughter in your hand, and walk upon the terrace. The King's seeing you at this time he will understand, and he is more likely to be touched by a hint of that delicate sort than by any direct application.'[2]

'Terracing' was a Windsor institution; every summer Sunday and on other fine evenings, the King processed up and down the South Terrace to the strains of one of the royal bands, smiling, nodding and talking animatedly, the Queen on his arm and his family in due order behind. It was a colourful occasion. The King and other members of his household would be wearing the Windsor uniform of dark blue and gold turned up with red which he had designed himself, while the Queen and Princesses would be elegantly clad, often in matching robes. Dorothy Wordsworth was so charmed by what she saw on her visit in 1792 that she fancied that she was 'treading upon Fairy-Ground, and that the gay company was brought there by Enchantment'.[3] Carriages of great lords lined Castle Hill but the Terrace was open to anyone; Charles Knight describes how as a boy he would sit on the wall listening to the bands, more cynically than Dorothy wondering 'at garters upon gouty legs, and at great lords looking like valets in the Windsor uniform'.[4] On another occasion, Dr Burney was to comment on the way the highest in the land mingled with farmers, servants, and tradespeople, suggesting with a similar enthusiasm to Dorothy Wordsworth that all were 'in Elysium'.[5]

But in 1786 Dr Burney's visit was uncomfortable and dispiriting. The King and Queen did not speak to him; Fanny, distressed for her father, wrote, 'There is nothing that I know so very dejecting as solicitation'. It proved that the post her father coveted had already been offered to someone else.[6] The only consolation for the Doctor was the singular attention paid to his daughter. Fanny, standing apart from him, had, in embarrassment at the real reason for her presence, tried to escape notice by pulling her hat over her face, but she was recognised. The King asked, 'How goes the Muse?' and unable to hear her reply disconcertingly 'put his head quite under my hat'.[7]

She was soon to discover the reason for this attention when an offer was made of a position as Keeper of the Robes to Queen Charlotte. A vacancy had been caused by the retirement of Mrs Hagedorn, one of the two German women who had travelled from Mecklenberg with Queen Charlotte at the time of her marriage. The other was Mrs Schwellenberg (the 'Mrs' was honorary), who would in effect though not in title be her superior. Fanny would be paid £200 a year, have her own apartment, maid and footman, and the use of a carriage. The offer was brought by Mr Smelt; to his mortification Fanny showed no excitement, even when he pointed out the great distinction of being picked 'in preference to the thousands of offered candidates, of high birth and rank', and suggested how the post would enable her to help her family, especially her father. But Fanny knew that she would lose control of her own life and be parted from what she valued most, family and friends. She would be able to receive visitors only by permission, every day would be a work day and there would be no holidays. It was a daunting prospect. Had her father opposed the appointment it might have been refused, but he was 'in raptures', foreseeing all his dreams of advancement fulfilled, and honours for the whole family.

Fanny had always found it hard to resist her father's wishes; she loved him, felt she owed him her duty, and was dependent on him for her livelihood. To have gone against his hopes would have obliged some alternative proposal for her means of living, but what prospects were there? The life of Mary Wollstonecraft at this time shows that independent living for a woman was possible, but, as she later wrote, 'Few are the modes of earning a subsistence, and those very humiliating'.[8] Mary found work as companion to a disagreeable old lady, as a teacher and a governess, but she had a self-confidence lacking in Fanny. In Fanny's later novel, *The Wanderer* (1814), the destitute heroine takes these kinds of employment – as music-teacher, sempstress and companion to a disagreeable old lady – and is humiliated in all. Only if Fanny could have informed the Queen that she was about to be married could she have escaped. She wrote a long letter to Charlotte Cambridge, setting out the situation and asking her to 'let me know which you wish to strengthen – my courage in making my real sentiments openly known, or my fortitude in concealing what it may be right I should endure'.[9] But if this was an appeal to Charlotte's brother George it fell on deaf ears.

In despair Fanny bowed to the 'inevitable'. Grateful acceptance was sent to the Queen, a public announcement was issued in the press, and delighted letters of congratulation were received, or exchanged among their friends. For Mrs Delany, totally unaware of Fanny's true feelings, the event brought 'great satisfaction', while Hester Chapone wrote to Mrs Delany of these 'honours she [Fanny] so well deserves'.[10] Edmund Burke, calling to offer congratulations and finding her out, left a card:

MR BURKE
To congratulate upon the Honour done by
THE QUEEN TO MISS BURNEY, –
And to HERSELF[11]

Even Mrs Piozzi, hearing the news in Italy, found the appointment cause for rejoicing, though not without a sly dig at the status of her former friend: 'What a glorious Country is ours! where Talents & Conduct are sufficient to draw mean Birth & original Poverty out of the Shades of Life, & set their Merit to ripen in the Sun'; she ignored the caveat from her informer that 'the attendance is so constant . . . as to render it by no means a pleasant situation'.[12] Resigned to her fate, Fanny set about preparing her wardrobe, but it must have been bitter to compare herself with her recently married sister, Charlotte. She wrote telling her that 'I am now *fitting out* just as you were, and all the maids and workers suppose I am going to be married, and snigger every time they bring in any of my new attire'.[13] It was in images of marriage and its attendant duties that she now saw her new life; perhaps she remembered Mrs Delany and her forced wedding.

On the morning of Monday 17 July Fanny set off for court accompanied by her complacent father and their equally complacent friend Mrs Anna Ord, a wealthy widow. They travelled to Windsor in Mrs Ord's coach, with Dr Burney's acting as baggage train, and Fanny tried to control her feelings. When they reached St Albans Street Marianne rushed out excitedly to greet them, but even Fanny's usual pleasure in seeing Mrs Delany was checked. They waited at the old lady's house for the summons to Queen's Lodge, then Fanny on her father's arm set out up the hill. It was only a short distance, but lengthy in distress; Dr Burney told Leonard Smelt that Fanny 'turned pale, her lips quivered, and she found herself so faint, that it was with the utmost difficulty she reached the portico'. Nevertheless, he added that he had never given any of his daughters away in marriage 'with the pride and pleasure I experienced in my gift of last Monday'.[14] Fanny was kindly received by the Queen, and she was afterwards able for her father's sake to restrain her agitation, seeing how thereby his doubts disappeared and 'his hopes and gay expectations . . . ran back at the first beckoning'.[15] After he had gone, Fanny steeled her nerves and resolved to 'make myself as happy as I can, & have done – if possible – with regrets'. Indeed, she admitted to Susan and Fredy Lock that 'all is far better than I could have expected or supposed'.[16]

She found that she had a pleasant apartment at the corner of the ground floor of the Lodge with a drawing-room and a bedroom, which afforded her some independence and privacy. The larger room had windows on two sides, the one at the front looking up to the Terrace and the Round Tower, and that on the side having a view over the Little Park. Her bedroom window overlooked the garden. The Queen had gone to some trouble to ensure Fanny's comfort, completely refurbishing the apartment at a total cost of just over £148, or the equivalent of nine months of her salary.[17] There were new carpets and curtains, while the chimney glasses had been newly polished and silvered and the frames regilded. In the bedroom a 'neat four Post Bedstead' was provided, with a 'fine white mattrass [sic] made remarkably thick & full by order of the best Curled Hair', a bolster 'fill'd with the finest and best seasoned Goose feathers', and a pillow of 'fine seasoned Down'. There was a mahogany basin stand with soap cups, a mahogany clothes press with '5 sliding Shelves and folding Doors', and a 'very neat Mahogany Ladys Dressing Table . . . the inside fitted up with every convenience'.

The most expensive item bought by the Queen was in the larger room, 'A neat Mah^y Bookcase, with scroll Pediment Sliding Shelves, and folding Doors glazed, a chest of Drawers under with Secretary drawer, fitted up very neatly inside with Sundry Drawers'. It cost 16 guineas. A 'Mahogany Reading Desk on a Pillar & Claw made to rise occasionally' was another item of furniture which must have been selected especially for Fanny. Though she was to worry about inviting guests, enough seating was provided for a party: a reupholstered sofa and chairs, and '6 splat back Chairs the frames very neatly Japan'd the seats stuffed with best curled Hair with deep Borders'. Perhaps this grand new furniture was some consolation, but it must have added to Fanny's sense of the strangeness of it all. In time she was to discover her apartments at the other royal residences. At Kew her rooms were 'small, dark and old-fashioned', but at St James's Palace her two rooms were again 'newly and handsomely furnished'.[18] Even better, she had a private staircase which would enable friends to visit her there.

Meanwhile, there were new faces and new names to learn at Windsor. Mrs Schwellenberg seemed on first impression to be 'a woman of understanding, and fond of conversation' despite having a poor command of English. Fanny immediately liked Major William Price, one of the King's equerries; he helped her over matters of etiquette – as Mrs Schwellenberg did not – and she was always to be glad to find him in waiting.[19] She encountered the older Princesses, and the royal governesses, Lady Charlotte Finch and Miss Martha Goldsworthy ('Lady Cha' and 'Goully' to their charges). In all their faces Fanny felt that she observed amazement that she should have been chosen for this appointment.

If she was right, it would more likely have been because she was known as a novelist, than for her lack of rank. Despite the tales of women of fashion and rank soliciting for the post in their thousands, the position of Keeper of the Robes was not one for an aristocrat and neither before nor after Fanny's period of service was it filled by anyone of high birth. Fanny was a strange choice because, as she wrote, Queen Charlotte had 'a settled aversion to almost all novels, and something very near it to almost all novel-writers'.[20] Like many of her contemporaries the Queen thought most novels frivolous and liable to corrupt; her daughters were not allowed to read a novel without her permission, though it was granted for *Evelina* and *Cecilia*. It has been suggested that the post was given to please Mrs Delany, or to recompense Dr Burney for his recent disappointment.[21] However, the Queen told Mrs Delany that 'I was led to think of Miss Burney, first by her books; then by seeing her; then by always hearing how she was loved by her friends; but chiefly by your friendship with her.'[22] If this was so then it seems that in choosing Fanny the Queen was choosing, if not a friend, then someone with whom she could find a sort of companionship and enjoy the kind of serious conversation for which she had told Mrs Delany she yearned. Moreover, Queen Charlotte was only eight years older than Fanny; both were small and neither noted for beauty. These are small points, but such physical interactions can matter.

Fanny began her court career with a little private rebellion; she had been advised, though she does not say by whom, against writing about her doings to outsiders, but she saw no reason why there should be a ban on 'a simple account of inoffensive actions' if she avoided all reference to politics and the private opinions of the royal family.[23] She knew she could trust to her sister Susan's discretion. She therefore began at once to journalise, each day setting down 'minutely faithful' memorandums of the previous day's activities, and writing up her finished 'pacquets' as and when she had time. Fredy became a reader too, and both she and Susan sent long accounts of their own doings in exchange. It was always a secret activity, and Fanny's journals could not be regularly sent. She does not explain the arrangements but they would be likely to have travelled – sometimes well after the events they recorded – when Fredy visited her, or when the Locks sent a servant with a gift. Nobody at court ever suspected this narration of her day-to-day affairs.

Daily life must have seemed extraordinary to Fanny at first, though the routine varied so little that she quickly settled into it. 'Keeper of the Robes' was in practice an arcane title, giving dignity to a position which amounted to little more than that of dresser. Fanny found that she must rise at six, to dress herself and to await a summons to the Queen's dressing-room at any time after seven. Together with the Wardrobe Maid, Mrs Anne Thielcke, she would then help the Queen into her morning gown. Afterwards she could return to her rooms for breakfast, with a book for company (the first was the newly published *Lakes of Cumberland and Westmoreland* by William Gilpin, lent her by Mrs Delany, and it carried her far away in imagination). After breakfast she devoted herself to preparing her own clothes, writing her journal, or walking in the Park. At a quarter to twelve came the call for the main dressing session, at which Mrs Schwellenberg would also be in attendance; twice a week this call would be an hour earlier for 'curling and craping' the Queen's hair. About two hours of freedom followed, used by Fanny for 'talking' with her friends.

The main meal of the day was taken at five o'clock in the ground-floor dining-room assigned to the women of the Queen's household. They might also be asked to entertain visitors to the King and Queen since the royal family dined in private, sometimes with women as guests but never men; they were not allowed to sit in the presence of the Queen. The dishes served at the attendants' table were the leftovers from the King's table 'renewed & re-fitted out', which sounds poor fare, but even the royal leftovers could be fit for a banquet.[24] Meals were not served in courses but rather as Chinese meals today, with a variety of dishes both savoury and sweet from which the diners could make a choice. On one of her first evenings Fanny was diverted by the sight of a gluttonous German officer whose eyes lit up at the sight of turtle on the table. It is unlikely that Fanny had a portion of this rich dish: all she ever mentions is being helped to 'greens'. William Lock once said that 'he saw her surrounded with the profusion of that sumptuous table, dining, *as a Mouse would*, upon three crumbs'.[25] She shared such abstemiousness with the King who likewise preferred plain fare; there is a mocking cartoon by Gillray of 1792, entitled 'Temperance Enjoying a Frugal Meal', which shows him tucking into a boiled egg while the Queen relishes a forkful of sauerkraut, an ornate jug of 'Aqua Regis' standing beside them.

After the meal coffee was served in Mrs Schwellenberg's apartment directly above Fanny's (she did not like coffee and usually sat looking at her cup), then at eight o'clock there was a return to the dining-room to drink tea, in the company of the equerries. Every evening at this time there would be a musical performance in the concert room; Fanny could hear it through the dining-room walls, and though it was almost always the works of Handel, she was glad not to be deprived of music. After the tea ceremony Fanny was left 'unremittingly' in the company of Mrs Schwellenberg, this the first word in her published journals to suggest that she was finding the company of her superior uncongenial. The evening concluded with supper – in Fanny's case 'a little fruit' – before her final call to the Queen which took place between eleven and twelve at night. She would afterwards fall asleep as soon as she had blown out the candle. The days were long, and though they were punctuated by periods of leisure these were unpredictable: 'sometimes I have not two minutes when I expect two hours, at other times I have two hours where I expected only two minutes'.[26]

She had to reconcile herself to being summoned to the Queen by a bell, 'so mortifying a mark of servitude', and she was not always ready: *run, gallop* and *fly* are words she uses to describe the rush to attendance, sometimes not fully dressed. Once when an unusually early summons made her race from her room inappropriately capless, gloveless and carrying her girdle, she encountered – oh horror! – 'one of the Windsor uniforms' (an equerry). Nearly seventy years later it was claimed by Mrs Delany's great grand-niece, Lady Llanover, that Fanny had been 'utterly unfit . . . for any place requiring punctuality, neatness, and manual dexterity', and that the Queen 'used to complain to Mrs Delany that Miss Burney could not learn to tie the bow of her necklace on court days without giving her pain by getting the hair at the back of the neck tied in with it'.[27] Lady Llanover was hostile to Fanny, as will emerge later, but it may be true that Fanny was clumsy with neck fastenings since she was short-sighted yet forbidden by etiquette from using spectacles.[28] Wearing gloves, as she would have done all day except when eating, would hardly have improved her manual dexterity.

There were other tasks with which Fanny was trusted. One was looking after the Queen's favourite dog, Badine; another was mixing her snuff. One day the Princess Royal brought the Queen's snuffbox with the request that she prepare some; the finely powdered and delicately perfumed tobacco required moistening for use.[29] It was not something she had ever done before, so she was glad when the King complimented her, saying, 'Miss Burney, I hear you cook snuff very well!' Princess Augusta laughed and asked for a pinch, but Princess Elizabeth exclaimed, 'Miss Burney, I hope you hate snuff? I hope you do, for I hate it of all things in the world!'[30] The Queen's addiction to snuff does not otherwise feature in Fanny's journals, though after she left court Mrs Piozzi claimed, without naming her source, that she 'takes off her Mistress to divert M[rs] Locke', which was 'grossly ungrateful'.[31] Fanny was a good mimic and could have given a mocking impression of royal snuff-taking, but since she does not do so in words it seems unlikely that she did so in actions.

However, dog-sitting and snuff-cooking were small duties: it was the daily toilette which was her principal concern. Fanny would willingly have admitted that had the Queen been looking for someone with whom to discuss clothes and fashion she could hardly have made a more unfortunate choice than herself. Unlike Mrs Delany, whose artistic eye was caught by fashion details, she rarely mentions it, and seems from her fiction to have seen it as vulgar to comment on dress. In *Evelina* it is a sign of the lack of refinement in the heroine's city cousins when they quiz her about what she is wearing: 'This apron's your own work, I suppose, Miss? But these sprigs a'nt in fashion now. Pray, if it is not impertinent, what might you give a yard for this lutestring [silk]? – Do you make your own caps, Miss?'[32] Indeed, readers learn very little about the appearances of any of her heroines, whether tall or short, dark or fair, let alone what they wear. On the rare occasions when clothing is described, and especially when colour is mentioned, it is usually a sign of moral error; thus in *Camilla* the heroine gazes guiltily at the expensive elegance of her outfit for a ball:

> Her robe was everywhere edged with the finest Valencienne lace; her lilac shoes, sash, and gloves, were richly spangled with silver, and finished with a silver fringe; her ear-rings and necklace were of lilac and gold beads; her fan and shoe roses were brilliant with lilac foil, and her bouquet of artificial lilac flowers, and her plumes of lilac feathers, were here and there tipt with the most tiny transparent white beads, to give them the effect of being glittering with the dew.[33]

It is an attractive description, but is written to highlight Camilla's dreadful extravagance. It does, however, show that Fanny could recognise elegance – this was the sort of costume she would have seen and handled at court.

In her journals Fanny highlighted her lack of instinct for the rituals of dressing when she told Susan and Fredy that it was a relief to find that in the morning the garments were handed to her in the proper order by Mrs Thielcke, the Wardrobe Maid, for 'I should never know which to take first . . . and should run a prodigious risk of giving the gown before the hoop, and the fan before the neckerchief'.[34] Mrs Thielcke had another vital role. She had to rise even earlier in the morning in order to 'dress' the Queen's hair and help her into her undergarments.[35] There was rank in dressing, and the Wardrobe Maid, who earned £30 a year compared to Fanny's £200, was at a more menial level than a Robe-keeper, while above the middle order came the posts of highest class, the Bedchamber Women, Ladies of the Bedchamber, and Mistress of the Robes, whose duties were more ceremonial than practical and who received £500 a year for them.

As all women then, the Queen would first have put on a short-sleeved shift of fine soft linen which reached just below the knee; its main function was to protect the precious, unwashable silks of the outer clothing from being soiled by contact with the body. Knitted silk stockings, usually white, were worn gartered just above or below the knee. Then came the stays – the Queen had her own stay-maker – of linen or silk brocade stiffened with whalebone; cut high under the arms and laced tightly behind, they both flattened and thrust up the bust and extended to low on the stomach. The Princess Royal and Princess Elizabeth were both curious to know if it was true that Fanny had once split a whalebone in her stays while coughing: it was. When her stays were fitted the Queen was ready to ring the bell for Fanny.

Fashioned to lift out the robe, the hoop was also made with a framework of whalebone, and was tied round the waist, though by 1786 the bulky, clumsy hoop was out of date for normal wear, and the padded 'bum-roll' was the fashion. But the Queen maintained the dress-style worn on her first arrival in England and the hoop was obligatory wear for court appearances: it was a clever way of making fashion leaders like the Duchess of Devonshire conform to *her* dictates. Though not as extreme as earlier in the century when the extraordinary rectangular or fan shapes of the hoop obliged women to shuffle sideways through the door it was still an awkward garment, especially when getting in or out of sedan chairs: since women did not yet wear drawers, a sudden gust of wind could be embarrassing.

For formal court appearances the dress which went over the hoop was an open robe, worn over a petticoat (not then a word for an undergarment); the edges, called 'robings', were turned back, and richly decorated, while the triangular gap left in the bodice was filled in with a stiffened stomacher – the court beauty was armour-plated. As many as 22 yards of expensive silk were needed to make these court robes, or 'sacques', in which the material fell from a double box pleat at the back of the neck, at this date sewn into the bodice but creating trains which swept the ground behind and required careful management. Sleeves were three-quarter length and adorned with layers of lace ruffles.

But in the morning the Queen was more informally arrayed in 'undress', another confusing word to us, especially as it could consist of a 'night-gown' or 'bed-gown' for *day* wear. An undress gown was looser and more comfortable than formal wear. In the early months of Fanny's service the Queen was particularly attached to her 'white dimity great-coat' (dimity was a strong cotton and linen twill), a newly fashionable dress with overlapping collars which buttoned down the front. So enthusiastic was the Queen for this easy-to-wear garment that she repeatedly declared that 'someone' should write a poem about great-coats. Since clothes were of so little interest to Fanny her Muse was 'not so kind as ever to make me think of the matter again when out of her sight', but after what amounted to a royal command she did produce some verses on the subject. They begin:

> Thrice-honour'd Robe! Couldst thou espy
>   The form that deigns to show thy worth;
> Hear the mild voice, view the arch eye,
>   That calls thy panegyric forth;
>
> Wouldst thou not swell with vain delight?
>   With proud expansion sail along?
> And deem thyself more grand and bright
>   Than aught that lives in ancient song?[36]

The dressing ritual continued with the neckerchief, a gauzy scarf with its ends tucked into the corsage; in the 1780s it was worn puffed out for the 'pouter pigeon' look. Gloves or mittens covered the lower arm and heads were always covered too, with caps, hats, or both. Last to be put on were the shoes, not then pairs but 'straights', usually made of material lined with kid and with a low heel; at Christmas 1786 the Queen presented Fanny with 'two pieces of black stuff, very prettily embroidered, for shoes'. When the Queen had been handed her fan, that essential piece of a woman's equipment then, the dressing was complete.

For Fanny the twice-daily performance was tedious; she many times notes the presence of the word 'toil' in 'toilette'. Most time-consuming was the hairdressing session, which could last two hours or more: no wonder the Queen wanted some intelligent conversation. The account which Evelina gives to her guardian when she is prepared for her first London ball describes the process, and gives a good idea how Fanny herself felt about it:

> I have just had my hair dressed. You can't think how oddly my head feels; full of powder and black pins, and a great *cushion* on the top of it. I believe you would hardly know me for my face looks quite different to what it did before my hair was dressed. When I shall be able to make use of a comb for myself I cannot tell for my hair is so much entangled, *frizled* they call it, that I fear it will be very difficult.[37]

Evelina was published in the 1770s, and this 'high' head-dressing was, like the hoops, an outmoded fashion by the 1780s when height had given way to width, though still with plenty of frizzing and stiffening of curls with wire or paste, but the old style was again maintained at court. The coiffure was also beribboned and bejewelled, and a little lacy cap might perch on top or for court occasions ostrich feathers; when Fredy's daughters, Augusta and Amelia, were later to be presented to the Queen, Fanny warned them to be careful not to brush her face with their feathers as they curtsied. Both men and women powdered their heads; the powder, made of starch, was normally white but could be coloured, and was applied to hair or wigs by powder puff or blower. A sheet was spread on the carpet and the Queen put on a powdering robe and sent Fanny away for this part of her toilette, which could be messy. Charlotte Albert, daughter of the Queen's hairdresser, once cut off all her hair and wore a cap 'to escape the disgrace . . . of not being tidy with powder'.[38]

Charlotte married one of the King's pages and, as Mrs Papendiek, was prompted to write her own memoirs after the publication of Fanny's. Many years had passed since the events she described and her chronology is unreliable; her claim that she had been 'Miss Burney's friend' at court may also be doubted since Fanny never mentions her, though she refers a number of times to her father. Mrs Papendiek probably inflated what was only acquaintanceship. Nevertheless, she writes interestingly on some of the social details which Fanny in her day-to-day journalising had no need to explain; moreover, she was as much interested in fashion as Fanny was uninterested, and had a clear memory both of what was worn and the dresses she made or altered for herself.

All through her life, though unconcerned with the niceties of fashion, Fanny spent a great deal of her time in dress preparation, so much so that Mr Cambridge senior once remarked that Miss Burney had no time to write for she was always working at her clothes. How much of her wardrobe Fanny made for herself is not clear, but she would certainly have made some if not all of her dresses, as even the Queen and Princesses did. Though they required vast lengths of material, dresses were sewn up using simple running stitches which could easily be unpicked, so that the pieces could be used as patterns for another robe, or the dress recreated in a new style. Mrs Papendiek tells how during a ten-year period she regularly new-made a 'puce satin' gown, and says that 'a silk gown would go on for years, a little furbished up with new trimmings – and a young woman was rather complimented than otherwise when she exhibited care of her possessions, and might, with no discredit to herself, appear time after time in the same attire'.[39] Fanny would likewise have restyled her gowns – though none would surely have been puce – and friends and relations helped her by creating frills and furbelows to achieve the transformations.

New, or apparently new, clothes were often needed at court; Fanny discovered that for each of the many royal birthdays and other anniversaries not just one but two new outfits were required. This she learnt on the Princess Royal's twentieth birthday in September 1786, two months after her arrival at court. The Princess came to the Queen's dressing-room, and the King brought the younger Princesses there to greet their sister. Three-year-old Princess Amelia showed off her own finery and examined all the new dresses of her sisters, then, looking with surprise at Fanny's everyday great-coat, exclaimed, 'And won't Miss Burney be fine, too?'[40]

Fanny did have a new dress for later in the day, though it had been the cause of some resentment. One day Mrs Schwellenberg had called her to her room and, with little tact, announced, 'The Queen will give you a gown! The Queen says you are not rich'. Fanny found her manner highly offensive and answered proudly that she had two new gowns and did not require another. Now it was Mrs Schwellenberg's turn to take offence: 'Miss Bernar . . . I tell you at once, when the Queen will give you a gown, you must be humble, thankful, when you are the Duchess of Ancaster!' (the Mistress of the Robes).[41] Fanny was obliged to swallow her pride and accept the gown, which proved to be of lilac tabby ('tabby' was the strongest and simplest type of silk weave).

As Mrs Thrale had found, Fanny was touchy on the subject of money. Hester's gift of silk may also have been a length of lilac tabby, for at

Streatham they had played the game of likening each other to different kinds of creature or object and as a silk Fanny had been labelled 'lilac tabby'.[42] Perhaps she remembered these things and they added to her discomfort. But on the evening of the Princess Royal's birthday she put the gown on and was complimented by the King, who called out, 'Emily should see Miss Burney's gown now, and she would think her fine enough'. Miss Burney remained sensitive about it, however. Next month when the Queen received a present of 'the most beautiful double violets' and gave her a bunch to take to Mrs Delany and another to keep for herself, Fanny 'quite longed to tell her how much more I valued such a gift, presented by her own hand, than the richest tabby in the world by a deputy!'[43] No wonder that ten years later Camilla's ill-starred dress is lilac-coloured.

CHAPTER FOUR

Assassination Attempt

Good God! How great an escape! – I am sure the whole Nation must feel it.[1]

Divinity might no longer hedge a King but his life was circumscribed by rigid protocols designed to protect both his person and his dignity. Discreet coughs and smothered sneezes apart, Fanny had to learn a variety of dos and don'ts: do not move close to royalty unless summoned; in an encounter in passage or street retire to the wall and stand 'dead still'; do not pass an open door if royalty is within; face forwards at all times; walk away backwards, and so on. But in the world outside the court these codes of conduct offered only limited protection. On 2 August 1786, only two weeks after Fanny's arrival at court, a woman called Margaret Nicholson tried to stab the King under the guise of presenting him with a petition.

That evening Fanny had been looking for an excuse to leave the tea table so that she could visit Mrs Delany, when the Mistress of the Robes, the Duchess of Ancaster, and her daughter, Lady Charlotte Bertie, came in. They were introduced to Fanny, but were clearly agitated and called Mrs Schwellenberg away. This gave Fanny her opportunity to go to her room for her cloak, but there she found the French reader to the Princesses, Madame de la Fite, who exclaimed, 'Have you heard? – *O mon Dieu! – O le bon Roi! O Miss Burney! – what an horreur!*' The visit to Mrs Delany was abandoned, and a little later Fanny heard the whole story from the Duchess of Ancaster, who had been present when the King came back to Windsor. She set it down for her friends:

> You may have heard it wrong; I will concisely tell it right. His carriage had just stopped at the garden-door at St James's, and he had just alighted from it, when a decently dressed woman, who had been waiting for him some time, approached him with a petition. It was rolled up, and had the usual superscription – 'For the King's Most Excellent Majesty'. She presented it with her right hand; and, at the same moment that the King bent forward to take it, she drew from it, with her left hand, a knife, with which she aimed straight at his heart!
>
> The fortunate awkwardness of taking the instrument with the left hand made her design perceived before it could be executed; – the

King started back, scarce believing the testimony of his own eyes; and the woman made a second thrust, which just touched his waistcoat before he had time to prevent her; – and at that moment one of the attendants, seeing her horrible intent, wrenched the knife from her hand . . .

While the guards and his own people now surrounded the King, the assassin was seized by the populace, who were tearing her away, no doubt to fall the instant sacrifice of her murtherous purpose, when the King, the only calm and moderate person then present, called aloud to the mob, 'The poor creature is mad! – Do not hurt her! She has not hurt me!'[2]

The King continued with the Levée, while the Spanish Envoy hurried to Windsor in case false rumours reached the Queen. But she knew nothing until the King walked into the room, cheerfully declaring 'Here I am! – safe and well, – as you see! – but I have very narrowly escaped being stabbed!' He asked if his waistcoat had been cut; it had not, though as he said 'nothing could have been sooner done, for there was nothing to go through but a thin linen and fat'.

The King was right about Margaret Nicholson. She was a wretched creature, whose sad life illustrates the harsh struggle for survival of single women. Aged about forty, she was born in Stockton-on-Tees in County Durham where her father was a barber, and had come to London as a twelve-year-old to enter service; at some date she had been seduced and abandoned by a valet-de-chambre. She had worked as a sempstress for millinery and mantua-makers (dressmakers), and more recently had been taking in 'plain work' while lodging with a Mr Fisk, a bookseller in Marylebone Lane, who used to hear her muttering to herself. Investigators found incoherent letters to the King in her room, apparently making a claim on the throne. She said that she had only wanted to terrify him into granting her petition which, apart from the heading, was blank. The weapon, an old dessert-knife with a cracked ivory handle, was worn to a point but the blade was so thin that it bent when pressed against a palm and did not penetrate the skin. She had been well attired in a black silk cloak over a flowered muslin dress, with a black bonnet covering a white morning cap with blue ribbons, but it proved that these 'decent' clothes were all that she possessed, and her entire wealth amounted to one silver sixpence and three halfpennies. After examination by the Privy Council she was pronounced 'deranged in her faculties', and sent to be confined for life in Bedlam.[3]

The Queen and Princesses shared none of the King's coolness. The Princesses wept, while the Queen 'could only, from time to time, hold out her hand to the King, and say, "I have you yet!"' Mrs Schwellenberg's certainty that the attempt must be part of some conspiracy did not help. Lamentation and rejoicing alternated, and there was 'not a dry eye in either of the Lodges'. But the King would not allow any change from normal routine. Next day Fanny wrote to her father:

> Without one guard, – or any Attendant but the usual Equerry, last night, in defiance of bad weather, the King was firm to show himself upon the Terrace, – such trust, after such an attack, – is it not proof of innate & superior fortitude? – The poor Queen & Princesses, with pale cheeks & swollen Eyes, accompanied him. – And again this morning to early prayers.[4]

Mrs Delany was shielded from the news the previous evening, but next day she wrote Fanny a note of her shock (using a pencil as her sight was now so poor that she could not find the ink-well with a pen).

Though the King had been in no real danger from Margaret Nicholson the circumstances showed how easy it would have been to kill him, and public reaction was as much to do with what might have happened as what actually did. One consequence of the assassination attempt was that the King was invited to Oxford a fortnight later to receive the congratulations of the University on his escape, and Fanny was told that she was to be in attendance on the Queen.[5] For this new experience Mrs Schwellenberg, in her brusque way, offered only the advice that it would not signify who she was or what she wore since she would be accompanying the Queen:

> You might go quite without no, what you call, fuss; you might take no gown but what you go in: – that is enough, – you might have no servant, – for what? – You might keep on your riding-dress. There is no need you might be seen. I shall do everything that I can to assist you to appear for nobody.[6]

In the early stages of Fanny's court service her lack of social confidence showed itself both in her constant fear of causing offence and also in her readiness to feel affronted; the Oxford visit was to be marred by a belief that she was indeed being treated as 'nobody'.

On this visit the King and Queen were accompanied by their three elder daughters, and they were the guests of Lord and Lady Harcourt at their seat at Nuneham Courtenay, just south of Oxford. George Simon, second Lord Harcourt, who later became Master of the Queen's Horse, had married his cousin Elizabeth Vernon, a Lady of the Bedchamber.[7] Lady Harcourt was perhaps closest of anyone to being a friend to Queen Charlotte, who had been wary of forming relationships which might cause resentment among the nobility or take a political interpretation. Confidence between the two women developed to the point where Lady Harcourt could say to the Queen, 'I should like to tell you something, but pray promise never to let the *Queen* know it', and the Queen laughingly agree.[8]

The King, Queen and Princesses set off for Nuneham on the morning of 12 August, but Fanny and Margaret Planta, her travelling companion, did not leave Windsor till late afternoon. Fanny described Nuneham as 'one of those straggling half-new, half-old, half-comfortable and half-forlorn mansions, that are begun in one generation and finished in another'; in fact, although wings had been added rather piecemeal to the original structure, the house had only been built that century and today is still an elegant Palladian mansion.[9] Her words do, however, reflect the half-uncomfortable, half-comfortable nature of her experience of it. Unfortunately, when their coach drew up at the portico, no one, not even a servant, came out to greet the two women and to help them into the house. If it had not been damp, Fanny, beginning to bristle at seeming to be 'a guest uninvited, a visitor unlooked for', would have remained outside, but Miss Planta urged that they search for their rooms.

Inside they wandered the passages, encountering only 'gold-braid saunterers' who could not or would not help. They took temporary refuge in a parlour but abandoned it when Fanny feared that the royal family might enter.[10] Every minute increased her indignation at their inhospitable reception and she was not appeased when they eventually met with Lady Harcourt. She asked Miss Planta to introduce her to Fanny and greeted her courteously though hurriedly, promising that her sisters, the Miss Vernons, would attend to her needs. Fanny responded with a 'cold' curtsey. Nor did the Miss Vernons appear. The wanderers found the Princesses in their apartment and they were sympathetic, Princess Elizabeth insisting that Fanny abandon her scruples and *sit down* and talk with her. When eventually they located their own apartment Fanny refused to be drawn from it, even when the call came for supper. Miss Planta, a more seasoned courtier, found Fanny's distress comical, nevertheless she good-naturedly, and with the sacrifice of her own supper, kept her company. Matters improved when Lady Harcourt paid a civil visit, and later the Queen informed Fanny that she and Miss Planta were to belong to the royal party next day. She asked Miss Burney what she had brought to wear and Fanny was glad she could reply 'a new Chamberry gauze', instead of the 'nothing but what I have on' of Mrs Schwellenberg's advice.[11]

Fanny was too ready to take offence at Nuneham, but she was placed in an embarrassing position. Her mistake was to assume that on a royal visit things would run smoothly; entertaining King George III was not like receiving Queen Elizabeth I and her entourage but it was still a formidable undertaking. Those servants Fanny suspected of insolence were probably merely ignorant. Fanny began to recognise Lady Harcourt's problems when she discovered that even in her own home she could not, unaddressed, speak to royalty, or, uninvited, enter a room where royalty was. Next day Lady Harcourt found occasion to apologise fulsomely, excusing her sisters on the grounds that one of them was ill, and blaming the confusion on Major Price. This was so obviously absurd that Fanny was not mollified. Lady Harcourt may in fact have been covering up for the Queen: a letter to her from the Queen asks 'if my bringing Miss Planta & the Princesses Maid Servant will not be inconvenient', but makes no mention of Miss Burney, so perhaps no one knew she was coming.[12]

Before the party left for Oxford next morning (Fanny had had to be up at six o'clock to have her hair dressed) a service of thanksgiving for the King's deliverance was held in the chapel; it was built on a little hill in the grounds in the form of a Grecian temple, and Fanny admired 'its plainness and elegance'. She was calmed by the service, and the sense of grievance finally left her in the interest of the day's expedition:

> The city of Oxford afforded us a very noble view on the road, and its spires, towers, and domes soon made me forget all the little objects of minor spleen that had been crossing me as I journeyed towards them; and indeed, by the time I arrived in the midst of them, their grandeur, nobility, antiquity, and elevation impressed my mind so forcibly, that I felt for the first time since my new situation had taken place a rushing in of ideas that had no connection with it whatever.[13]

According to the *Oxford Journal*, 'a vast concourse of people' greeted the royal party's arrival at half-past one, but 'a decent Decorum was universally observed'.[14] The first stop was the Sheldonian Theatre for the University address; it was 'exceedingly crowded, and their Majesties, on their Entrance, seemed highly pleased with the splendour of the Appearance'.[15] The King, Queen and Princesses were seated, but all else stood while listening to the Vice-Chancellor. When he spoke of the danger to the King, Fanny wrote that the Princesses wept, the Queen wiped tears from her face with her fan, and once again there was not a dry eye to be seen; the *Oxford Journal* confirms her words: 'The Audience . . . as well as the royal visitors conspicuously displayed their tender

Feelings during the reading of the Address'. The King responded with his own short speech of thanks, delivered in a voice which must have been unlike his normal speaking manner for it surprised Fanny with its 'ease, feeling, and force'. He declared that 'The University of Oxford may ever depend on my inclination to encourage every branch of science, as the more my subjects are enlightened, the more they must be attached to the excellent constitution established in this realm'.[16]

After an organ had 'anthem-ed, and voluntary-ed' the assembly for some time, the mood changed, at least for Fanny, as she was diverted by watching the professors and doctors taking turns to kiss the royal hand:

> Some of the worthy collegiates, unused to such ceremonies, and unaccustomed to such a presence, the moment they had kissed the King's hand, turned their backs to him, and walked away as in any common room; others, attempting to do better, did still worse, by tottering and stumbling, and falling foul of those behind them; some, ashamed to kneel, took the King's hand straight up to their mouths; others, equally off their guard, plumped down on both knees, and could hardly get up again; and many, in their confusion, fairly arose by pulling His Majesty's hand to raise them.[17]

Walking backwards out of the royal presence was an art which Fanny herself had not yet acquired, especially in a sacque, but the Oxford expedition proved a learning experience in a number of ways. Later in the day she watched a demonstration by a master of what she satirically called 'the true court retrograde motion'. In Christ Church College, where they visited the picture gallery, Fanny had been admiring a Holbein portrait of King Henry VIII when King George III entered and forced her into awkward retreat. Lady Charlotte Bertie had been similarly trapped, but she was equal to the occasion. Despite nursing a painful twisted ankle she swept out of the room, 'perfectly upright, without one stumble, without ever looking once behind her to see what she might encounter; and with as graceful a motion, and as easy an air, as I ever saw anybody enter a long room'.[18] Fanny herself sought the safety of the wainscot from which she crept backwards a few paces at a time, frequently pretending to admire some portrait in order to disentangle her heels from the train of her dress.

The tour round the colleges excited her; she had never been to Oxford before, though her father had acquired his doctorate there, and she felt little tiredness, absorbed by the old buildings, the libraries and works of art, and wanting to miss nothing. At one point the Duchess of Ancaster cried sympathetically, 'Poor Miss Burney! I wish she could sit down, for she is unused to this work. She does not know yet what it is to stand for five hours following, as we do'. But Fanny knew that she was relatively fortunate in this respect and that her post would not involve her in such lengthy standing; Duchesses and Countesses paid for their high places in the hierarchy by being required to stand immobile behind the seats of the King and Queen throughout ceremonies, performances of plays, concerts and so on. At a concert in Worcester in 1788 Lady Harcourt was feeling so ill from flu that she 'was forced to ask permission to resign her place to Lady Pembroke', permission that would not have been granted – *could* not have been granted Queen Charlotte would have said – had Lady Pembroke not also been a Lady of the Bedchamber.[19] Being of a lower rank was of some advantage to Fanny then as she had a seat. In fact, this Oxford visit was to be the only occasion in her court career when Fanny performed a ceremonial role and Miss Burney, Keeper of the Robes, is indeed listed as part of the official train in the *Oxford Journal*.

Fanny discovered another drawback to the attendants' life: there was no provision for refreshment. At Trinity College, where they arrived at about three o'clock, 'an elegant Repast was upon the Tables', but not for the attendants, who had to stand still in a semicircle and watch the royal family eat.[20] Whisper of their famished state reached the 'worthy Doctors' and in a buzz of further whispering a rescue plan was conceived, taking into account that to eat in the presence of the royal family was as impossible as to sit down:

> Major Price and Colonel Digby . . . seeing a very large table close to the wainscot behind us, desired our refreshments might be privately conveyed there, behind the semicircle, and that, while all the group backed very near it, one at a time might feed, screened by all the rest from observation . . .
>
> This plan had speedy success, and the very good Doctors soon, by sly degrees and with watchful caution, covered the whole table with tea, coffee, chocolate, cakes, and bread and butter.
>
> The further plan, however, of one at a time feasting and the rest fasting and standing sentinels, was not equally approved; there was too much eagerness to seize the present moment, and too much fear of a sudden retreat, to give patience for so slow a proceeding. We could do no more, therefore, than stand in a double row, with one to screen one throughout the troop; and, in this manner, we were all very plentifully and very pleasantly served.[21]

Colonel Stephen Digby, the Queen's Vice-Chamberlain, was two years later to play an important part in Fanny's life at court; it was typical of him to show concern for the well-being of the attendants. As Fanny and Miss Planta wandered through another college, Digby came up behind and whispered that there was a small parlour nearby, belonging to the Master, where she could take some rest. Miss Planta was desperately tired, so for her sake rather than her own Fanny agreed. Once they were seated, Digby produced from his pocket a paper with some apricots and more bread and butter, but suddenly the door opened and the Queen and attendants entered. For one of the few times in her journals a very sharp note enters Fanny's comments:

> Up we all started, myself alone not discountenanced; for I really think it quite respect sufficient never to sit down in the royal presence, without aiming at having it supposed I have stood bolt upright ever since I have been admitted to it.
>
> Quick into our pockets was crammed our bread, and close into our hands was squeezed our fruit; by which I discovered that our appetites were to be supposed annihilated, at the same time that our strength was to be invincible.[22]

She must have been infected by the disputatious air of Oxford.

Of the other basic physical need Fanny never makes mention. At the palaces the Queen employed 'necessary women' for the sanitary arrangements in both the private and public apartments, and there were water closets, at least for the royal family. As early as 1703 Celia Fiennes, the indefatigable sightseer who never left a door-handle unturned, had discovered and marvelled at them in Queen Anne's house at Windsor (which became Queen's Lodge): each closet had 'a seate of easement of marble with sluces of water to wash all down'.[23] But flush toilets did not become efficient until the nineteenth century, and even royals often made do with close-stools and chamber-pots (called jordans). After a royal visit to Wilton House in 1778 a Dr Eyre wrote: 'The Blue Closet within was for her Majesty's private purposes, where there was a red new velvet Close Stool, and a very handsome China Jordan, which I had the honour to produce from an old collection, & you may be sure, I am as proud as Punch that her Majesty condescended to piss in it.'[24] For Fanny to allude to bodily functions of this nature is unimaginable; even to her sister there is never the most veiled reference to menstruation, for example. So what facilities were available at Oxford for the courtiers to relieve themselves can only be guessed. Possibly there was a closed carriage with a close-stool, though since they had nothing to drink for most of the day none might have been needed. It was an aspect of royal service that did require management, however, since no one could leave the royal presence without permission; some of those present may have known of the woman in the previous reign who had reached a point during a Drawing-room when she could no longer hold her water and a huge puddle consequently spread from under her skirts almost to the feet of the Princess of Wales (the King's mother).[25]

Despite its inauspicious beginning, the Oxford visit became a happy memory for Fanny. Often during the day she wished her father could have been among the Doctors, and she was able to write to him with unforced enthusiasm that 'It was, – in one word, – *delightful* to me', and of her wish that she could have 'seen my dearest father among all the good fat Doctors who followed the Vice Chancellor with the address'.[26] All ended as pleasantly as it had begun distressingly. The following day the royal family paid a visit to Blenheim Palace where they were saluted on arrival by 'the firing of eleven cannon', but this time Fanny was left behind at Nuneham.[27] There she was taken on a tour of the house and gardens (laid out by Capability Brown) by the two Miss Vernons, with whom she now made her peace. They worked assiduously to entertain her, and Fanny willingly acquitted them of inhospitality. She had received a further apology, this time from the Countess's sister-in-law, wife to General Harcourt, and since she had found Mrs Harcourt a tiresome rattle at the breakfast table she was happy to lay responsibility for the indignities of her arrival at this lady's door.[28] Far better to blame someone she did not care for than those to whom she now felt drawn.

CHAPTER FIVE

Royals, Rituals, and Retainers

[I] resolved . . . to settle myself in my monastery, without one idea of ever
quitting it; – to study for the approbation of my lady abbess . . . and to
associate more cheerily with my surrounding nuns and monks.[1]

Shortly before Christmas 1786, the Reverend Charles de Guiffardière, the
Queen's French reader, spoke to Fanny about the Queen's official
birthday celebrations in January, and then, in words which must have
chilled her, added:

'You have now nearly seen the whole of everything that will come
before you: in a very short time you will have passed six months here,
and then you will know your life for as many, and twice and thrice as
many years. You will have seen everybody and everything, and the
same round will still be the same, year after year, without
intermission or alteration.'[2]

Christmas came, and Fanny wanted no one to wish her 'what was so far
from possibility – a merry Christmas'. The separation from family and
friends was a never-healing wound, and she still felt the humiliation of
her 'servant' status. Even the words the Queen used to dismiss her
attendants, 'Now I will let you go', suggested bondage. Queen Charlotte
was – in so far as consciousness of their positions allowed it – considerate,
encouraging Fanny to take exercise for her health, and looking for
occasions to send her to Mrs Delany. After the Queen's death in 1818
Fanny wrote that 'From the time of my first entrance into her household
her manner to me was most kind and encouraging', but at the time
Fanny found that her manner was not invariably kind.[3] She records a
surge of 'republican feelings' one day when the Queen seemed unwilling
to accept her reason for being missing when wanted, that she had been
informed that Her Majesty had gone with the King to Windsor. Fanny
later confessed to Stephen Digby that she was initially distressed by the
'inequalities' in the Queen's behaviour until she accepted these
inconsistencies as 'the effect of a royal education and Court system'.
'Kindness, like places,' she sourly commented, 'must be portioned out.'[4]

Some days of illness in the New Year gave Fanny the chance to reflect, to see that her lot was better than many another's, and to resolve to accept it for what it was. She was touched when the King came to enquire personally whether she would be well enough for the Birthday. Fanny was not acquisitive but, apart from the tabby silk where it was the manner of giving that offended, she treasured presents she received from her royal mistress which showed appreciation of her services; her New Year gift was a set of 'very beautiful white and gold china for tea, a coffee-pot, cream-jug, and milk-jug, in forms remarkably pretty'.[5] Later gifts included a mahogany writing-box, a gold pen and inkstand, and a gold enamelled pocket watch and chain.

It was gratifying that as she grew less stiff herself the Queen sought to engage her more in conversation, though she was conscious now of being a member of the royal household and did not, as she might have done, note down anything indiscreet. As recorded in her own style by Hester Piozzi, the actress Sarah Siddons who came to court to read to the royal family told her that 'our Queen was not one of those who let the Maids comb Secrets out of her Head, & that She certainly had no immediate & personal Partiality for Fanny Burney'.[6] But the Queen *did* confide in Fanny and was never betrayed – on her return to court after her resignation Fanny was to write that she had 'the pleasure to find the whole Household firmly persuaded I shall regard the secrets of the Royal *House* to be as sacred now I am at large, as when I was one of the inmates'.[7] The Queen took pleasure in their conversations and when Mrs Delany commented that Fanny 'wants so much drawing out', she replied, 'Yes, but she's very well worth it'.[8] This Fanny could not forbear passing on to her 'equally blind partialists', Susan and Fredy. Watched and derided by caricaturists, it must have been difficult for Queen Charlotte to relax and be humorous, but she could make a joke: the Princess Royal's birthday on 29 September coincided with Miss Goldsworthy's, and in 1788 the Queen asked Fanny to go and fetch the 'two Michaelmas geese'.[9]

Though her taste in literature was narrower than Fanny's, the Queen, an avid book collector, liked to discuss her reading, not of course fiction but letters, biographies, scientific works or books of travel, and especially works of a religious or moral nature. She lent Fanny books, though some brought little pleasure: of one called *Filial Duty* by a Mrs Scott she drily wrote, 'I think I have seldom perused anything that has contained less to surprise'. But surprise, even shock awaited her when she borrowed a book as yet unread by the Queen, Horace Walpole's tragedy *The Mysterious Mother*. He had promised Fanny a copy next time she visited his home at Strawberry Hill. To her horror, she found that the mother's mysterious secret was an incestuous relationship with her son; when she returned the book to the Queen she was 'earnest in my hopes that she would never deign to cast her eye upon it'.[10] (Surely she must have looked into it as soon as she had given Miss Burney leave to depart?)

The Queen's life was controlled by ritual and timetable quite as much as her Robe-keeper's; her cage might be gilded, but it was still a cage. The rigid patterning is illustrated by the diary she kept of her daily activities. Unfortunately, most of the Queen's personal papers were destroyed after her death and only two diaries survive from the period of Fanny's office, dark blue, neatly written exercise books, interleaved with blotting-paper, which cover the second half of 1789.[11] The entries show why Fanny worried so much about punctuality, for exact times are Queen Charlotte's preoccupation – her days ticked by with the regularity of a metronome. Any entry can be taken as typical; that written at Windsor on 28 October 1789 is unusual only in its afterthought, a reminder that terrible events were unfolding in France:

> We breakfasted by 9 after Early Prayers. ½ Hour after the Princesses Walkd, & at 10 The K^g set off for London. I went into my Room where I staid till 12 then playd upon the Harpsichord till ½ after one, then Dressd & ½ Hour after two Mr de Luc came & read to me till 4 then we went to Dinner. ¼ after five we went Upstairs & drank Caffé, & at Six the Princesses went to their Masters, L^{dy} Holderness to Her room & I playd with Mr Horn upon the Harpsichord till ½ Hour after seven when the K^g arrived, the Music begun immediately. The three Younger Princesses, L^{dy} Courtown & Miss Townsend came at 8. We drank Tea, & the K^g playd with Monsieur de Budé & I playd with L^{dies} Holderness, Courtown & C. Finch. The Princesses workd. We parted at 10. Suppd & retired at 11. L^{dy} Courtown & Miss Townsend staid supper.
>
> To Day the K^g gave Audience to the Duke of Orleans, who is not come in a public Capacity but brought only a Private Letter from the French K^g.
>
> Very Fine all Day.[12]

The retired, staid life of the King and Queen evidenced here caused amazement to foreigners; ironically, a French diplomat thought that 'the want of splendour and gaiety had an ominous aspect, that tended to revolution'.[13]

The only evidence in these diaries that Fanny was ever present is implied in the word 'Dressd'; she could still have been in the room when

André de Luc came to conduct his reading. He was Swiss, scarcely able to 'speak four words of English' according to Fanny, which makes his appointment as English reader strange. But the Queen shared with de Luc an enthusiasm for natural science (with her precise mind she might have made a fine scientist herself). That autumn he installed a rain gauge and three thermometers for her – the Queen always noted the day's 'Wheather' in her diary – so some of their time together may have been spent in scientific discussion. She had a musical talent as well, with a sweet singing voice, and as the diary reveals played the harpsichord, sometimes accompanying the King on the flute, but she may have lacked his passion for Handel for she never elaborates on the phrase 'the Music begun' [sic] of the evening concerts. No day was complete without some card-game; commerce, piquet, cribbage, and 'reversi' are named in these diaries.[14] Any stakes would have been small ones, however, for though it was an addiction of fashionable high society the King disapproved of gambling.

The three elder Princesses also led very structured lives (unlike their unruly brothers), and had to observe the rules of etiquette with respect to the King and Queen – when the Princess Royal had tried to help Fanny by looking for her rooms at Nuneham she returned unsuccessful for 'the King was that way, and so, you know, I could not go past him'. The 'work' they undertook in the evening was not scholastic but with the needle, and they had helped create some of the furnishings of Queen's Lodge. This domesticity of the English royal family was often mocked, though the fairy-tale beauty of the sisters could only arouse admiration. Fanny tried to differentiate between them, praising 'the Princess Royal for figure, the Princess Augusta for countenance, and the Princess Elizabeth for face'.[15] With the beauty went unassuming charm, friendliness and lively spirits. Fanny came to love them all, though because they lived in the Lower Lodge at Windsor she saw less of the three younger siblings, Princesses Mary, Sophia and Amelia.

Mary and Sophia she first met on the morning of the assassination attempt. Princess Mary was 'capering upstairs' when she saw Fanny, whereupon she stopped and 'inquired how I did, with all the elegant composure of a woman of maturest age'.[16] A little later Princess Sophia came to her room; Fanny had been looking after Badine and the Princess had come to retrieve the dog's basket, 'curtseying and colouring' as she asked for it. The youngest princess, Amelia, became for Fanny, as for everyone else, a special favourite; a few days after these encounters Fanny went with Mrs Delany to watch the procession on the Terrace to celebrate her third birthday:

It was really a mighty pretty procession. The little Princess . . . in a robe-coat covered with fine muslin, a dressed close cap, white gloves, and a fan, walked on alone and first, highly delighted in the parade, and turning from side to side to see everybody as she passed: for all the terracers stand up against the walls, to make a clear passage for the Royal Family, the moment they come in sight.[17]

Fanny's heart was taken for ever when the little girl put up her face to her to be kissed.

In the more informal setting of the White House at Kew Amelia discovered in Miss Burney someone with whom to play games. One day in November when she and Mr Smelt were pretending to drive the Princess about in a phaeton the King came into the room, causing the usual scattering and an immediate end to the Princess's fun. This did not please the child who began at once 'Miss Burney! – come! why don't you play? – Come, Miss Burney, I say, play with me! – come into the phaeton again! – why don't you, Miss Burney?' A whisper that she could play no more did nothing to quieten her:

'But why? why, Miss Burney? – do! do come and play with me! – You must, Miss Burney!'

This petition growing still more and more urgent, I was obliged to declare my reason, in hopes of appeasing her, as she kept pulling me by the hand and gown, so entirely with all her little strength, that I had the greatest difficulty to save myself from being suddenly jerked into the middle of the room: at length, therefore, I whispered, 'We shall disturb the King, ma'am!'

This was enough; she flew instantly to His Majesty, who was in earnest discourse with Mr Smelt, and called out, 'Papa, go!'

'What?' cried the King.

'Go! Papa, – you must go!' repeated she eagerly.[18]

Papa took her into his arms but still she struggled, calling out 'Miss Burney! Miss Burney! take me! – come, I say, Miss Burney! – Oh Miss Burney, come!' In his own time the King took his departure and the game resumed. Not long afterwards Fanny gave the little girl a present of a pincushion, which 'ingenious' Fredy had made. 'Her delight was excessive,' Fanny reported, though today we might not think a pincushion suitable for a three-year-old. Fanny herself received a gift from the Princess of a tiny egg-shaped ivory box containing a perfumed sponge.[19]

A few weeks later, Princess Augusta was to open the ball at St James's Palace to celebrate the Queen's official birthday on 18 January, a duty normally carried out by the Princess Royal, who on this occasion was ill; Princess Augusta invited Fanny to watch from the Lord Chamberlain's box.[20] It was another day when everyone had to be new dressed. The Queen's preference was for neatness and simplicity but she recognised that appearance was part of her function and had, in the year just ended, paid milliners, mercers, laceman, mantua-maker, glover, shoe-maker, staymakers, hoopmaker and trimming-maker a total of nearly £4,500.[21] It was her jewelry, however, which enabled her truly to outshine other women at the court. On their marriage, George III had presented his Queen with a magnificent collection, including a stomacher decorated with Brazilian diamonds worth £70,000.[22] In her early appearances she had glittered with diamonds, worn round her neck and wrists, on her head, from her ears, and sewn all over her robes, of such a quantity and size that she earned a reputation, never lost, for inordinate fondness for jewels. But she told Fanny that though she had been dazzled at first, that was soon over:

'Believe me, Miss Burney, it is a pleasure of a week, – a fortnight, at most, – and to return no more! I thought, at first, I should always choose to wear them; but the fatigue and trouble of putting them on, and the care they required, and the fear of losing them, believe me, ma'am, in a fortnight's time I longed again for my own earlier dress, and wished never to see them more!'[23]

The bulk of the jewelry remained in town in winter and at Windsor in the summer, but the box with the 'travelling jewels' was entrusted to Fanny. This responsibility was to bring a troubled end to the birthday ball.

The day began with peals of bells rung alternately from St Margaret's Westminster and St Martin's in the Fields, and these continued all day. At noon the guns of Hyde Park and the Tower fired a salute, and in the evening the streets of the capital were brilliantly illuminated. During the afternoon members of the government, the nobility, and foreign ambassadors flocked to a Grand Court at St James's Palace to congratulate the Queen on the day. As at the twice-weekly Drawing-rooms, they stood round the walls (no chairs were provided) and her Majesty circled the room, speaking to everybody in turn. Afterwards there was a struggle in the dusk to find sedan-chairs or carriages, and it was reported in the *Morning Chronicle* that 'several of the light-fingered gentry' had taken advantage and relieved the rich and famous of their watches and purses. The royal family then retired to dine at the Queen's House, returning to St James's for the ball, which began at nine o'clock.

As far as Fanny was concerned, the day she had spent with milliners and mantua-makers to make ready her own attire had been one of 'wasteful toil'. The Drawing-rooms and these special occasions she found very wearisome; she had to begin her own 'full hair-dressing' at six in the morning and set out for London in the early hours but, even in the middle of winter, was forbidden by etiquette from covering her court gown with a cloak. Impatient with the whole proceeding, she does not describe her robe for the birthday, but whatever it was it received the Queen's approval and the Princesses also 'spoke very kind words . . . about my frippery on this festival'. The rituals of the occasion required that a Bedchamber Woman hand the Queen her gloves and fan, and tie on her necklace (belying Lady Llanover's claim that on court days Fanny mistied it). While they were being summoned Fanny was given the office of holding her train: this she knew she should consider a great honour, but it left her feeling like a stage mute.

As she had been bidden, Fanny watched the dancing from the spectators' box, using her opera glass so that she could see clearly. She felt she could understand from 'the motion of the Queen's lips, and the expression of her face . . . the gracious and pleasant speeches she made to all whom she approached'; she would have been far more interested to know what she said than she was to observe what she wore, though she does note that the Queen's dress was 'extremely simple, the style of dress considered'. That comment was also made by the reporter for the *Morning Chronicle* who declared that the Queen's 'amiable smiles of cheerfulness and benignity' were ornament enough for the occasion. The King's suit was of 'a rich puissé embroidered', and the two Princesses' dresses of 'cream-coloured satin, richly trimmed with gauze and blue foil'.[24] It was a pity that there was no handsome Prince to lead the eighteen-year-old Princess Augusta into the first minuet, the Prince of Wales being on such bad terms with his parents that he did not attend.[25] Instead, the Princess opened the ball with her uncle, the Duke of Cumberland, resplendent in crimson and gold.[26] The stately minuets which customarily opened a ball were followed by more lively country dances. The first of these went to the tune of 'Good morning to your Night-cap', with which hint the *Chronicle* reporter 'quitted the ballroom and retired to rest', but Fanny remained as instructed till after the second country dance shortly before midnight, when she slipped away to attend the Queen in her apartment and take charge of her jewelry.

Outside, however, there were neither servant nor sedan-chair as expected. Uncertain what to do, Fanny returned to the waiting-room where her agitation attracted the attention of a young clergyman; he insisted on handing her into the hire-chair which was eventually found for her. Then her problems really began. The brick-built St James's Palace, begun in the reign of Henry VIII and added to by later monarchs, was a maze of courts and passages, and to her distress Fanny realised that she had no idea where the Queen's apartment was. All she could say was that it was 'near the park'. Her companion looked at her in astonishment:

'Ma'am,' said he, 'half the palace is in the park!'

'I don't know how to direct,' cried I, in the greatest embarrassment, 'but it is somewhere between Pall Mall and the park.'

'I know where the lady lives well enough,' cried one of the chairmen, ''tis in St James's Street.'

'No, no,' cried I, ''tis in St James's Palace.'

'Up with the chair!' cried the other man, 'I know best – 'tis in South Audley Street; I know the lady well enough.'

Think what a situation at the moment! I found they had both been drinking the Queen's health till they knew not what they said, and could with difficulty stand. Yet they lifted me up, and though I called in the most terrible fright to be let out, they carried me down the steps.[27]

Luckily Fanny's clergyman-friend came to her rescue. After enquiring for directions, he told the chairmen to follow him, but they refused his orders and to Fanny's terror entered a blind alley and ran their poles against a wall. She grew even more frightened when after backing out they reached a court where sentries threatened to run a bayonet through anyone going further, and she screamed again to be let out. It took an exorbitant half a crown before the men would leave, and still Fanny was in a plight – in her court finery, at midnight, in the rain, with a stranger, and totally lost. Finally, the pair found an open door and Fanny discovered someone within who could direct her. She took leave of the clergyman 'with a thousand acknowledgements for his benevolence and services', and was just in time for the Queen.

With another would-be gallant she was much less pleased. On her journey back to Windsor, Fanny was accompanied by the Reverend de Guiffardière, known as Giffy to the Princesses, and found it uncomfortable to be closeted alone with him for three and a half hours. He was not the 'serious, silent, quiet, and observant' man she had at first thought, but importunate, intrusive and insensitive to rebuff, to be given the nickname 'Mr Turbulent' in correspondence with Susan. Page after page of her subsequent journals were concerned with this reverend gentleman's antics as he acted out an apparently desperate attachment to her. Never taking no for an answer he would push his way into her room then refuse to leave, make 'oeuillades' at her from behind the Queen's back, or snatch her hand for a kiss. He was a big man, over 6 feet tall, which made the posturings the more ridiculous. Susan expressed herself 'both scandalised and frightened' by his behaviour, though Fanny thought his declared attachment was more to her books than to herself. It seems likely that he could not resist teasing her by playing the fictional hero (Delvile is the hero in *Cecilia*):

> I . . . told him I must run & Dress, or be again not ready, through his fault. He quite disregarded me, & vowing he would be heard, he followed me to my Room, calling out 'I *must* speak with you! I am bursting, I am crammed, – I am BeDelviled & Ceciliad, – all over, & through & through . . .
>
> 'Stay, stay,' said he, 'I beg of you, & let me speak to you a little first! – I can never see you – never get a sight of you for a moment, – & I think of nothing else; – I can never find you, – read of you! – never have you an instant out of my Head, night or day! –'
>
> I knew all this meant Cecilia, which he is still reading . . . I knew, 'twas the Book, not the Writer, he was thus worshipping.[28]

That Giffy enjoyed teasing is seen from the baiting to which he subjected Princess Augusta when a possible match with a Danish prince was talked of; she lost patience and snapped 'How can you be such a fool!'[29] Fanny might have taken a lesson from her.

For the household attendants such as de Guiffardière, the social centre of the day was the evening tea table, presided over by Mrs Schwellenberg or Fanny in her absence, when the men joined the women. Most of these men were the King's equerries, some of whom became good friends to Fanny: Major William Price and Colonels Philip Goldsworthy, Francis Edward Gwynn, and Robert Fulke Greville. Unlike robe-keepers, equerries served for only three months at a time, and one of the aspects of the tea-hour which Fanny at first disliked was that these 'Windsor uniforms' were always changing (but if her own employment had been similarly rotated she might have liked it well).

The equerry who comes most vividly to life in her journals is the middle-aged Colonel Goldsworthy, brother of Martha Goldsworthy, the

Princesses' sub-governess. Fanny relished his dry wit, exercised in grumbling at his duties though there was no one more loyal to the King. Susan, who nicknamed everyone at court in case her letters were seen by prying eyes, called him 'Colonel Glum'. His woeful mock-complaints not only amused Fanny but also spoke for herself:

'After all one's labours, riding, and walking, and standing, and bowing – what a life it is? Well! it's honour! that's one comfort; it's all honour! royal honour! – one has the honour to stand till one has not a foot left; and to ride till one's stiff, and to walk till one's ready to drop, – and then one makes one's lowest bow, d'ye see, and blesses one's self with joy for the honour!'[30]

Colonel Goldsworthy warned Fanny of the perils of the winter to come, counting all the draughts, enough 'to carry a man of war', which would assail her between her room and the Queen's. He entreated her to stay away from early morning prayers in the Castle chapel or suffer the regular fate of Queen, Princesses and attendants, who 'drop off; one after another, like so many snuffs of candles; till at last, dwindle, dwindle, dwindle – not a soul goes to the chapel but the King, the parson, and myself; and there we three freeze it out together!'[31]

For a collector of characters, Colonel Goldsworthy was a gift. A day or so later he came in so weary after hunting that he would not have spoken a word, until teased into resuming his theme by Marianne Port:

'After all the labours . . . of the chase, all the riding, the trotting, the galloping, the leaping, the – with your favour, ladies, I beg pardon, I was going to say a strange word, but the – the perspiration – and – and all that – after being wet through over head, and soused through under feet, and popped into ditches, and jerked over gates, what lives we do lead! Well, it's all honour! that's my only comfort! Well, after all this, fagging away like mad from eight in the morning to five or six in the afternoon, home we come, looking like so many drowned rats, with not a dry thread about us, nor a morsel within us – sore to the very bone, and forced to smile all the time! and then after all this what do you think follows? – "Here, Goldsworthy," cries His Majesty: so up I comes to him, bowing profoundly, and my hair dripping down to my shoes; "Goldsworthy," cries His Majesty. "Sir," says I, smiling agreeably, with the rheumatism just creeping all over me! but still, expecting something a little comfortable, I wait patiently to know his gracious pleasure, and then, "Here, Goldsworthy, I say!" he cries, "will you have a little barley water?" Barley water in such a plight as that! Fine compensation for a wet jacket, truly! – barley water! I never heard of such a thing in my life! Barley water after a whole day's hard hunting!'

'And pray did you drink it?'

'I drink it? – Drink barley water? no, no; not come to that neither! But there it was, sure enough! – in a jug fit for a sick-room; just such a thing as you put upon a hob in a chimney, for some poor miserable soul that keeps his bed! just such a thing as that! – And, "Here, Goldsworthy," says His Majesty, "here's the barley water!"'

'And did the King drink it himself?'

'Yes, God bless His Majesty! but I was too humble a subject to do the same as the King! – Barley water, quoth I! – Ha! Ha! – a fine treat truly! – Heaven defend me! I'm not come to that, neither! bad enough too, but not so bad as that.'[32]

The Colonel claimed that the comfort of his life was the half-hour around the tea table, but for Fanny this time was often made miserable by the domineering presence of Mrs Schwellenberg. Elizabeth Juliana Schwellenberg might be compared with John Brown or the Munshi in the reign of Queen Victoria: beloved of the monarch but hated by the household. Born in 1728, she was nearly twice the age of the Queen when she came over with her from Mecklenberg-Strelitz, and she must have been something of a mother-figure for the seventeen-year-old girl. But as a foreigner she was suspiciously regarded in England and thought to influence the Queen improperly. Peter Pindar mocked her in his satiric poem 'The Lousiad', which describes her as having been placed by the Queen in 'a most important sphere/INSPECTRESS GENERAL of the Royal Geer [sic]'. The poem tells how the King discovers a louse in a dish of peas and calls to Mrs Schwellenberg for each head and 'filthy jowl' of cook and scullion to be shaved:

> To whom the DAME, with elevated chin,
> Wide-staring eyes, and broad, contemptuous grin:
> 'Yes, sure as dat my soul is to be sav'd,
> So sure de dirty rascals sal be shav'd.'[33]

There was enough truth in the portrayal to be wickedly effective.

Fanny respected her superior's fierce loyalty to her mistress while irritated that she regarded the slightest hint of criticism as a treasonable offence; Stephen Digby had fallen foul of her by wishing that the Queen's name had not been linked in a newspaper paragraph with that of Marian Hastings, wife of Warren Hastings, the impeached former Governor-

General of India. Marian was a close friend of Mrs Schwellenberg, who never forgave 'Colonel what-you-call' for his impudence.[34] This aggressive devotion had its counterpart in bullying behaviour to subordinates. Diffident Fanny was only too easy to intimidate, though on occasions she may have over-reacted to a blunt, tactless manner. Like Giffy, Mrs Schwellenberg did not tell her own story, but other members of the court also experienced her splenetic outbursts. She suffered severely from asthma and when she had a bad attack Fanny felt compassion, but illness made her temper worse; Peggy Planta once lamented, 'Ah Miss Burney, if Mrs. Schwellenberg was not so sick – and so cross – how happily we might all live!'[35] Even Mrs Delany was not exempt from rudeness, and Fredy was so incensed by the treatment of Fanny that she fantasised about punishment (the masculine pronoun is used, like Susan's nicknames, in case the wrong person read her letter):

> I am most afraid for her [Fanny] when she is frightened by the odious Monster's savage violence . . . I want to throw him out of the window and from hence into a Blanket & out of that into the Horse Pond.[36]

Yet Marian Hastings kept a miniature portrait of her, encircled with pearls, and told a visitor that she would 'never forget that Miss Schwellenberg was my benefactress, giving me dresses and linen when I left for East India'.[37]

Fanny thought her jealous: jealous of a rival for the Queen's esteem and for the attention of the equerries. Another reason may have been financial. When Fanny was engaged by the Queen her annual salary was set at £200; for years both Mrs Schwellenberg and Mrs Hagedorn, Fanny's predecessor, had been receiving £127 a year, and Mrs Schwellenberg was not given an increase.[38] It is said she was offered one and refused it, but consciousness of her sacrifice could have coloured her attitude to Fanny. There may have been a touch of jealousy in Fanny too: in the Queen's dressing-room the two chattered away in German and Fanny felt excluded.

If she could have asserted herself more Fanny might have prevented some excesses of behaviour, but it was not in her temperament. Her only defence was silence. Since it was resented if she spoke to the equerries at the tea table, she voluntarily put herself into Coventry and was the more miserable – 'in her presence little *i* am fairly as one annihilated' she wrote, the lower case emphasising how crushed she felt.[39] Mrs Schwellenberg ignored her in company, yet nevertheless expected her to be in attendance in her apartment, not as 'her visitor at my own option, but her companion, her humble companion, at her own command!'[40] Fanny disliked card-games but she learnt piquet, Mrs Schwellenberg's favourite, and used playing or not playing as a strategy in her handling of this difficult woman. Nicknaming her enemy was another way to relieve her feelings: she was La Présidente, the Lady of the Manor, and Cerbera, a feminised form of Cerberus, the multi-headed dog who guarded Hades. The equerries called her 'Schwelly' but she only pretended to mind their teasing: 'comical men! They bin bears!'[41] She had her favourites, though Colonel Goldsworthy was not one of them. He disliked her and was inclined to feign sleep at her tea parties. This once led to a ludicrous exchange after illness had left Fanny in charge:

> A few evenings after her confinement she very gravely said, 'Colonel Goldsworthy always sleeps with me! sleeps he with you the same?'
>
> In the midst of all my irksome discomfort, it was with difficulty I could keep my countenance at this question, which I was forced to negative.
>
> The next evening she repeated it. 'Vell, sleeps he yet with you – Colonel Goldsworthy?'
>
> 'Not yet, ma'am,' I hesitatingly answered.
>
> 'Oh! ver vell! he will sleep with nobody but me!'[42]

It no doubt gave Fanny satisfaction to hold her English up to ridicule; the Queen's German accent and her interjections of 'So!' are never mocked.

One of Schwelly's eccentricities was her choice of pet:

> What a stare was drawn from our new equerry the following evening, by Major Price's gravely asking Mrs. Schwellenberg after the health of her Frogs! She answered they were very well, and the Major said, 'You must know, Colonel Gwynn, Mrs. Schwellenberg keeps a pair of Frogs.'
>
> 'Of Frogs? – pray what do they feed upon?'
>
> 'Flies, sir,' she answered.
>
> 'And pray, ma'am, what food have they in winter?'
>
> 'Nothing other.'
>
> The stare was now still wider.
>
> 'But I can make them croak when I will,' she added; 'when I only go so to my snuff-box, knock, knock, knock, they croak all what I please.'
>
> 'Very pretty, indeed!' exclaimed Colonel Goldsworthy.[43]

Giffy gleefully told Fanny that Mr de Luc was catching flies to supply the
frogs; she also recorded Mrs Schwellenberg's enthuasiastic tea table
description of their 'dulcet croaking . . . their ladder, their table, and
their amiable ways of snapping live flies'.[44] In presenting her in this way
Fanny creates a figure who seems to step from a Grimm's fairy-tale, an
impression apparently confirmed by the only surviving pictorial images of
Mrs Schwellenberg, in caricatures. Thomas Rowlandson shows her in a
cartoon of 1788 as fat and frumpish, with heavy eyebrows and large jaw;
she thrusts her huge bosom forcefully forwards and wears a man's
buckled shoes. The image is grotesque and unkind, and if Fanny saw it
she would have recognised the grossness, yet might have allowed herself a
secret smile. For a sensitive woman who disliked confrontation, daily
intercourse with a domineering and unpredictable personality was
oppressive, sapping to the spirit. But, of course, Fanny has had her
revenge: in her journals Mrs Schwellenberg emerges as a witch, her frog-
familiars probably transformations of some poor hapless attendants.

CHAPTER SIX

Visits and Visitors

Madame la Fite said . . . that, nothing remaining upon earth good enough to console me for les Lockes and Mrs. Phillips, I was fain to travel to the moon for comfort. I think it was very well said.[1]

While Fanny was writing copiously about those she met at court, almost none of them, residents or visitors, were recording their own experiences of the shy little woman they encountered, apart that is from the respectful Charlotte Papendiek, in whose case it is Fanny who is silent. In one instance, however, a meeting between Fanny and another diarist led to impressions being recorded by both.

Sophie von la Roche was like Fanny a writer, some twenty years her senior, cousin of the German novelist and poet Cristoph Martin Wieland. In 1771 she produced the first novel by a woman in German, called in English *The History of Lady Sophia Sternheim* and published in 1776. Written in epistolary form it can be compared with *Evelina* (1778), telling of a young woman who, like Evelina, moves from a simple country life to the fashionable world; there she meets an upstanding English lord (first cousin to Fanny's Lord Orville) and the villainous Loveill (closer to Richardson's Lovelace than Fanny's Sir Clement Willoughby). The novel lacks the comedy and satiric bite of *Evelina* and Fanny does not seem to have read it, but a heroine who 'at a luxurious table eats nothing but an apple and drinks nothing but the water' would surely have been one after her own heart.[2] Sophie had subsequently written more novels and journalistic pieces and just as Fanny had been admired by Dr Johnson, so Sophie was by Goethe. In the autumn of 1786 she came to England, keeping a diary of her experiences for her daughters. Sophie was an Anglophile, excited by her visit to London, the 'city of Newton and Addison', and in admiration of almost everything she saw. It is hard to believe that all was quite so orderly, clean, and efficiently run as she suggests, but her journal presents a vivid picture of the great city, describing everyday sights which Fanny would have taken for granted but which had formed the background to her daily life when she lived 'in the world' rather than in her present 'monastery'.

Sophie met Fanny through Marie-Elizabeth de la Fite, French reader to the Princesses, who had translated *Sternheim* into French. What better than to introduce the German novelist to her famous English counterpart? Fanny's dislike of meeting anyone new was intensified when pressed on her with the fervour of Madame de la Fite, but she reluctantly agreed to join a tea party to which Madame la Roche had been invited (she had married a Frenchman). Thus we can read of the same event from two perspectives, Sophie's totally enthusiastic, Fanny's mainly irritated and amused. John Bull to the core, Fanny was ready to be critical of foreign ways; she expressed astonishment when after a rapturous meeting between Mesdames la Fite and la Roche she discovered that they had never met before, only corresponded. Fanny preferred restraint and did not relish the embraces and ardent protestations of regard with which it was next her turn to be favoured. Two other women joined the tea party, and if Fanny had known that beneath her effusive manner Sophie was critical of their fussy court hairstyles she would have warmed to her more. Even so, she admitted that 'could I have conceived her character to be unaffected, her manners have a softness that would render her excessively engaging'.[3] Sophie, however, had no reservations: Miss Burney was perfection, 'a true ideal in figure, culture, expression, dress and bearing'.[4] The occasion had been for her 'a picture, too, of a first-class English tea-party', the ladies sipping their tea (tea imported from China and drunk from small bowls) and sewing 'fine bands of muslin' for dress trimmings.

Looking back on her English visit, Sophie recalled as one of its highlights listening to Miss Burney tell the story of Captain Cook's death, and the heroic part played by her brother-in-law, Molesworth Phillips: 'Dear noble Burney! How well you told this tale! How pleasant your voice sounded, and the delicate flush upon your countenance as our gaze was fixed upon you!'[5] When someone said that Cook had fulfilled his mission and that it was time for him to die, Sophie relished Fanny's ironic answer: 'That is a very sublime way of considering Cook's death'. This sentence has been doubly translated – from the French which they spoke because Sophie's English was poor, and then from Sophie's German into English; nevertheless, it rings true and, short though the sentence is, represents a rare occasion when Fanny's words are recorded by someone other than herself. In her own account, Fanny was seeking to amuse Susan and Fredy so she emphasised what she found comic, getting some of the details wrong probably because of speaking French. She thought that Sophie had only been three days in London and had chosen as her only sightseeing trip thus far to go to Bedlam. Sophie had indeed added

Bedlam, then a tourist attraction, to her impressive list of visits (she may have told the company of seeing Margaret Nicholson composedly reading Shakespeare, while several discarded pens lay on the floor from her continued attempts to write to the King).[6]

According to Sophie, at the end of the tea party the ladies 'very courteously expressed a desire that I would call on them'. According to Fanny, Madame la Fite 'proposed bringing her to the Lodge'.[7] They arrived next afternoon in her absence and she was not too pleased to find them inspecting her books (*Sophie*: 'she has a very choice book collection, from which I should steal Samuel Johnson's *Dictionnaire* of the best thoughts and passages from English poets'). Of the ensuing conversation, which lasted till it was time for dinner, Sophie wrote:

> My whole discussion with Miss Burney was extremely pleasant, and it is certainly doubtful whether her personal grace, her mental accomplishments or her modesty merit first place, but all noble-minded rational beings would delight in her acquaintance and feel at home with her.[8]

Fanny records listening sympathetically to Sophie's narration of her life-story, but the focus of her account was the pantomime which followed, when Madame la Fite attempted to persuade Fanny to invite them to dine at the Lodge. Fanny tried to explain that she was not at liberty to ask anyone: 'But the Queen, my dearest ma'am – the Queen, if she knew such a person as Madame la Roche was here.' Fanny was embarrassed but could not respond. 'It rains! – *Que ferons nous! . . . La pauvre Madame la Roche! Une telle femme!*' ('What shall we do! . . . Poor Mme la Roche! Such a woman!') Dinner was announced – Fanny declared herself not hungry. Madame la Fite, however, was starving, and begged 'a bit of bread and a glass of water'. Hard-heartedly Fanny sent for some, while Sophie stared out of the window murmuring about the lateness of her coach, no doubt ordered for *after* dinner. None of this performance gets into Sophie's diary; she is writing for her daughters and her welcome must be unequivocal.

Despite her irritation, Fanny would have liked to have obliged Madame la Roche but felt herself unable to do so; she noted that Miss Planta, who had eaten a lonely dinner, approved her action, though Peggy Planta was always obligingly ready to agree with Miss Burney. It had never been made clear to Fanny how much liberty she had to issue invitations, a part of her problem generally about what she might or might not do. She even worried about letters: could she 'risk' correspondence with the writer Madame de Genlis, as urged once again by Madame la Fite? Fanny had met and liked her, and admired her writing, but she was disturbed by rumours that she was mistress of the Duke of Orleans.[9] After some agonising, Fanny sought advice from Mrs Delany who in turn sent her to the Queen. In view of the tales circulating, Queen Charlotte thought it 'unsafe and indiscreet to form any connection with her'.[10] So no letter was written.

Worrying about whom she might invite to the Lodge, Fanny again applied to the Queen, who this time advised her to consult Leonard Smelt. From him she received directives to 'see nobody at all but by appointment . . . see no fresh person whatsoever without an express permission from the Queen' and, except for her father and Mr Lock, to receive '*no men – none!*'[11] That monastic dictate startled even Fanny. Her worries, and the advice she received, seem absurdly overscrupulous today, but it is easy to criticise from a more liberated age and from outside the stuffy atmosphere of the court. Even so, Fanny could surely have taken a more relaxed attitude and not incurred royal displeasure; but since she had always had an older man, her father or Daddy Crisp, to advise her, she felt much more comfortable with an 'oracle' to consult; it is notable that she supplies all her heroines with such advisers.[12]

A further rule stipulated that attendants could not leave court without permission, though provided there were no clashes with Fanny's duties it was usually granted. Indeed, one November day while at Kew the Queen ordered a coach to take her to Chessington where her father was staying. Her feelings were coloured by regret for Samuel Crisp, but the arrival of their Fanny in a royal coach made for a great occasion for all her other old friends. On her return Fanny stopped to see her Aunts Ann and Rebecca, her father's sisters, at Kingston; they were so astonished that they 'took me for my own ghost'.[13] When in London she could sometimes call at home, or be visited in her apartment at St James's Palace. Fredy was one such visitor, once smuggling in a decanter of barley water and a tin saucepan under her hoop (but why was secrecy necessary?) Fanny even went to the theatre with the Locks on occasion.

During her court years Fanny also sometimes joined the royal party at the theatre, though she was not of it and therefore had a seat. She shared the King and Queen's enthusiasm for the stage and, like them, loved to laugh at a comedy; there is a cartoon of the King and Queen convulsed with laughter in the royal box while equerries stand behind looking loftily superior to such foolery. Fanny was equally willing to weep at a tragedy, but the royal couple's preference was for comedy and they attended about ten comedies for every tragedy.[14] The King enjoyed plays like Sheridan's *The Rivals* and *The School for Scandal* (despite his dislike of the author's Whig politics) and his preference in general was for contemporary dramas. In early 1787 Fanny attended two new plays; one was Elizabeth Inchbald's *Such Things Are* at Covent Garden, which she talked over with the Queen afterwards, the other *Seduction* by Thomas Holcroft at Drury Lane, 'a very clever piece, but containing a dreadful picture of vice and seduction in high life'.[15] This performance was memorable for the consternation caused her when during the Epilogue she heard a couplet in praise of *Cecilia*. The royal box was opposite and all looked directly at her, the King raising his opera glass and laughing, while Fanny retreated behind her fan. The King later said that he could not help taking a peep at her, as he thought it would show him how she had looked when her father first discovered her writing.[16]

The actress Sarah Siddons told Fanny that she wished she could play Cecilia on stage, when she visited Windsor that August, summoned to Queen's Lodge to give a play-reading. Mrs Siddons was the leading tragic actress, famed for such roles as Lady Macbeth, and Jane Shore in Nicholas Rowe's play of that name; Fanny once told Mrs Thrale that she had been 'half-killed' by her performance as Belvidera in Thomas Otway's tragedy, *Venice Preserv'd*.[17] When the Queen asked her to entertain Mrs Siddons in her apartment before the reading, Fanny welcomed the opportunity to meet the actress. But she found Mrs Siddons difficult to talk to as she seemed to maintain her on-stage presence even in private:

I found her the Heroine of a Tragedy, – sublime, elevated, and solemn. In face and person, truly noble and commanding; in manners, quiet and stiff; in voice, deep and dragging; and in conversation, formal, sententious, calm, and dry.[18]

Had she not had Mrs Delany with her, Fanny would have sought an adjoining room to listen to the reading of the Restoration comedy *The Provok'd Husband* by Vanbrugh and Cibber, even though she did not feel that Mrs Siddons was a natural comedienne. Perhaps on this occasion it did not matter – the first time Fanny met Dr Johnson the talk was of David Garrick who had been disappointed when he gave a command reading at Windsor of one of his comedies. He had carefully prepared for the performance but no one laughed and applause was muted; Garrick afterwards said, 'It was as if they had thrown a wet blanket over me'.[19]

Fanny was to have a similar experience herself in 1790, when she was asked by the Queen to read a play after recalling that Mrs Delany had praised Fanny's readings of Shakespeare. Fanny was presented with a one-act comedy to read to an audience consisting of the Queen, the three elder Princesses and Lady Courtown; the Queen invited Fanny to sit down and suggested that Lady Courtown draw close as 'Miss Burney *has the misfortune* of reading rather low at first'.[20] By this date Fanny had grown used to reading to the Queen and she did her best, but her task was not made easy by her audience, who worked impassively at their different occupations – knotting, spinning and drawing – and neither laughed nor commented on what they heard. Fanny was called on twice more, on the last occasion to read *The Rivals*; it too was received with 'respectful solemnity' and Fanny could understand Garrick's frustration. How their Majesties could laugh uproariously in the theatre yet discourage laughter at home is difficult to comprehend, but Fanny was told it was the etiquette – 'Nobody is to comment, nobody is to interrupt'. On no other subject did she write at greater critical length about the royal family than on this, believing that 'They none of them do justice to their own minds, while they enforce this subjection upon the minds of others'.[21]

Dull and hidebound as the court was in this and other respects, at least in their encouragement of science the King and Queen were progressive. Queen Charlotte was a knowledgeable botanist; she continued the development of Kew's botanical gardens (begun by the King's mother) guided by Joseph Banks, ship's botanist on Cook's first expeditionary voyage to the Pacific.[22] Banks brought back from South Africa the beautiful blue and orange 'Bird of Paradise' flower, established it in Kew's hothouses, and named it *Strelitzia reginae* in the Queen's honour. Fanny met him when he visited the court in 1788, the year he was made President of the Royal Society, but she found him unsociable, commenting tartly that 'If instead of going round the world he had only fallen from the moon, he could not appear less versed in the usual modes of a tea-drinking party'.[23] She took some interest herself in botany, one of the occupations of her leisure hours being to make 'plant impressions'. These were turned into patterns, presumably for furnishing or fashion accessories; one such was sent to Sophie after Madame la Fite came begging for a lock of hair for her friend, or failing that 'a morsel of an old gown, the impression of a seal from a letter, two pins from my dress – in short, anything' as a keepsake.[24]

Another scientist who came to court was the astronomer William Herschel. Fanny found him much more agreeable than Banks, 'a delightful man; so unassuming with his great knowledge, so willing to dispense it to the ignorant, and so cheerful and easy in his general manners'.[25] The King, who was intensely interested in astronomy and had his own telescopes, had appointed Herschel Royal Astronomer following his discovery in 1781 of the planet Uranus (initially named 'Georgium Sidus' by the astronomer). Herschel brought his telescopes to Windsor and settled in nearby Slough with his chief assistant, his sister Caroline. He was paid £200 a year, the same as Fanny – 'Never bought Monarch honour so cheap', it was said.[26] But the King gave him £2,000 to construct a 40-foot telescope, watching the progress with interest; when the great wooden tube was lying on the ground he encouraged the Archbishop of Canterbury to follow him through it with the words, 'Come, my Lord Bishop, I will show you the way to Heaven'.[27] Fanny also walked through the 5-foot diameter tube when her father took her to see it in December 1786, 'and it held me quite upright, and without the least inconvenience; so would it have done had I been dressed in feathers and a bell hoop'.[28] Probably she exaggerated: to walk through upright with a high head and feathers she would have needed to be under 4 feet tall.

On an earlier occasion Herschel had come to the Castle to show the King the new comet which his sister had discovered. Princess Augusta came to Mrs Schwellenberg's rooms to invite her and Fanny to view it too, and though Schwelly declined, Fanny was delighted to leave off playing piquet and go to the garden:

We found him at his telescope, and I mounted some steps to look through it. The comet was very small, and had nothing grand or striking in its appearance; but it is the first lady's comet, and I was very desirous to see it. Mr. Herschel then showed me some of his new-discovered universes, with all the good humour with which he would have taken the same trouble for a brother or a sister astronomer; there is no possibility of admiring the genius more than his gentleness.[29]

Fanny wanted to meet Miss Herschel, and got her chance the following autumn on a visit with Mrs Delany. She found her 'very little, very gentle, very modest, and very ingenuous'.[30] Had she learnt more about Caroline's devoted service in her brother's cause, the hours spent grinding lenses, the copying (not unlike her own for her father), the nights endured in bitter cold or damp, Fanny would have admired her even more. She had hoped to see the moon that night but it was hidden; instead she witnessed the beauty of the planet Saturn and its attendant rings.

Fanny wanted to see the moon because Herschel's claim that he had discovered active volcanoes on its surface was the talk of the tea table. This was one of Herschel's few mistakes: he did not realise that the moon has no atmosphere so combustion is impossible.[31] Fanny had heard Colonel Goldsworthy and a new equerry, Colonel Robert Manners, scoff at the volcanoes; hearing that André de Luc supported Herschel, Manners exclaimed, 'Oh, as to Mr. de Luc, I'd no more trust him than anybody: if you was only to make a little bonfire, and put it upon a hill a little way off, you might make him take it for a volcano directly!' In this case, the scoffers were right, though his error has not diminished Herschel's reputation.[32]

Some of Herschel's discoveries about the universe had implications for its age which would disturb orthodox religious belief, heralding the nineteenth-century 'Age of Doubt'. On the other hand, the opinions of the elderly antiquarian Jacob Bryant, a man whose company was equally sought by the King, were rooted in past belief.[33] For Bryant the date 3949 BC signified, as the publication the *Royal Kalendar* announced annually in capitals, THE CREATION OF THE WORLD. Fanny too was fond of the old man and several times invited him to dinner (with permission), leading the Queen to call him her 'old Beau'. He had a fund of entertaining anecdotes, but Fanny also enjoyed the more serious discussion of the Bible. Evidence of the state of the natural world which challenged the Biblical account of creation was already being produced, ideas which were troubling to a traditionalist such as Fanny, so discussion with a man who sought to prove 'the truths of creation according to Moses' was reassuring.[34] Bryant lived at Cippenham near Windsor and Mrs Delany took Fanny to visit him there; amid all the ancient volumes in his book-lined study she discovered copies of *Evelina* and *Cecilia*, which she found surprising for a man said to know 'all things whatever up to Noah, but not a single thing in the world beyond the Deluge!'

Bryant's other passion was his spaniels, of which he kept a large number, treating them as a tribe of unruly children:

'Come, now, be good! Be good, my little fellows! – don't be troublesome! Don't jump up on Mrs. Delany! Miss Burney, I'm afraid they are in your way. Come, my little fellows, keep back! – pray do. There! – there's my good dogs! – keep back!'[35]

Some of the inevitable puppies made their way to court. When in June 1787 one was presented to the royal family, Colonel Goldsworthy left them 'to kiss and hug it' while he slipped away to swallow a quick dish of tea. But he was summoned back before he could finish it, and went away grumbling, 'What! already! without even my tea! Why this is worse and worse! – no peace in Israel!'[36]

At this time Fanny had not long recovered from a serious illness, so severe that Esther, Susan and Fredy came in turn to Queen's Lodge to nurse her. She had suffered from bouts of fever before, its exact nature impossible to diagnose now. Susan, in a letter to her father, wrote of a return of severe pain in her head which she believed to be 'rheumatic'.[37] Fanny was given a 'Blister for her Back' by the King's apothecary, Robert Battiscombe; a standard treatment then, blisters were made from cantharadin, an insect product which is an irritant to the skin, causing inflammation and blistering and, theoretically, drawing out the poisons in the body. Blisters were painful and it is not surprising to find that Fanny's night thereafter had been a disturbed one. Susan's letter is breathless, written in haste to tell Dr Burney of the honour of the Queen's coming to Fanny's apartment to ask after her. Susan confessed herself confused, embarrassed, even dismayed when she answered a rap at the door and found the Queen outside, three little dogs yapping round her skirts. No doubt the Queen also wanted to have a look at her Robe-keeper's sister, whom she later pronounced unlike her in appearance.

The benefit of illness for Fanny was that she had been allowed a convalescence at Norbury Park; it was a pity that it was only by being ill that she could get leave of absence. She did not write about it as she did not need to, but there she would have enjoyed the hospitality of Fredy and her family, taken walks on the wooded slopes in their spring glory, and played with her niece and nephew, Fanny and Norbury Phillips. But she was back at court before the next great date on the royal calendar, the King's birthday on 4 June. It followed the pattern of the Queen's birthday, and Fanny made sure that she knew where to go this time. This birthday was a happier occasion than the Queen's for there had been a reconciliation with the Prince of Wales, from his point of view no doubt in anticipation of the return to England of his brother and childhood companion, Frederick, Duke of York.

Despite being his father's favourite the Duke, who reached his twenty-fourth birthday in 1787, had been out of the country for seven years; for over a year he had been pleading to be allowed to return to England. At last permission was granted and on 2 August 1787 Fanny watched him leap from his carriage on arrival at Windsor, to a joyous welcome from his father. Later she went to the Terrace with Marianne:

It was indeed an affecting sight to view the general content; but that
of the King went to my very heart, so delighted he looked – so proud
of his son – so benevolently pleased that every one should witness his
satisfaction.

The Terrace was very full; all Windsor and its neighbourhood
poured upon it, to see the Prince, whose whole demeanour seemed
promising to merit his flattering reception; gay, yet grateful –
modest, yet unembarrassed.[38]

Next day, having travelled through the night from Brighthelmstone
(Brighton), the Prince of Wales arrived for his own reunion with his
brother. When he came again for a family dinner at Kew, Princess
Augusta told Fanny, 'There never had been so happy a dinner since the
world was created'. Sadly, this harmony was not to last.

Fanny watched one morning as the Prince and the Duke went off
arm in arm, but she later listened to Leonard Smelt, their former
deputy-governor, talking of his fears for the Duke under the influence of
his brother. The Duke of York needed no brother to lead him astray,
however; though less ostentatiously riotous, he was already well versed
in gambling, womanising and drinking. Absence from England had
helped to keep such things hidden, though the King was willing to turn
a blind eye to his favourite's failings as he never was with his eldest
son. The Prince of Wales returned to Windsor for his twenty-fifth
birthday on 12 August, and his equerries, Colonels St Leger, Hulse and
Lake, appeared at the tea table where, in Mrs Schwellenberg's absence,
Fanny presided. They had their own wild reputations and Fanny was
uncomfortable in their presence until she realised that they were silent
and ill at ease too. She wondered if they feared being 'inserted in a
book' by her.

Two days later it was Fanny's turn to be worried. One of the Duke of
York's equerries proved to be the caricaturist Henry Bunbury:

So now we may all be caricatured at his leisure! . . . A man with such
a turn, and with talents so inimitable in displaying it, was a rather
dangerous character to be brought within a Court![39]

The last two decades of the eighteenth century were the heyday of the
political and social caricature. Buyers, or merely onlookers, crowded
around the windows of specialist London print-shops, gawping and
giggling at scurrilous, often scatological pictures of their leaders. It

amazed foreigners that within a stone's throw of St James's Palace the most licentious caricatures of the King and his ministers were on public display.[40] There was no redress for those ridiculed, though one favourite target, the Prince of Wales, might buy up a whole print run and the plate too. The most famous caricaturists of the day were James Gillray and Thomas Rowlandson, both professional artists trained at the Royal Academy; the amateur Henry Bunbury avoided personal attack and confined himself to fairly gentle satire of fashionable behaviour, so Fanny need not have worried.

Bunbury had recently published one of his best-known works, *The Long Minuet at Bath*, a scroll of posturing dancers, and another 'long joke', *The Propagation of a Lie*, was published in December 1787; Fanny was given a copy by Colonel Gwynn's wife Mary, Bunbury's sister-in-law. Eighteen men express in gesture and look their horror, delight, boredom or rage at the 'lie', whatever it is, with corresponding exclamations such as 'O Fye', 'Ha Ha', 'Heigh ho', and 'The Devil!'.[41] Bunbury was a devotee of the theatre, chatting endlessly to Fanny about plays and players, and his figures all have a look of dramatic posture. He was a jovial fellow; nevertheless, his presence at court agitated everyone, everyone that is except Mrs Schwellenberg 'who is happy that he cannot caricature her, because, she says, she has no *Hump*'.[42]

The summer of 1797 passed as agreeably for Fanny as her court life could, and there was a week's visit from Susan and Fredy in the autumn, but the chilly winds of winter also brought irritable blasts from her superior. The account of a coach journey from St James's to Windsor then is probably the best-known instance of Mrs Schwellenberg's unkindness to Fanny. On the journey there she had insisted that the window be kept down on Fanny's side – possibly she feared an asthma attack in an enclosed, airless coach. The biting wind caused a painful inflammation of Fanny's eyes; it did not encourage her to hear that inflamed eyes had been Mrs Hagedorn's winter problem, and her maid Goter told her that '*all the servants in the house had remarked I was going just the same way!*' Before the return journey Miss Planta came to Fanny's room to announce her hope that Mrs Schwellenberg would be left behind, but one of the London household exclaimed, 'Oh, for Heaven's sake don't leave her behind; for Heaven's sake, Miss Burney, take her with you!' Fanny's father, concerned at the state of her eyes, had told her to draw up the window regardless of opposition, and Fanny had the support of Mr de Luc, travelling with them on the three-hour journey. But he was in trouble as soon as he pulled up the glass:

'Put down that glass!' was the immediate order.

He affected not to hear her, and began conversing.

She enraged quite tremendously, calling aloud to be obeyed without delay. He looked compassionately at me, and shrugged his shoulders, and said, 'But, ma'am —'

'Do it, Mr. de Luc, when I tell you! I will have it! When you been too cold, you might bear it!'

'It is not for me, ma'am, but poor Miss Burney.'

'Oh, poor Miss Burney might bear it the same! Put it down, Mr. de Luc! without, I will get out! put it down, when I tell you! It is my coach! I will have it selfs! I might go alone in it, or with one, or with what you call nobody, when I please!'

Frightened for good Mr. de Luc, and the more for being much obliged to him, I now interfered, and begged him to let down the glass. Very reluctantly he replied, and I leant back in the coach, and held up my muff to my eyes.

What a journey ensued! To see that face when lighted up with fury is a sight for horror! I was glad to exclude it by my muff.[43]

De Luc suggested that Fanny change places with Miss Planta, but Fanny declared she was always sick if she rode backwards. Temporary sickness would surely have been preferable to eye damage, but Fanny opted for martyrdom. She did debate with herself whether to rebel as her father had urged, but was unable to face an open quarrel. A bizarre moment occurred when Schwelly suddenly brought out cake and Fanny found herself accepting a slice, but it was not a peace-offering; over the next weeks the hostility to Fanny continued, until her eyes recovered and the visible sign of unkindness was no longer a reproach. Yet Miss Planta informed her that everyone thought that she was better treated by Mrs Schwellenberg than anyone else.

January 1788 brought another celebration of the Queen's birthday, and Fanny had a little celebration of her own. Mrs Ord, who had accompanied her to court and was perhaps realising the isolation to which her appointment condemned her, arranged a special assembly at her home for all Fanny's old friends. Among them were Sir Joshua Reynolds, the widowed Mrs Garrick, the Blue Stockings Mrs Montagu, Mrs Boscawen and Mrs Chapone, Mr Cambridge senior (not his son), and Horace Walpole whom Fanny was glad to see despite *The Mysterious Mother*. Of an earlier meeting that year he had told the writer Hannah More that he found Fanny looking 'so cheerful and agreeable, that the Court seems only to have improved the ease of her manner, instead of stamping more reserve on it, as I feared', though he went on to say that 'what slight graces it can give, will not compensate to us and the world for the loss of her company and her writings'.[44] Cheerful and agreeable she may have been in greeting her old friends at Mrs Ord's, but 'all was so short! – so short!' Hester Chapone shook her hand, only half joking when she said, 'I hope you are not always to appear only as a Comet, to be stared at, and then vanish? If you are, let me beg at least to be brushed by your tail, and not hear you have disappeared before my telescope is ready for looking at you!'[45]

CHAPTER SEVEN

The Death of Mrs Delany

What a character is Mrs. Delany's! – how noble throughout! – how great
upon great occasions! – how sweet, how touching, how interesting upon all!
Oh, what should I do without her here?[1]

Writing to her sister Charlotte a year after her appointment at court, Fanny told her:

> Sweet Mrs Delany continues delightfully well, & my best & dearest solace in this land of strangers, – for such it is to me, compared with the lands I forsake for it.[2]

The passing of time only added to Fanny's sense of alienation from family and friends. She had just become godmother to Charlotte's first baby, another Charlotte (who became the first editor of her journals), but she could not go to her sister and could only beg to learn 'how round she is, how plump, how fair, – in what she resembles Papa, & what she has stolen from Mama'. Another godchild, five-year-old Fanny Phillips, dictated to her mother a letter of protest:

> King George Rex, I am much obliged to the queen for letting Aunt Fanny come the last time to Norbury when we did not expect her: but I don't know what is the reason that she is so fond of her as not to let her come again when I asked her. So now I hope *you* will let her come to stay, and to sleep at Norbury, and to never go away as long as she lives, because I love her so much and Mama loves her so much too – I send my love to the queen and to Aunt Fanny and to the King. Adieu – I am . . . your humble respectful servant Fanny Phillips.[3]

The letter was never delivered; had it been, the King would surely have laughed, and perhaps the little petitioner would have won a few days of her aunt's company.

It was hard on Fanny with her love of small children to have to miss these early years of her nieces and nephews, and even to Mrs Delany, her 'earthly angel', she could not speak of this kind of loss; Mrs Delany still rejoiced in her appointment, and Fanny could not repay that pleasure by 'painting, to her, its interior sadness'. So well indeed did she hide her real feelings, that after she had been ill again in the spring of 1787 Mrs Delany wrote to a friend that 'Miss Burney now only wants time to restore her to strength and her happy occupation, which she delights in'.[4] She did, however, know all about her troubles with Mrs Schwellenberg, and sympathised fully. Though at first she urged Fanny to assert herself more she seems to have realised the impossibility for Fanny of snubbing the tyrant of the tea table.

All at court were aware of Mrs Delany's great age as she approached her eighty-eighth year. It had earlier been the subject of one of Colonel Goldsworthy's outbursts, provoked by Madame la Fite, when in her broken English she tried to explain that as she had been born in 1700 Mrs Delany belonged to the last century:

'In the last century, ma'am! – What do you mean by that? Would you make the good old lady out to be two hundred years old?'

She explained herself so extremely ill, that not a creature was brought over to her opinion, though it was afterwards proved that she was right, and that the year 1700, in which Mrs. Delany was born, belonged to the last century . . .

'1700 belong to 1600!' cried the Colonel indignantly – 'why then I suppose Friday belongs to Thursday, and Wednesday to Tuesday! Bless us! here's such a set of new doctrines, a man won't know soon whether he's alive now or was alive the last age!'

Madame la Fite now attempted a fuller explanation, but was so confused in her terms, and so much at a loss for words, that, though perfectly right, the Colonel looked at her as if he thought her half mad.

'Oh dear, yes, ma'am! yes,' cried he, bowing with mock submission, 'I daresay it's all very right! only it's a little new – that's all! – 1700 makes 1600! – Oh, vastly right! . . .

'*Mais, monsieur –* sir – if you will give me leave – *si monsieur veut bien me permettre —*'

'Oh no, ma'am, don't trouble yourself! I am not worth the pains; I am quite in the dark in these things. I was franking a parcel of letters yesterday, and I thought I franked them all for this year; but I suppose now I franked them all in the last century!'[5]

Fanny worried about the prospect of Mrs Delany's death, though she herself welcomed its approach, only sorry in the knowledge that it would bring distress to those who loved her. But she urged her friend to accept its inevitability: 'You must let me, my dear Fanny, you must let me go quietly,' she told her. Fanny knew it must be so, but that did not make it any easier to contemplate: 'Oh, how shall I do now without her?' was the question she could not answer. It was not simply that she found the house in St Albans Street a refuge from the exigencies of her superior; there was a sweetness of temperament and a quality of intellectual refinement not found elsewhere among her court acquaintances. It has sometimes been suggested that it was presumptuous of Fanny to claim close companionship with a woman whose social level was above hers; culturally, however, the one-time friend of Swift and the one-time friend of Johnson were equals, and each found in the other a companion of the mind and spirit. Fanny was taken fully into Mrs Delany's confidence, shown her letters and papers and the memoirs compiled at the behest of the Duchess of Portland; this uses disguised names, Mrs Delany calling herself 'Aspasia' after the witty and learned woman who entertained Socrates at her salon in Athens.[6]

The intimacy between the two women led to a 'secret' project. Mrs Delany had told Fanny so many interesting stories which were not in the memoirs that Fanny suggested 'filling up the chasms, and linking the whole together'. The aim was to produce a 'history of her whole life', adding what had been so far unrecorded of her earliest and later memories. Mrs Delany liked the idea and they began one day by spreading out all the old letters on the table in Fanny's apartment. Then, in the midst of the activity, the King walked in:

> Dear Mrs. Delany was quite frightened, and I felt myself pretty hot in the cheeks. He immediately asked what we were about? Neither of us answered. 'Sorting letters?' cried he, to me. 'Reading some, sir,' quoth I.[7]

Unusually for the King he did not pursue the matter, but the next time he interrupted them they were ready to tell him that they were selecting letters, some to keep, others to burn, 'preserving only such as were ingenious, without possible hazard to the writers or their family'; the King grew used to finding them at their work, only saying, 'Well, who are you reading now?'

In 1832, when Fanny as Madame d'Arblay published her *Memoirs of Dr Burney* and wrote of the joint design, Marianne questioned her account of events and wrote to her great-aunt's old servant Anne Astley, by then Mrs Agnew; about the burning of letters and help with the autobiography Mrs Agnew replied:

I doubt the truth of it, with *good reason,* for more than a fortnight before we left St. James's place I was employed upon them every morning in examining and burning a large box of letters, which grieved me to destroy, as some of them were written by the first people in the world; but *I was obliged to obey,* and observed at the time that the box of letters (containing hundreds) would have been a fortune to anybody were they published. '*That is what I want to prevent,*' was the answer. But if Madame D'A. happened to look over one letter or MS., that *was enough* for an authoress to *build upon!*[8]

The accusation, that Fanny as a writer of fiction felt herself licensed to embroider the facts, is a serious one. Mrs Agnew, unlike Lady Llanover who printed her letter thirty years later, had no axe to grind with Fanny, but she believed from her own memories that Madame d'Arblay's version of events was wrong. Fanny in her own old age was capable of manipulating the truth (claiming, for example, that the routine duties belonging to dress were solely the concern of Mrs Schwellenberg). But she based what she wrote about Mrs Delany in the *Memoirs* on her journals, and there could be no reason then why she should make up stories. Both women could be right, if it is assumed that Mrs Delany selected some letters to keep before she moved to Windsor and asked her maid to destroy the rest, an interpretation supported by Fanny's saying that they spread 'all' the letters on her table, impossible if there were hundreds. Moreover, Mrs Delany's remark that she wanted to prevent some unknown person publishing her letters after her death has nothing to do with a 'secret' plan to add to the already existing autobiography. Mrs Agnew's own memory after all those years was not perfect; she denied that Fanny had the right to call herself Keeper of the Robes, a title she thought belonged only to Mrs Schwellenberg.

The biographical project was begun in 1786 and Fanny wrote then that the childhood section was proceeding 'pretty well'. However, nothing of Mrs Delany's childhood experiences survive into her published autobiography, and whatever was written was probably later lost. The problem was that the time when the two could be alone together was limited, particularly since when Mrs Delany came to Fanny's apartment she was almost invariably 'carried off' to the King and Queen. A year after they had begun their project Fanny records that they had returned to it, but were soon interrupted: 'The good King and his charming little daughter [Princess Amelia] came, as usual, to rob me of my venerable Biographer.'[9] Probably Fanny should also be blamed for the lack of progress, for it is only in January 1788 that she recorded that she had finished reading Mrs Delany's memoirs – and wondered again, 'Oh, what should I do without her here?'

Fanny's company was valued by the old lady for the sake of her great-niece as well as herself. Georgina Mary Ann Port was then in her seventeenth year, and Mrs Delany saw Fanny (though twice her age) as an exemplary companion for her. During her Christmas visit two years earlier, Mrs Delany had written to the girl's mother, saying that 'Miss Burney . . . is a most valuable acquaintance, and *on Mary's account*, as well as my own, I am happy to have as much of her company as I can'.[10] Mary, or Marianne as Fanny called her, was the eldest of eight children of the only daughter of Mrs Delany's much-loved sister Anne (who had never known her granddaughter). From the age of seven she had spent long periods with her great-aunt, and for some years had lived exclusively with her, being educated and introduced into society by her and, as Mrs Delany's sight deteriorated, reading and writing her letters. Fanny liked the high-spirited girl and in Mrs Schwellenberg's absences would invite her to help perform the rituals of the tea table. To such invitations Marianne would hasten 'with good-humoured delight'. She, more than anyone, could rouse Colonel Goldsworthy from a fit of gloomy silence and, when the cat was away, Fanny, Marianne and the equerries enjoyed evenings of banter and laughter.

Colonel Robert Manners, the 'tall and extremely handsome young man' who took up his duties in the spring of 1787, was another who responded to Marianne's good looks and vivacity. He was a Member of Parliament as well as an equerry but something of a clown, quite seriously complaining to Fanny that whenever he had something to say in the Commons William Pitt, the Prime Minister, always managed to say it first. Colonel Goldsworthy picked up on a maladroit remark, perhaps reacting also to attentions to his own favourite:

> The Ascot races were held at this time; the Royal Family were to be at them one or two of the days. Colonel Manners earnestly pressed Miss Port to be there. Colonel Goldsworthy said it was quite immaterial to him who was there, for when he was attending royalty he never presumed to think of any private comfort.
>
> 'Well, I don't see that!' cried Colonel Manners, – 'for if I was you, and not in my turn for waiting, I should go about just as I liked; – but

as for me, as it happens to be my own turn, why I think it right to be civil to the King.'

We all looked round; – but Colonel Goldsworthy broke forth aloud – 'Civil, quotha?' cried he: 'Ha! ha! civil, forsooth! – You're mighty condescending! – the first equerry I ever heard talk of his *civility* to the King! – "Duty," and "respect," and "humble reverence," – those are words we are used to, – but here come you with your civility! – Commend me to such affability!'[11]

The younger Colonel laughed and did not take offence at, or perhaps did not recognise, the sarcasm. He appeared to enjoy being a buffoon; he was tone deaf, unable even to manage 'God Save the King' in tune. One evening he reduced Fanny and Marianne to fits of laughter by singing a solo at Marianne's request, producing 'such shocking, discordant, and unmeaning sounds' that after only one verse Colonel Goldsworthy cried out 'There, – there's enough! – have mercy!'[12]

This is innocent, if schoolboyish, fun, but in the unnatural, cloistered atmosphere of the court, such apparently carefree occasions could have their undercurrents of feeling, and jealousy and tittle-tattle were a hazard of court life. When Major Price began to ignore her in company, Fanny learnt that Colonel Manners had been teasing him about his friendship with her, though he continued to speak kindly where there were no observant eyes. She regretted the change, but recognised that 'when once a report of this sort has gained Ground . . . all comfort is at an end between those on whom it falls'.[13] Manners enjoyed mischief-making and plagued Mrs Schwellenberg; as Marianne's admirer he may have been the original source of the story, maliciously offered seventy years later by her daughter Lady Llanover, that Fanny was so vain of her personal charms that she 'became convinced that all the equerries were in love with her, although she was continually the object of their ridicule, as they discovered her weaknesses and played upon her credulity for their own amusement'.[14]

It is unfortunately common in institutions for groups to mock the foibles of individual members of it. Another of Lady Llanover's claims, that Fanny was laughed at when she answered the King's enquiry about her health by saying that '*the little machine has not yet quite ceased to vibrate*', may be true, as she can be found referring to herself as 'the little machine'.[15] But if some or all of the equerries laughed at Fanny for occasional grandiloquence they did not necessarily do so in contempt, and Fanny's day-to-day journalising does not support the allegation that she thought herself the centre of their amorous attentions. It is true that there seems to have been a general archness between the women of the household and the Windsor uniforms, and the equerries are often referred to as 'Beaus' in the journals, but when Mrs Schwellenberg presided over the tea table Fanny effaced herself and said nothing, and at first when she was absent Fanny tried to avoid standing in for her, hoping to spend the time instead with Mrs Delany. To her surprise she found that the old lady disapproved of her plan and she had to assume the presidency of the tea table after all.

As has been said, what Fanny disliked about meeting the equerries was the way they came and went. No sooner had she got to know one of them than he disappeared and was replaced by someone unfamiliar. One new equerry whom she tried to avoid meeting at first, especially since his acquaintance was pushed by Mr Turbulent, was Colonel Greville. He was a man of her own age, and once met she found in him someone with whom she could have serious conversation; she described him as 'sensible, well-bred, modest, and intelligent', attributes which are borne out by his own diary writings.[16] Fanny was aware that Greville was drawing his chair up beside her and choosing her company, but he was an honourable man and cannot be suspected of pretending an attachment in order to ridicule the Robe-keeper among his fellow equerries afterwards.

According to Fanny, the serious-minded Greville considered Marianne a 'flighty female'; she found him 'stiff and proud'.[17] Fanny thought disapprovingly that in discovering the power of her beauty the young girl was receiving 'too much admiration'; from the autumn of 1787 the unpublished parts of the journals suggest that it was on Marianne that court gossip centred. Her great-aunt worried about what would happen to the girl when she herself died. She hoped to see her niece settled in a good marriage, and an opportunity had seemed to present itself when Mr and Mrs Lock came, with Susan, on their visit to Fanny in September 1787, bringing with them their eldest son William. After their return Susan told Fanny of an exchange between William and his mother:

'Were you not delighted with Mrs. Delany, my William?' asked his sweet mother.

'Yes,' said he, smiling, with great meaning, his full assent. We all then joined in speaking our admiration of this very extraordinary and most charming lady.

'And there is,' said Mr. William, 'something very pretty in Miss Port.'[18]

This response from the normally reserved young man pleased his parents, and Mrs Delany and her niece were invited to Norbury Park. Fanny thought that Mrs Delany 'would almost *die* with joy' if a match could be brought off between Marianne and William.[19] It is a measure of the old lady's anxiety about Marianne that she was prepared to undertake the visit. During their stay William, a talented amateur artist, was noticeably attentive to the beautiful Miss Port. He showed her his drawings and explained his work as he had never done before to visitors. A friend of Fredy's observed to Susan, 'Do you see how William is smitten?'[20] Susan, however, was far from happy. She had heard of Marianne's coquetry with the equerries, and had christened her the 'Friskitten'. She watched her closely, commenting severely that Marianne was 'as flattering with her eyes as she could contrive to make them and I believe she is not a novice at that art'. The prospect that she might marry the heir to Norbury Park filled Susan with 'dread and alarm' (were the shades of Norbury to be thus polluted?), the only hopeful sign being that on the day the visitors left William went off to the races rather than stay to say goodbye. He was 'smitten', but not totally enamoured.

As it turned out the match was never made. It seems that in an exchange of letters between Norbury and Windsor, Fanny, who was much more sympathetic to Marianne than Susan, felt in honesty compelled to tell Fredy something of what had been developing at court. For Marianne had fallen deeply in love, not with the handsome young soldier but the crusty old one, not the clown Robert Manners but the jester, Philip Goldsworthy. More than thirty years her senior, he was old enough to be her father; perhaps it was because she had seen so little of her actual father that she found Goldsworthy so attractive. Fanny very much hoped that a marriage would take place, 'for such steps has she [Marianne] ventured that she will otherwise be deeply mortified, & poor Mrs. D. thinks even disgraced'.[21] But unfortunately for Marianne, though Goldsworthy allowed Mrs Delany to believe that he would marry the girl, he had no real inclination for matrimony.

On 1 January 1788 Fanny hastened to Mrs Delany's for her 'annual benediction', and comforted herself that the old lady looked so well that it seemed as if she could easily live to be a hundred. Despite her failing sight she wrote Fanny a letter in her own hand at Easter, 'full of all the spirit, affection, fancy, and elegance with which she could have written at twenty-five'. But Mrs Delany's health was fragile. After a summons to meet the King and Queen at Kew she returned to her house at St James's Place with a chill; it turned to pneumonia and by early April she was dangerously ill. She had made miraculous recoveries before, and on 13 April it seemed that she would cheat death again. But a day later she was sinking, and on 15 April she died. Fanny and Marianne were at her bedside:

> She had just given me her soft hand; without power to see either of us, she felt and knew us. Oh, never can I cease to cherish the remembrance of the sweet, benign, *holy* voice with which she pronounced a blessing upon us both! We kissed her; and, with a smile all beaming – I thought it so – of heaven, she seemed then to have taken leave of all earthly solicitudes. . . . She would not bid us farewell – would not tell us she should speak with us no more – she only said, as she turned gently away from us, 'And now – *I'll go to sleep!* – But oh, in what a voice she said it! I felt what the sleep would be; so did poor Miss Port.[22]

She was buried in St James's Church, Piccadilly, where her memorial tablet can still be seen.

Fanny grieved deeply for the loss of her friend and for some time could think or write of little else. Reason told her that the old lady's death was in the course of nature, and faith instructed her that it was for a greater happiness in another world, but her heart found it difficult to accept the loss in this one. Harder hearts at court criticised her for mourning too much and too long, but it was not a selfish grief. She was very concerned for Marianne, giving what solace and advice she could, and she worried about Mrs Delany's servants, *her* dependants not the King's. She spoke to the Queen on behalf of Mrs Astley, and was overjoyed when she heard that his Majesty had agreed to pension her in the Windsor house; Fanny also managed to find a position for the footman, Joseph.

Mrs Astley brought a message which moved her greatly; she had been instructed by her mistress to say, 'how much comfort I must always feel in reflecting how much her latter days had been soothed by me'.[23] Fanny was also remembered in her will, receiving one of Mrs Delany's own paintings, medallion portraits of the King and Queen, and her choice of a mosaic flower. Perhaps she treasured most of all the edition of Shakespeare's plays which Mrs Delany had herself given her two nights before her death, saying that 'she had never received so much pleasure from him in any other way as through my reading'.[24]

In accordance with Mrs Delany's wish, guardianship of Marianne passed to her elderly bachelor uncle, Court Dewes of Wellesbourne in Warwickshire. For some reason Marianne was reluctant to return to her

natural home; she had been away from it for a long time, but the
company of her younger sisters would have been better for her than that
of a man described as being of 'ungenial nature, with no liking for the
society of young people'.[25] However, Marianne was still hoping that Philip
Goldsworthy would come forward to claim her. It was said at a later date
that his sister Martha Goldsworthy intervened to prevent the marriage;
certainly someone poisoned the Queen's mind against the girl, for she
was allowed only a brief farewell visit to Windsor before she was packed
off to Warwickshire, parting from Fanny with floods of tears.[26] Fanny
condemned Goldsworthy's behaviour both towards Marianne and
Mrs Delany, resenting the selfish conduct of 'him who so little weighed
their peace, or ought else but his own immediate gratification . . . that he
authorised all outward Reports, & all inward expectations'.[27] One sad
aspect of this sorry affair was Fanny's loss of respect for the Colonel.

Despite rebuffs, Marianne continued to cherish her dreams, pouring
her heart out to Fanny in her letters. In one reply Fanny told her in
measured words that Colonels Goldsworthy and Manners had enquired
after her 'and desired their compliments when I wrote', but put the
emphasis on Colonel Manners. He had said that the '*Ascot Races* made
him feel quite melancholy from recollecting how all was broke up since
we had them last year'.[28] She tried to discourage Marianne from writing
to either of them, prudent counsel with which her great-aunt would have
agreed:

> As you ask my advice about your correspondents – I must give it you
> honestly – I cannot wish you to *renew any* yourself. I think those only
> who seek it can be worthy of it from you. I have always been a little
> proud for my dear Marianne, and I feel no inclination to be less so.[29]

In July, when the court moved to Cheltenham for the King to take the
waters and society followed in its wake, Marianne came there too with her
relations (an aunt by marriage was daughter of Cheltenham's
magistrate). No doubt she hoped that if she could see Colonel
Goldsworthy again the match could be made, but according to Fanny it
was here that he 'fairly, & openly, & even formally, gave her up'.[30]

Fanny was herself placed in a difficult position at Cheltenham, given
'*advice*' – a euphemism for an order – not to receive Marianne in the
royal residence.[31] To hide this from the girl Fanny pretended that she
could not invite anyone at all because the house was so small. Marianne
felt that an exception might have been made for her and Fanny agreed;
she thought it 'cruel' but could not say so. Even after Marianne was

respectably married to someone else the King and Queen seemed unable
to forgive her for attempting to marry a court favourite; in 1790 when the
young woman appeared on the Terrace with her baby she was pointedly
ignored. Fanny 'grieved, & felt redoubled tenderness for her'.[32]

Rejected by the man she loved, and believing herself a burden to her
relations, Marianne had accepted an offer from a middle-aged man she
scarcely knew, Benjamin Waddington, and they were married on
17 February 1789. Fanny was at that time cut off from any direct contact
with her because of the King's illness, but she felt very anxious about the
wisdom of the decision; she was relieved when a year later she heard news
of the birth of a daughter and rejoiced in Marianne's declaration that
'she could now forget every sorrow, if her darling might be spared to
her'.[33] Sadly this child (the baby snubbed at Windsor) lived only a few
weeks. Marianne Waddington was to bear seven daughters but tragedy
dogged her life; only three of her girls lived to young adulthood and only
two beyond that. Despite Fanny's fears, indicated at the time of the
marriage by sententious letters urging wifely duty, Marianne proved a
loyal not a 'flighty' wife. But she never forgot Philip Goldsworthy and
years later was still seeking news of him from Fanny.[34] Hers was an
unhappy story, leaving a residue of bitterness which was to affect Fanny in
old age and even beyond the grave.

After Mrs Delany's death, Fanny and Marianne swore a vow of eternal
friendship. Inevitably the nature of that friendship changed as time went
on; at first Fanny saw herself *in loco Delaniae*, offering sympathy but also
moral guidance as Marianne poured out her misery about Philip
Goldsworthy. When Marianne acquired the status of a wealthy wife the
position altered, and at the time when Fanny's novel *Camilla* was published in 1795 she acted as Fanny's benefactress, earning her gratitude
for her canvassing for the subscription list. Two decades on she became a
confidante to Fanny in her worries about her son Alex and his lack of
social graces; she invited Alex to stay and her daughters, especially
fifteen-year-old Augusta, took him in hand, teased and tamed him a little.
But the relationship with Marianne always had its prickly aspects, with
Marianne quick to take offence if Fanny was neglectful of their
correspondence, wrote only short letters, or failed to inform her of
important news (Fanny defended herself robustly: *she* had received brief
or no letters too, and she did not feel that a relationship should stand or
fall on prompt letter-writing). Afraid for what might happen after Fanny's
death, Marianne was understandably anxious to have the letters
concerning Philip Goldsworthy returned for burning; Fanny agreed but
was dilatory in carrying out the promise, excusing herself on the grounds

of having boxes and boxes of letters to sort out for the *Memoirs* that she was compiling of her father. These were eventually published in 1832, her eightieth year.

There are many reasons why it might have been better if the *Memoirs of Dr Burney* had never been written, one of them being the termination of good relations with Marianne. Old age had clouded Fanny's judgement; she eulogised Mrs Delany but had the indiscretion to write of her relationship with the Duchess of Portland that 'unnumbered were the little auxiliaries to domestic economy which her Grace found means to convey to St James's Place'.[35] Fanny meant to suggest the strength of the friendship but her words had implications of patronage which she would not have liked said of herself. Further offence was caused by the stress laid on her own relationship with Mrs Delany at the end of her life, a tactlessness probably caused by her consciousness of Marianne's wish not to have attention drawn to herself at this period. Mrs Waddington also disputed her account of the circumstances of Mrs Delany's death. In this Fanny drew her information from her journals which inevitably described it from her own point of view; in the highly charged atmosphere of a death bed it is difficult to be objective.

Worse was to follow, after Fanny's own death. When she was editing the *Diary & Letters of Madame d'Arblay*, Charlotte Barrett was aware of the sensitivity of Mrs Waddington and others to finding themselves or their relations identified in the publication, so names were disguised. Marianne Port was referred to simply as 'a friend', and her name represented with a dash. However, the offence caused by the *Memoirs* seems not have been erased. In 1860 the first three volumes of Mrs Delany's autobiography and letters were published by Marianne's daughter, Augusta Lady Llanover, and inevitably comparison was made in reviews with the *Diary & Letters*. Lady Llanover seems to have been incensed by reference to Madame d'Arblay as an 'undeniable authority . . . who had *honoured* Mrs Delany by *her notice*', the very italics bristling with offence.[36] In editing the second series of volumes she dipped her pen in vinegar to produce the most hostile criticism of Fanny anywhere to be found. Madame d'Arblay, she suggests, was at best a fantasist, at worst a liar, who insinuated herself into Mrs Delany's favour with assumed deference and sympathy. She protests her aversion to 'throwing discredit upon the dead, especially upon an individual who may have been known to persons still living', but never reveals either that she herself had known Fanny (who once called her 'my dear and bright little Friend'), or that she had had a warm friendship with her son, Alex. He had nicknamed her 'Puss', and Fanny was reminded of her mother at the same age.[37]

Possibly some resentment with Madame d'Arblay was created in Augusta at that time, for there must be some personal explanation beyond the family annoyance to explain such very sharp claws in later life.

While Fanny was in Cheltenham in 1788 she read an article by Giuseppe Baretti which was highly abusive of Mrs Piozzi; she was horrified, but wrote 'It can hardly hurt her – it is so palpably meant to do it'.[38] The same can be said of Lady Llanover's hostile remarks, and it is true that Fanny's reputation has not been diminished by anything she wrote. Nevertheless, print is a preservative and anyone reading Mrs Delany's letters will encounter the attack on Fanny's integrity. No one would have been more saddened by it, or of the breakdown of friendship between the two families, than that remarkable woman Mary Granville, Mrs Delany.

CHAPTER EIGHT

Taking the Waters

Now, my dearest friends, I open an account which promises at least all the charms of novelty, and which, if it fulfils its promise, will make this month rather an episode than a continuation of my prosaic performance.[1]

Not long after his fiftieth birthday in June 1788 the King suffered what he described as 'a pretty smart bilious attack'. His doctor, Sir George Baker, recommended taking the waters at Cheltenham and Lord Fauconberg, a Lord of the Bedchamber, offered to lend the summer residence which he had built there for his own medical purposes. It was sited on a rise with fine views of the surrounding countryside.[2] The house could only accommodate a small party, but Miss Burney was among those chosen to accompany the King, Queen and three elder Princesses. The chance to get away from Windsor routines, Cerbera, and the empty house in St Albans Street, caused Fanny's spirits to rise, a cheerfulness reflected both in the vigour of her writing and her haste to set pen to paper:

> So now for yesterday, Saturday, July 12.
> We were all up at five o'clock; and the noise and confusion reigning through the house, and resounding all around it, from the quantities of people stirring, boxes nailing, horses neighing, and dogs barking, was tremendous.[3]

The party travelled through Henley and Oxford along a route lined by the curious and loyal:

> All the towns through which we passed were filled with people, as closely fastened one to another as they appear in the pit of the playhouse. Every town seemed all face; and all the way upon the road we rarely proceeded five miles without encountering a band of most horrid fiddlers, scraping 'God Save the King' with all their might, out of tune, out of time, and all in the rain; for, most unfortunately, there were continual showers falling all the day.[4]

This was a rare opportunity to see Majesty in the flesh since the King and Queen normally spent their weeks circling between Windsor, Kew and

London. The royal tour was therefore of sufficient novelty for newspapers of the day to follow its progress; the Cheltenham episode was to be of important personal consequence for Fanny, but a part of the interest of her journals is that her account of day-to-day experiences from within the royal household can be set beside that of *The Gentleman's Magazine*, which kept a diary of the King's public activities.

To prepare Fauconberg Lodge for its royal occupants it was said that workmen had been 'literally turning the House out of windows, breaking Holes in the walls, spoiling the Papers, Stucco &c', but nothing could make the property any larger.[5] Fanny found herself living far more intimately with the royal family than she did elsewhere, conscious that the King might pop his head round a door at any moment to ask a question or make a joke, and alerted by the barking of the dogs to every royal entrance and exit. When she went into the first-floor room which was to serve the Queen both for dressing and drawing-room Fanny exclaimed, '*This*, ma'am! . . . is *this* little room for your Majesty?' The Queen replied with a laugh, 'Oh stay till you see your own before you call it little!' Fanny discovered her bedroom on the top floor, so tiny that there was room for no more than a bed, chest of drawers, and three small chairs. But it compensated for its size with a beautiful view over the countryside to the hills beyond.[6]

The ground-floor accommodation consisted only of the royal dining-room, the King's dressing-room, and behind it the housekeeper's room; this was allotted to Fanny as her 'parlour'. Its windows with their checked curtains looked out into the kitchen courtyard, and she appropriated a drawer which had held table-linen for her books and papers. There was no room for the men in the party and they, including Fanny's servant Jacob Columb, were lodged in the town. She was not allowed her maid Goter, and it was awkward to have no help with her own dressing, royal attendance at the wells being so early that she had to be up before five to prepare herself for the Queen's call. The first morning, however, was a Sunday, and the royal family went to service at the parish church while she and Miss Planta were busy 'fagging', unpacking and preparing their clothes. Next morning the King, Queen and Princesses were reported to have been drinking the waters at half-past five. Fanny and Peggy Planta tried them too, but once was enough for Fanny who found their taste 'very unpleasant'.

Cheltenham Spa then consisted almost entirely of a single well-paved street, but its fame grew greatly as a result of the royal visit. The medicinal spring had been identified some seventy years earlier when pigeons were observed pecking at the salty deposits; when people took to drinking the water the farmer started charging a fee. Then in 1738 the land came into the ownership of the enterprising Henry Skillicorne; he covered the spring with a brick canopy, pumped up the water, laid out a tree-lined walk from the town and built an assembly room nearby. Patrons were attracted by the cure-all properties claimed for the waters, though they were thought particularly effective in treating stomach disorders. Later analysis showed that the water was largely a solution of Epsom salts, so its main effect was purgative; jokes and cartoons illustrated the risks of immediate effect.[7] No wonder that the Queen abandoned her early morning attendance at the wells, which must have been a relief to Fanny.

The King, however, was enthusiastic, drinking a pint and a half every day except Sunday, and enjoying the vigorous exercise which was recommended to follow the drinking. On horse or on foot he roamed the countryside, often quite alone and unrecognised; one man with whom he fell into conversation asked if he had seen the King who was said to dress 'very plain'. He replied, 'Aye, as plain as you see me now'.[8] In contrast, on an official visit to Stroud to watch cloth being made, some 50,000 people thronged to see and cheer him.[9] He also travelled with his wife and daughters on sightseeing trips to Gloucester and Tewkesbury, and visited the homes of local dignitaries. In the evenings the royal party promenaded on the Walks just as on the Terrace at Windsor, or attended what Fanny called the 'village theatre' which soon boasted itself the Theatre Royal.

Fanny began the visit hopeful that she would have much more time to herself than at Windsor, free from the compulsion of the daily tea table. Miss Planta, the only other member of the household to be living in the Lodge, was planning to spend her time walking for her health. After the death of Mrs Delany, Fanny suffered from having no intimate woman friend at court; though Peggy Planta was much her own age, 'good, and sensible, and prudent, and ready for any kind office', Fanny did not find her a very stimulating companion.[10] Susan called her the Wallflower. But Fanny's plan to enjoy her own company, at least until the arrival of Marianne Port, was frustrated. On the first evening Fanny had gone downstairs to look for Columb and give him orders for tea on the upstairs landing for Miss Planta and herself, when he came to say that Mr Digby asked to speak with her. With Lord Courtown, the Treasurer of the Household, he had come to beg that for this day only they might join her for tea. Next day, he promised, they would arrange to take it at their lodgings and would not disturb her. How strange, thought Fanny, that the first person she should meet at court who understood her preference for solitude should be the one for whom her resolution to attain it wavered.

Colonel the Honourable Stephen Digby, born in 1742, belonged to a family first mentioned in Domesday Book, owning estates in the Midlands, south of England and Ireland. Their principal seat was Sherborne Castle in Dorset, though the Castle itself was a ruin and the family lived in a house built on the estate by Sir Walter Ralegh; the extensive grounds had recently been landscaped by Capability Brown. Stephen was one of a family of six brothers of whom Edward was 6th and Henry 7th Lord Digby (Earl Digby from 1790); another brother, Robert, became a successful Admiral, and another the Dean of Durham. Stephen was probably educated at Eton, though no record of him exists there.[11] At the age of eighteen he entered the army, serving in Germany, Gibraltar and Ireland until 1778, when he resigned his commission with the rank of Lieutenant-Colonel.[12] Thereafter, he was first appointed Groom of the Bedchamber to the Prince of Wales, then in 1783 the Queen's Vice-Chamberlain. He was liked and trusted by the King and Queen and had a number of friends at court including the Harcourts and Colonel Greville, but by the time of the Cheltenham expedition he planned to retire, telling Fanny that the exertions of royal attendance were not suited to his 'turn of mind'. In 1771 he had married his cousin, Lady Lucy Fox-Strangways, daughter of the Earl of Ilchester, and they had four children; Lady Lucy was granddaughter of Sir Stephen Fox, Charles II's Paymaster-General, and cousin of the politician Charles Fox who in turn was grandson of the Duke of Richmond and descended from Charles II. The title 'Mr' Digby, so frequently found in the journals, scarcely does justice to his web of aristocratic connections.

These bare facts give little sense of the man. Contemporary references to him in early life are hard to find, but it is clear that Stephen was strongly attached to his family and his childhood home, where he was known as 'Ste'. He returned regularly to Sherborne Castle while in the army, and in the Castle Game-books (in which social events as well as statistics of game bags are recorded) the brothers made bantering entries about each other. In October 1767, for example, Robert reported that 'Ste would not go [to Montacute] lest Miss Philips shd. not think him handsome, having scratched his face by a fall', and in January 1770, 'Ste riding down the Lawn like a Goosecap tumbled down backwards like a sack of oats', adding 'If you would know how a Goosecap rides, you may suppose a silly girl upon a mans saddle'.[13] Stephen got his own back by reporting that Robert's dogs had failed to catch a hare. A close relationship with his mother is confirmed by letters written at the time of her death, and by the feeling recorded by Fanny when he spoke of her.[14] Stephen's letters reveal a curious feature of his handwriting: writers then made the long stroke of a *d* upwards and curving backwards, but he takes the curve right round into a snail shape. It is an affectation (lost in his later hand) perhaps on a par with sensitivity about a scratch on his face.

There is a portrait at Sherborne Castle by Sir Joshua Reynolds which shows Stephen as a young man; his face reveals the family features of long aristocratic nose, dark eyes and eyebrows, and rather small mouth.[15] The hair is lightly curled and powdered and he is wearing a scarlet military jacket. But he looks scholar more than soldier, serious, sensitive, and strikingly pale. Though this pallor probably owes more to fading paint than to natural complexion, it does seem appropriate for a man who was dogged by ill health during the time when Fanny knew him.

She met Stephen Digby when she first went to court, and he was attentive to her needs on the Oxford expedition, but shortly afterwards he had taken his leave of her because of the illness of his wife. From time to time thereafter Fanny heard how she was suffering 'death by inches' from breast cancer, devotedly nursed by her husband.[16] She died on 16 August 1787. On his return to court Digby had aged; he was thin and haggard, his hair had turned white and some of his front teeth were missing (though from the frequency of Fanny's references it seems he retained a beguiling smile). But grief had changed more than his appearance. He had become excessively melancholy, convinced that after youth happiness was unachievable, a theme he often returned to in conversations with Fanny. She could not accept that God had created the world to be a place of misery for mankind, though she made allowance for his ordeal. In Digby, however, Fanny found someone sympathetic to her mourning for Mrs Delany, and he also took a practical interest in her well-being, urging her to take walks for her health and to look after her diet. Despite his pessimism, Fanny was glad to have discovered someone of 'gentleness, good breeding, and delicacy', with whom she could converse on serious subjects.[17]

The request for tea was readily granted though Fanny was not quite comfortable about abandoning Miss Planta on the upstairs landing. Afterwards Digby asked if he might stay a little longer, and though it was an embarrassment when the King put his head round the door and exclaimed, 'What! Only you two?', she considered that their remaining together was a declaration of liberty for both. The King wanted a letter written and Digby asked permission to do it in her parlour, afterwards saying 'Will there be any – impropriety – in my staying here a little longer?' His very use of the word shows a consciousness that others might think so, but Fanny had too much enjoyed his company to send him away. Nothing further was said about independent arrangements for tea, and next morning Fanny found that the gentlemen were also to breakfast with her and Miss Planta. Digby busied himself with the seating arrangements, placing himself next to Fanny.

During the rest of the Cheltenham stay Digby showed increasing inclination to remain in the parlour with Fanny. She also became aware of a
significant difference between his behaviour in company, and alone with
her: in general company he talked freely, even jestingly, but when they were
alone he frequently lapsed into gloom. She would sit sewing through long
brooding silences, which she attributed to the approaching anniversary of
his wife's death. A week after their arrival Digby caught a cold and was
confined to his lodgings with a swollen face; he was still too unwell to accompany the King and Queen when they went to Tewkesbury. Great, therefore,
was Fanny's surprise when she was told that he was in the house and asking
for her. She was glad to receive him though he looked very ill, and they
conversed on his favourite topics of 'Death and Immortality, and the assured
misery of all stations and all seasons in this vain and restless world'.[18]

This was not the only time that Digby came to see Fanny when claiming
to be unfit for his royal duties. He had scarcely recovered from this illness
when Colonel Gwynn reported at breakfast that his companion would be
unable to join the royal family on their visit to the Earl of Coventry's seat
at Coombe:

> Soon after the King came into the room and said, 'So, no Mr. Digby
> again?'
> 'No, sir; he's very bad this morning.'
> 'What's the matter? His face?'
> 'No, sir; he has got the gout. These waters, he thinks, have brought
> it on.'
> 'What, in his foot?'
> 'Yes, sir; he is quite lame; his foot is swelled prodigiously.'
> 'So he's quite knocked up! Can't he come out?'
> 'No, sir; he's obliged to order a gouty shoe and stay at home and
> nurse.'[19]

For the royals the visit to Coombe was made memorable by the antics of
local young farmers who 'having previously found their way into the
Earl's cellar, came forth in high spirits, and one of them, newly married
. . . would kiss his bride in the King's coach'.[20] Despite remonstrances
from the coachmen, others followed suit; luckily his Majesty was amused
by what he saw as harmless behaviour.

The departure for the day of the royal family gave Fanny a chance to
rest and relax; around midday, however, she heard Miss Planta scream, 'Is
it possible? Mr. Digby?' Soon he was rapping at the parlour door and
hobbling in, stick in hand and with one foot encased in a great cloth

shoe. When Columb came to ask Fanny at what time she should dine, 'a ghost could not have made him stare more' than the sight of the supposedly stay-at-home courtier ensconced in his mistress's parlour.

It is easy to feel sympathy for Digby, in pain, alone in his lodgings, and probably going over in his mind the harrowing events of the previous year. His discontent with his post had increased when he heard that the King intended to stay an extra week at Cheltenham and to travel back to Windsor on the very anniversary of his wife's death. Yet as he limped across the summer fields to Fauconberg Lodge he appears to have been anticipating more than sympathetic company. He had begun to read favourite poetry and other literature aloud to Fanny, an activity both would have been aware as more fitting to the role of would-be wooer than grieving husband. Indeed, when he appeared so unexpectedly in her parlour Fanny was reading from a novel he had lent her called *Original Love Letters, Between a Lady of Quality and a Person of Inferior Station*; it purports to be genuine letters offering, Digby said, 'nothing but good sense, moral reflections, and refined ideas' (and there is certainly nothing scandalous in a novel whose lovers are destined for winding-rather than bridal sheets).[21] But the title made Digby nervous, and he needed reassurance that no one would come in and catch him 'reading love-letters to Miss Burney'. Later Digby begged that he might dine with her and Miss Planta, despite the need to hobble back and forth from his lodgings again in order to dress. Miss Planta was astonished when told they would have a 'beau' for dinner:

> 'Well,' she exclaimed, ''tis the oddest thing in the world he should come so when the King and Queen are away! I am sure, if I was you, I would not mention it.'
> 'Oh yes, I shall,' cried I; 'I receive no visitors in private; and I am sure if I did, Mr. Digby is the last who would condescend to make one of them.'
> Such was my proud, but true speech, for him and for myself.[22]

After dinner Miss Planta took herself and whatever private thoughts she had for her usual walk, while Digby and Fanny went out onto the porch to enjoy the air. The golden evening light falls not only on the landscape when she writes:

> And here, for near two hours, on the steps of Fauconberg Hall, we remained; and they were two hours of such pure serenity, without and within, as I think, except in Norbury Park, with its loved

inhabitants and my Susan, I scarce ever remember to have spent. Higher gaiety and greater happiness many and many periods of my life have at different times afforded me; but a tranquillity more perfect has only, I think, been lent to me in Norbury Park, where, added to all else that could soothe and attract, every affection of my heart could be expanded and indulged.[23]

For the first time in two years Fanny expresses contentment of spirit; in a rapturous continuation of the passage in the unpublished journals she suggests that Digby shared with her an 'inward peace'.[24]

Reading of this evening's events and seeing the implications Susan was to comment: 'Surely it was a little mad – a little crazed! – come to pursue his lecture! – What an interest in it he must have felt - - - - well well –'.[25] Like Susan, Fanny was not unaware of the possibilities of the developing situation though at the time she wrote with detachment, neither analysing nor speculating. A modern reader might be reminded of Anne Elliot and the grieving Captain Benwick who in *Persuasion* read poetry together at Lyme; like the fictional Anne, Fanny sensed that Digby was 'not inconsolable'.[26] But she was so sure that at present he was preoccupied with the past that she did not credit gossip, which she had heard before they left Windsor, that he was seeking to marry one of the Maids of Honour, Charlotte Gunning, daughter of a diplomat, Sir Robert Gunning.[27] Two remarks by Digby confirmed her opinion, firstly that he had told her that the position of Maid of Honour was 'one in which he would not place any person for whom he had the smallest regard', and secondly that he had declared that it would not be for Fanny's happiness to become versed in the classics – yet Miss Gunning was a noted scholar. Thus she dismissed what may have been intended as a friendly warning, when Colonel Gwynn asked her opinion of Digby remarrying:

'I think it very doubtful,' I answered, 'but I hope he will, for, whether he is happy or not in marrying, I am sure he will be wretched in singleness; the whole turn of his mind is so social and domestic. He is by no means formed for going always abroad for the relief of society; he requires it more at hand.'

'And what do you think of Miss Gunning?'

'That he is wholly disengaged with her and with everybody.'

'Well, I think it will be, for I know they correspond; and what should he correspond with her for else?'

'Because, I suppose, he has done it long before this could be suggested as the motive. And, indeed, the very quickness of the report makes me discredit it; 'tis so utterly impossible for a man whose feelings are so delicate to have taken any steps towards a second connection at so early a period.'

'Why, I know he's very romantic; but I should like to know your opinion.'

'I have given it you,' cried I, 'very exactly.'

However, you may believe I could not tell him what had passed about *Maids of Honour*.[28]

Had Fanny done so, Colonel Gwynn might have proposed a lovers' tiff in explanation. Next day she told the Queen of his visit and was naïvely surprised in that small household to discover that she knew already:

'But pray, ma'am,' very gravely, 'how did it happen? I understood Mr. Digby was confined by the gout.'

'He grew better, ma'am, and hoped by exercise to prevent a serious fit.'[29]

Fanny was covering up for Digby, and risking royal displeasure herself. She was later to excuse all such indiscretions in the grand statement that 'His noble and undisguised nature disdains precautions towards others, where he feels no necessity for them in himself'.[30] This was rather at odds with Digby's obvious anxiety not to be discovered reading the *Love Letters* or any other literature with Fanny. If a sound suggested someone might come into the room he would thrust the book behind him, and once he asked Fanny to put her manservant Columb on guard, in case the King and Queen returned unexpectedly. Though the reason given was a desire to avoid a reputation as an intellectual – with which Fanny concurred – it was all rather furtive. Digby wanted Fanny to write to him after his departure, and to demonstrate how safe her letters would be he took one which he had just received from his eldest son Charles, read it, then burnt it in the candle flame. If he could thus destroy a letter from one so dear to him, hers would not fall into the wrong hands (an action Fanny herself could never have undertaken in her later life with even the most trivial of her own son's letters).

Fanny did not spend all her time at Cheltenham preoccupied with Stephen Digby. Entertainments were being provided for the King and Queen, in some of which Fanny participated, though she does not seem to have watched the cricket matches the King organised to keep the servants fit, nor to have watched a conjurer cut a piece of silk from the Queen's dress and miraculously replace it.[31] But she went several times to the theatre with Marianne Port to see the popular comic actress Dora Jordan in plays; on the evening of the sojourn on the steps they attended Garrick's toned-down version of Wycherley's *The Country Wife*, though it was still too gross for Fanny's taste. But she admired Mrs Jordan, as did the King and Queen. They showed their appreciation of her powers to amuse some evenings later by sending the recovered Colonel Digby with a gift for her.[32]

For a while Cheltenham became synonymous with fashion; even those who could not travel to the spa vaunted tokens of it. It was reported that 'the Cheltenham cap – the Cheltenham bonnet – the Cheltenham buttons – the Cheltenham buckles – all the fashions are completely Cheltenhamised'.[33] But society was flocking to Cheltenham and Fanny met a number of old friends there. They included the Dean of Winchester, Dr Newton Ogle and his family, whose daughter Esther, a high-spirited girl of republican views who later became the second Mrs Sheridan (and was known to Fanny as 'Spotty'), here distinguished herself during one of the evening promenades by accidentally-on-purpose turning her back on the Queen. However, the gesture, if that was what it was, went unrebuked.

Though Fanny was never part of an official royal party, the Queen encouraged her and Miss Planta in some sightseeing, sending them one day to Gloucester, where they were taken to the Cathedral and then to the new gaol being built to the recommendations of the penal reformer John Howard.[34] Even so, Fanny found it inhumane: though each cell had light and air, no communication between prisoners was allowed and the aim seemed to be 'to show in how small a space . . . human beings can live, as well as die or be dead'. She preferred the infirmary with its combination of cleanliness and compassion. But she recommended both to the Queen and, whether as a consequence or not, while in Gloucester it was reported that their Majesties followed a visit to the Pin-manufactory with ones to the infirmary and gaol.[35]

Fanny and Miss Planta also went to Tewkesbury, where they saw the Abbey with its reminders of victims of the Wars of the Roses. On return Fanny was surprised to find her cousin Richard Burney waiting in the parlour; the Worcester branch of the Burneys, her father's brother Richard and his family, were looking forward to seeing her there when the King attended the city's music festival. Normally Fanny would have been pleased to see Richard, but she had declared that she could have no visitors and anyway, in riding clothes and with his hair neither curled nor powdered, Richard was unfit for royal eyes. After enough conversation for courtesy Fanny asked jokingly if 'he felt stout enough' to meet the King, explaining the situation. He was alarmed almost immediately by a knock on the door, but it proved only to be Digby, himself given something to stare at in this stranger – who hurried away before worse might befall him.

These events occurred on a day otherwise notable for the arrival of the Duke of York, for whom extraordinary preparations had been made. The King could not endure for his favourite to be lodged apart from him, so seeing a small wooden house at the edge of the town he had engaged an engineer to move it to the side of the Lodge. This had been achieved, to the marvel of everyone except his Majesty who was displeased that the operation took six whole days, thus removing the planned element of surprise.[36] After all this effort the Duke announced he could only stay one night, though he would spend all next day in Cheltenham and travel back afterwards. Digby commented, 'I wonder how these Princes, who are thus forced to steal even their travelling from their sleep, find time to say their prayers!'[37] With Miss Planta he gave Fanny some idea of just how disruptive the young Princes could be, and declared that no money on earth would now induce him to take a post with any of them.

After the Duke of York's flying visit a flu epidemic swept through the health resort and one after another of the household succumbed to it. Seeing Fanny drooping in the Queen's dressing-room, the King summoned the doctor already in attendance on the Princess Royal. The resulting 'consultation' illustrates the difficulties for humble beings in a royal environment:

'Now, Mr. Clerk,' cried he, 'here's another for you.'

Mr. Clerk, a modest, sensible man, concluded, by the King himself having called him, that it was the Queen he had now to attend, and he stood bowing profoundly before her; but soon observing she did not notice him, he turned in some confusion to the Princess Augusta, who was now in the group.

'No, no! it's not me, Mr. Clerk, thank God!' cried the gay Princess Augusta.

Still more confused, the poor man advanced to Princess Elizabeth.

'No, no; it's not her!' cried the King.

I had held back, having scarce power to open my eyes, from a vehement headache, and not, indeed, wishing to go through my examination till there were fewer witnesses. But His Majesty now drew me out. 'Here, Mr. Clerk,' he cried, 'this is your new patient!'

He then came bowing up to me, the King standing close by, and the rest pretty near.

'You – you are not well, ma'am?' he cried in the greatest embarrassment.

'No, sir, not quite,' I answered in ditto.

'Oh, Mr. Clerk will cure you!' cried the King.

'Are – are you feverish, ma'am?'

'Yes, sir, a little.'

'I – I will send you a saline draught, ma'am.'

'If you please.'

And then he bowed and decamped.[38]

The Princess Royal later kindly shared her own medicine with Fanny, who though ill was not excused attendances on the Queen. At teatime she crawled down to the parlour where Digby read her a sermon and, not altogether tactfully in view of her illness, talked of death and the after-life.

It was as well that she had more or less recovered two days later for the Worcester expedition, as there was a busy programme which involved rather more formal dressing than was required at Cheltenham. Fanny was able to see something of her cousins, but only during the concerts as her duties left insufficient time to visit them at home. Reports show that these concerts were splendidly staged in the Cathedral, where a throne canopied in crimson silk with a gold fringe was placed for the King under the great west window. Those who attended the first performance, devoted entirely to music by Handel, saw the tall figure of their sovereign in his Windsor uniform and with the diamond Garter star on his breast; the men of his suite wore the same uniform, while the Queen and her daughters were dressed in silver tissue gowns with bonnets of blue tiffany spotted with silver.[39] Packed into the four days were more concerts, and a ball, processions, a reception, levée, and visits to carpet and china manufactories. The King seemed tireless, but Digby must have felt even less enthusiastic about royal service when on the second morning his Majesty arrived at his lodgings at five-thirty and woke both him and Colonel Gwynn up. It was said they 'leaped out of their beds as if surprised in camp by an enemy'.[40]

On the evening of their return to Cheltenham Digby came to take his departure; Fanny already knew he intended to leave early to be at home with his children for the anniversary of their mother's death. He was in 'melancholy and moralising' mood as they spoke together, before he took his hat and prepared to go:

'We will say,' cried he, 'nothing of any regrets,' and bowed, and was hastening off.

The 'we', however, had an openness and simplicity that drew from me an equally open and simple reply. 'No,' I cried, 'but I will say –

for that you will have pleasure in hearing – that you have lightened my time here in a manner that no one else could have done, of this party.'[41]

Though limited by the final phrase Fanny was making as clear as she decorously could not just her gratitude but her liking for his company. He did not reply but bowed and went away, leaving Fanny 'firmly impressed with a belief that I shall find in him a true, an honourable, and even an affectionate friend, for life'.

Next day, however, Digby placed her in a difficult position. Just before dinner she received a note from him, sent express from Northleach some fifteen miles from Cheltenham. She copied it out for Susan and Fredy:

Her Majesty may possibly not have heard that Mr. Edmund Waller died on Thursday night. He was Master of St. Catherine's, which is in Her Majesty's gift. It may be useful to her to have this early intelligence of this circumstance, and you will have the goodness to mention it to her. Mr. W. was at a house upon his own estate within a mile and a half of this place. – Very truly and sincerely yours, S. Digby.[42]

St Katharine's was and is a charitable foundation in London's dockland.[43] Fanny's problem was that she knew such information ought to have been conveyed through a lady-in-waiting, not a robe-keeper. Then there was the wording of the close. 'Very truly and sincerely yours' – what would the Queen think of that? She was well aware that the Queen had shown a certain dryness in discovering Digby's presence at the Lodge when 'too ill' to accompany the royal party, or when she had learnt of her Vice-Chamberlain's plans for leaving Cheltenham not from himself but from Fanny. Yet Digby's wishes were paramount and she did not consider refusing to deliver the message.

Trying, therefore, to avoid a face-to-face encounter, Fanny asked Princess Elizabeth to give the Queen the news, without revealing her source. She was summoned to the royal presence nevertheless, and asked how long she had known Mr Waller; she had to confess that she did not know him at all and had been sent the news by Mr Digby. This reply was greeted with silence. Fanny quickly improvised – Mr Digby was in great haste – wrote on very small paper – the note was not fit to be shown to the Queen. Silence again. In the end Fanny had to fetch it, wishing she had burnt it, Digby-fashion, on receipt. The Queen read it aloud and Fanny thought that at the final phrase her tone altered and 'she seemed to look at [it] for a moment with some doubt if it were not a mistake'. But she handed it back with a bow, saying simply, 'I am very much obliged to Mr. Digby'. (His anxiety to inform the Queen of the vacancy was probably explained when the post, worth several hundred pounds, was awarded to him.) In her journals Fanny expressed no criticism of the courtier for exposing her to this awkward encounter. Her concern was how to word a letter to say she had carried out his commission, and she composed a short note which while wishing him and his family well carefully avoided both an opening and a close.

On 16 August the royal party left Cheltenham in the belief that the King was completely cured.[44] The High Street was crowded as they took their departure ('gentles' one side, 'commons' the other); among the onlookers was Marianne, with whom Fanny exchanged sorrowful looks. The return to Windsor meant joyful reunion for the King with his younger daughters, but for Fanny it was a 'most melancholy' experience. Her reunion, and her evening's tête-à-tête, were with Mrs Schwellenberg. The five weeks away had seemed a very long time; next day she wrote that she felt something like the Sleeping Beauty waking to a life exactly the same as it had been before. Unexpressed in the comparison was the knowledge that in the fairy-tale the awaking involved a prince: was someone about to rescue her from the palace?

CHAPTER NINE

Two Prisoners

Oh, my dear friends, what a history! The King, at dinner, had broken forth
into positive delirium . . . and the Queen was so overpowered as to fall into
violent hysterics. All the Princesses were in misery, and the Prince of Wales
had burst into tears. No one knew what was to follow – no one could
conjecture the event.[1]

Whatever fantasies Fanny may have been nourishing after Cheltenham
none came immediately to pass. Digby did not write. Two months later he
visited the court at Kew, yet did not seek her out till the second day, and
then neither referred to her note nor explained why he had not written.
She was hurt that so much intimacy seemed so soon forgotten, but
concluded that the difference in their rank made it unlikely he would
contemplate an alliance; she had been living in a dream and must wake
from it. The brevity of her note to him had been no encouragement to
correspondence, but throughout their relationship it seems that when
Fanny was out of Stephen's sight she was also out of his mind. However, a
situation was developing at court to absorb all her emotional energy. On
the very day when she saw Digby again, 17 October 1788, she also noted:

> Our return to Windsor is postponed till tomorrow. The King is not
> well; he has not been quite well some time, yet nothing I hope
> alarming . . .[2]

The King had been forced to summon his physician following another
crippling bilious attack. He was treated with alternating doses of laxatives
and laudanum, his indisposition put down to not having changed a pair
of wet stockings the previous day. The court was forced to remain at Kew,
which created difficulties since no one had any change of clothing. There
were no books to read, so 'in mere desperation for employment' Fanny
began to write a blank-verse tragedy. She can hardly have begun as
precipitately as the casual announcement in her journal suggests, but the
melancholy situation provided an incentive, and writing distracted her
from anxiety.[3]

It was a week before the King was well enough to return to Windsor, and this amendment was only temporary; other strange and frightening symptoms were appearing, most obviously a change of manner:

> I had a sort of conference with His Majesty, or rather I was the object to whom he spoke, with a manner so uncommon, that a high fever alone could account for it; a rapidity, a hoarseness of voice, a volubility, an earnestness – a vehemence, rather – it startled me inexpressibly; yet with a graciousness exceeding even all I ever met with before – it was almost kindness!
> Heaven – Heaven preserve him![4]

Fanny noted the curious nature of his condition, that with extreme restlessness went a physical weakness which made him walk 'like a gouty man' and require a walking-stick. 'My dear Effy,' she heard him say to Lady Effingham, 'you see me all at once an old man.'

The Queen grew more and more fearful; that same morning she had broken off from reading to Fanny and burst into tears:

> 'How nervous I am!' she cried; 'I am quite a fool! Don't you think so?'
> 'No, ma'am!' was all I dared answer.[5]

That night Fanny observed the Queen sitting wordless in her dressing-room while the King begged her again and again 'not to speak to him when he got to his room, that he might fall asleep'. On 3 November, Princess Sophia's eleventh birthday, a second doctor was called in. In distress of mind Fanny ceased writing her journal, though at some later date, realising the importance of events, she began keeping detailed memoranda to write up later, some notes made retrospectively. Other observers were to record their memories and immediate experience of this time, but no one catches better than Fanny the horror of the initial onset of the illness and the day-to-day fluctuations of hope and fear. However, she herself gets little mention in others' accounts, while for her continuing personal story she is virtually the only source.

The day of crisis was 5 November, heralded in her journal by 'Oh dreadful day!' The royal household had grown more and more shut in on itself: the Queen never left the Lodge, Fanny had given up her walks, and people coming to enquire found themselves turned away. At noon Fanny saw from her window that the King was setting off for an airing with his eldest daughter. He seemed all benign smiles yet his behaviour was disordered, climbing in and out of the carriage and bewildering the postillions with contradictory commands. Through the same window Fanny later saw Digby arrive, and since he was not expected knew it for a sign of the gravity of the situation. For the Queen's sake she was glad to see him, though her own feelings had been further confused when her ever-ready informant, Miss Planta – who always now named 'Mr. Digby' with a certain emphasis – told her that he had been confined with gout at Sir Robert Gunning's. She 'would now lay any wager he was to marry Miss Gunning'. He was still walking lamely when he entered Queen's Lodge.

That evening the two women dined together almost in silence; afterwards Fanny became aware of a total and unnatural stillness about the whole house:

> Nobody stirred; not a voice was heard; not a step, not a motion. I could do nothing but watch, without knowing for what: there seemed a strangeness in the house most extraordinary.
>
> At seven o'clock Columb came to tell me that the music was all forbid, and the musicians ordered away!
>
> This was the last step to be expected, so fond as His Majesty is of his Concert, and I thought it might have rather soothed him: I could not understand the prohibition; all seemed stranger and stranger.[6]

Colonel Goldsworthy and General Budé came in for tea, then Colonel Digby, who bowed silently to her. All were immensely grave but uncommunicative; Colonel Goldsworthy was called away and Fanny could hear him whispering in the passage. Finally she found herself alone with Digby and after a frighteningly long pause he asked her whether she knew 'how bad all was become, and how ill the King': at dinner he had broken out in 'positive delirium' throwing the whole family into hysteria. No doubt he also told her that the King had physically attacked the Prince of Wales, grabbing him by the collar and flinging him against the wall, but this was the sort of detail she would prefer to suppress in her later account. Digby spoke compassionately of the Queen and Princesses, then, in a restoration of the old intimacy, looked closely at her:

> 'How,' he cried, 'are you? Are you strong? are you stout? can you go through such scenes as these? you do not look much fitted for them.'
>
> 'I shall do very well,' I cried, 'for, at a time such as this, I shall forget myself utterly. The Queen will be all to me. I shall hardly, I think, feel myself at liberty to be unhappy!'[7]

When he left, Digby took her hand and exhorted her to keep herself 'stout and firm'.

That night she needed all her strength and courage. She waited in her room – 'alone, in silence, in ignorance, in dread' – till one o'clock in the morning, when a page summoned her to the Queen; she found her royal mistress 'pale, ghastly pale', her hand as cold as marble. Next morning Fanny rose at six, dressed by candlelight then, unable to bear the suspense, crept along a passage made gloomier by a penetrating fog. As she reached the dressing-room door she stopped, alarmed by the sound of men's voices inside. It proved to be Colonel Goldsworthy and the apothecary Robert Battiscombe, both of whom had sat there all night. Along the passages and in the ante-rooms the royal pages had sat up too; Fanny saw horror in every face. She hovered at the door till Miss Goldsworthy, seated on a stool beside the Queen's bed, said, ''Tis Miss Burney, ma'am':

> She leaned her head forward, and in a most soft manner, said, 'Miss Burney, how are you?'
>
> Deeply affected, I hastened up to her, but, in trying to speak, burst into an irresistible torrent of tears.
>
> My dearest friends, I do it at this moment again, and can hardly write for them; yet I wish you to know all this piercing history right.
>
> She looked like death – colourless and wan; but nature is infectious; the tears gushed from her own eyes, and a perfect agony of weeping ensued, which, once begun, she could not stop; she did not, indeed, try; for when it subsided, and she wiped her eyes, she said, 'I thank you, Miss Burney – you have made me cry – it is a great relief to me – I had not been able to cry before, all this night long'.[8]

Fanny heard how the King had come into her room in the middle of the night, candle in hand, opened the bed-curtains to see if the Queen was still there, and remained for almost half an hour. He was still in the next room with his doctors, talking unceasingly. Fanny was asked to listen and report what she could hear:

> Nothing could be so afflicting as this task; even now, it brings fresh to my ear his poor exhausted voice. 'I am nervous,' he cried; 'I am not ill, but I am nervous: if you would know what is the matter with me, I am nervous . . .'

This was what he kept saying almost constantly, mixed in with other matter, but always returning, and in a voice that truly will never cease vibrating in my recollection.[9]

It was considered that on this day the King came close to death.

More doctors were brought in, but all were completely at a loss. Today it is accepted that the King's derangement was caused by variegate porphyria, a genetically transmitted condition in which toxic chemicals damage the nervous system, producing drastic effects on body and mind.[10] This illness was not known to medical science until the 1930s so there was no possibility of accurate diagnosis by George III's physicians. They were left floundering, trying in turn their standard remedies of bleeding and blistering, cupping, emetics, purges and febrifuges to draw the ill humours from the body. Entries in Robert Battiscombe's memorandum book illustrate treatments ordered by the King's physician up to the night of crisis:

[Oct] 30   cuppd His Majesty
[Nov] 1   cuppd His Majesty again
       4   cuppd His Majesty again
       5   applied Blister to the Head
           Sate up in the night wth y[e] King
           Dr Warren & Heberden sent for express in the night.[11]

Cupping was the application to the skin of heated glass vessels which adhere and in cooling draw the blood to the surface, after which incisions were made to drain the 'infected' blood; like blistering it caused useless pain and distress. Because of their desperate rotation of remedies, Mrs Harcourt told her sister-in-law that the doctors 'seem to be amusing themselves . . . and feel no more for him than if he were a dog or a cat'.[12] Though there were days of apparent improvement the King's condition generally worsened. Only the physician Sir Lucas Pepys, an old social acquaintance of Fanny's, felt at all optimistic, accurately deducing from periods of lucidity that the King's mind was unaffected and that he would eventually recover.

The atmosphere of Queen's Lodge was one of extreme gloom; Fanny heard the Queen exclaim, 'What will become of me? What will become of me?' She could not eat and would not even dress – on advice she had moved to a room more distant from the King and wanted to maintain the fiction to him that it was because she was unwell. She passed the time 'walking backwards and forwards' till exhausted.[13] Fanny offered to take the place of Miss Goldsworthy who had become ill with sitting up at night, but the Queen thought her not strong enough. Between her times of attendance Fanny found herself alone in her room, so wrapped up in the atmosphere of misery that she could neither read nor write; in the midst of this 'living tragedy' her fictional one was set aside.

Fanny's sense of isolation would have been unendurable without Stephen Digby, who kept her informed of events. Their evening meetings were re-established in Fanny's apartment since the dining-room had been appropriated for the doctors; Digby declared that her room was 'his only refuge and consolation in this miserable house'. He had set aside his plans for retirement and gave devoted service; Fanny heard the Prince of Wales tell the Queen how it was Mr Digby who had managed to persuade the King to return to his bed one night after he had risen in extreme agitation:

> 'He came boldly up to him, and took him by the arm, and begged him to go to bed, and then drew him along, and said he must go. Then he said he would not, and cried, "Who are you?" "I am Mr. Digby, sir," he answered, "and your Majesty has been very good to me often, and now I am going to be very good to you, for you must come to bed, sir: it is necessary to your life." And then he was so surprised, that he let himself be drawn along just like a child; and so they got him to bed.'[14]

Such scenes took their toll on a man whose own health was doubtful: Digby told Fanny that he wished he could live without sleep. He was not hopeful about the outcome, unlike Fanny who never despaired. It was, however, easier for her to hope; Digby was spending as much as five hours at a time with the King and was witness to the full derangement. But pessimism was natural to his character: life was to be endured not enjoyed, and he offered Fanny his watchwords, 'Expect little, be humble, and pray'.[15]

Yet Digby's attention was not entirely focused on spiritual matters. One evening, after a soft tap, he entered and swiftly shut the door, so conspiratorially muffled up that Fanny did not immediately recognise him. He seemed flurried, telling her that he had come to warn her that the King, who was much better, had been making 'charges' and that she had come in for her 'share'. He had criticised his equerries for not being ready when wanted, adding that Digby was as bad, for 'he's just as late as the rest, for he's so fond of the company of learned ladies, that he gets to the tea-table with Miss Burney, and there he spends his whole time'. Fanny sat speechless, totally disconcerted. Digby hurried on, breathlessly identifying the other 'learned lady' as Miss Gunning, but vigorously denying the reports which had been circulating about them. Then he left, saying with a laugh which she could not echo, 'Well, since I have now got the character of being fond of such company, I shall certainly . . . come and drink tea with you very often'.[16]

This event is recorded by Fanny for 20 November; Colonel Greville in his day-to-day account of the King's illness records that around this time the King was praising some of his attendants and abusing others. Though there is a discrepancy of date (perhaps explained by Fanny's retrospective journalising) he notes on 23 November that 'Col. Digby . . . for the first time was a little in disgrace with H. M^y'.[17] He does not say why, but if the reason involved Miss Burney, Greville would have been too much the gentleman to say so. Again Digby's motives are unfathomable: was his concern only to warn her? Did he want to reassure her about Miss Gunning? Perhaps the idea of youthful flirtation and intrigue came as a relief from his arduous sick-room duties. But if he thought Fanny would be responsive he mistook her nature, for his news caused her consternation and she seriously considered whether she should now put a stop to his visits. However, he was her only 'social comfort' in the present miserable situation so, consoling herself that the charge was the innocent one of 'learning' not flirtation, she decided against doing so.

In any case she would not be staying much longer in Queen's Lodge. It had been decided that the King should be removed to Kew, where privacy could more easily be maintained than at Windsor; the Queen consented to the move only with the greatest reluctance, knowing how much the King disliked Kew and that he would object strongly to the transfer. It took place on 29 November, a day recalled with horror by Fanny:

> Terrible was the morning! – uninterruptedly terrible! all spent in hasty packing up, preparing for we knew not what, nor for how long, nor with what circumstances, nor scarcely with what view! We seemed preparing for captivity, without having committed any offence; and for banishment, without the least conjecture when we might be recalled from it.[18]

The Queen and elder Princesses left in tears at ten o'clock; Fanny and Miss Planta were to follow later. The King proved as angry with the proposed move as the Queen had anticipated and he adopted an effective tactic, refusing to leave his bed. Before she left for Kew herself, Fanny was aware of 'Princes, Equerries, Physicians, Pages – all conferring, whispering, plotting, and caballing, how to induce the King to set off'.[19] Threatened with force and bribed with a promise that he could see the Queen and Princesses on arrival, the King finally left with as much dignity as he could muster; servants and citizens despondently watched his carriage drive away. Digby galloped ahead to let the anxious Queen know he was on his way. But the promise to the King of seeing his family when he reached Kew was not honoured.

If the Palace of Kew was run-down and uncomfortable in summer, it was a cheerless, wretched place in winter. The King and his doctors were housed on the ground floor and all the rooms directly above were kept empty that he might not be disturbed by footsteps above, so the attendants could not occupy their usual rooms. Fanny found that her name had been chalked by the Prince of Wales on the door of a bare-boarded room, so thinly partitioned from Mrs Schwellenberg's that every word could be heard from one to the other; fortunately after a few days the Queen moved Fanny to another room. It was of a good size, more comfortable, and carpeted, but it was up two steep winding staircases and at the end of a long dark passage lined with the maids' rooms; one day Fanny broke her shin tripping over a bucket in the gloom. The greatest discomfort, however, was the cold. Digby, mindful as ever of health, ordered more carpets, and sandbags to block the draughts at doors and windows.

The days in Windsor had been terrifying but eventful, but with the household now established at Kew the dramatic urgency, at least for Fanny, disappeared, and her life became one of numbing boredom, its daily highlight the overnight bulletin which it became her responsibility to take to the Queen. To collect it she sheltered from the early morning cold in Mrs Schwellenberg's parlour on the ground floor. This, when found out, was seen as an unwarrantable intrusion, and next day Fanny found the doors locked against her. After standing instead in a freezing, dark, damp passage she was shivering so much when she delivered her message to the Queen that she intervened and the parlour was made free, but Fanny then had to bear the brunt of Cerbera's wrath.

As throughout his illness the King's condition fluctuated, now better now worse. There were days when Fanny could race to the Queen with good news; then 'the little fair gleam' would pass and all grow black again. She would try to soften bad reports without misrepresenting them; the Queen, however, was aware of the horrors of the King's worst days,

1a. Fanny Burney by Edward Burney, 1782. Fanny wears a black Vandyke dress with lilac sleeve inserts, white fichu, black hat, and a fashionable black velvet ribbon around her neck.

1b. Fanny Burney by Edward Burney, 1784–5. The dress is pale blue-grey with a deep pink bow, and she is shown with black gloves and shawl, and a Lunardi bonnet with brown ribbons.

1c. Watercolour believed to show Hester and Henry Thrale with the portrait of Dr Johnson commissioned by Henry Thrale for Streatham Park. Artist uncertain.

2a. Miniatures on ivory of George III and Queen Charlotte by Richard Collins based on portraits by Thomas Gainsborough of 1781 and 1782 respectively. The King wears the Windsor uniform; the Queen is in a black dress with white fichu.

2b. The Eldest Daughters *by Thomas Gainsborough, 1784. Charlotte, Princess Royal (centre) wears pale gold, Princess Augusta (left) turquoise, and Princess Elizabeth (seated right) pink; the dresses are trimmed with gold-threaded lace. Originally full-length, this portrait was cut down in Victorian times.*

3a. A Milliner's Shop *in Windsor by S.W. Fores, dated 24 March 1787. The Queen and one of the Princesses are seated to be served; the King stands by. There is a striking contrast between the Princess's fashionable dress in this drawing and the obligatory court attire in the one below.*

3b. View of the Ball at St James's on the Celebration of Her Majesty's Birth Night *(1786). The Princess Royal dances with the Prince of Wales. In 1787 Fanny took her place in the onlookers' gallery at the back.*

4a. A View of the Garden Entrance to St James's Palace *with Margaret Nicholson attempting to assassinate the King, 2 August 1786. She is on the King's left wearing a black bonnet.*

4b. A View of Fauconberg Hall in Cheltenham with their Majesties taking an Airing. *The steps where Fanny spent two hours talking with Stephen Digby can be seen. Her room was at the front of the house on the top floor.*

5a. *Mrs Schwellenberg leading the Queen, from Thomas Rowlandson's* The Prospect Before Us *(1788).*

5b. *The Honourable Stephen Digby as a young man by Sir Joshua Reynolds (date unknown).*

5c. Restoration Dresses *of April 1789 by S.W. Fores. These ladies display their loyalty on their heads, arms and sashes; one of them has a fan with a portrait of the King, another has GR embroidered on her shoes.*

6a. Royal Dipping *by John Nixon, 1789. A lively if fanciful representation of the scene at Weymouth. The King ensured that he was decently covered, and no doubt the dippers were more modestly attired too.*

6b. Plymouth Fort and St Nicholas's Island *(today called Drake's Island), seen from Mount Edgcumbe in 1779.*

7. A View of the court sitting on the trial of Warren Hastings *(Westminster Hall). The view is shown from the position where Fanny sat. The prisoner's box is immediately in front, guarded by two Yeomen. Members of the Commons Committee sit around their table in a box on the left (Edmund Burke in spectacles); lawyers for Warren Hastings on the right. The Peers sit in front, the judges on the woolsack in the middle, and the Lord Chamberlain's throne and royal boxes are at the far end.*

8a. General Alexandre d'Arblay, painted in Paris by Carle and Horace Vernet in 1817. He is shown wearing the medals with which he appeared before Queen Charlotte.

8b. A View of the Queen's Levée in the Pump Room at Bath *(1817). The Queen sits on a chair to drink a glass of the water. The Duke of Clarence stands in front of her, Princess Elizabeth behind.*

the wild ravings, eruptions of violence and, most hurtfully, both the animosity he had begun to express towards her and the crude longings for a respectable middle-aged woman of the court, Lady Pembroke. The cruellest aspect of the illness was its Jekyll-and-Hyde distortion of an honourable, temperate man. In one respect, however, the King did not change: he was constant in his loathing of his doctors, yet on 5 December, as Fanny learnt from Digby, he was introduced to yet more, Dr Francis Willis and his son Dr John, later joined by another son, the Reverend Thomas Willis.

Seventy-year-old Dr Willis, physician and cleric, ran an asylum in Lincolnshire and had been recommended by Lady Harcourt, whose mother he had treated; when the King discovered the old man's dual pursuits, he expressed strong regret that a man in a profession he admired should have adopted one which he detested.[20] Willis's method of curing the sick in mind was to establish mental control of them, and a battle for domination between patient and physician began. A strait-jacket, called a 'strait-waistcoat' then, had already been used in the King's wilder moments; Dr Willis employed it also as punishment for unacceptable behaviour. The King regularly had his legs tied to a bed-post, was gagged for uttering obscenities, and strapped into a restraining chair: he dubbed it his 'coronation chair'.[21] Fanny cannot have known much of this or she would not have liked the Willises as much as she did, finding them friendly, unassuming, and engagingly oblivious of court etiquette. They liked her too, old Dr Willis later saying that her 'good-humoured' face in a morning cheered him in his troubles with the London physicians. They regarded the Willises as country quacks, and there were daily squabbles over treatment and the wording of the bulletins.

As well as the direct worry about the King, the political crisis also caused acute anxiety. Fanny did not even like to write the word 'Regency', but the longer the King remained incapable of conducting public affairs, the closer Parliament came to establishing one. In pursuit of the Regency, the Prince of Wales' conduct and that of the Duke of York were widely criticised, though Digby told Lady Harcourt that the Prince had been naturally affectionate until leaders of the Opposition, who saw their own way to power, showed him where his self-interest lay.[22] Fanny had always been treated courteously by the Prince in their few personal encounters, but she was well aware of the indignation caused when he took control at Windsor, ignoring the Queen, and she shared the resentment of Leonard Smelt who was handed his greatcoat and told to leave the Lodge by the porter, on the express orders of the Prince. At

Kew, however, the Prince apologised to him, having, as Fanny wrote, 'the faculty of making his peace, where he wishes it, with the most captivating grace in the world'.[23]

Mr Smelt became a regular visitor to Fanny for news, and she was very glad to receive him, since at Kew she was more cut off than ever from those she loved. No visitors from the outside world were allowed, nor any visits to it. Her family and friends worried about her, her sister Charlotte offering her a home if she would but resign her position. But however drearily isolated her life Fanny could not abandon her post. Much of her day was spent in her room, her only company often the birds who thronged to her window-sill for scraps. She read, sewed, wrote letters and journal notes – and undoubtedly spent much of her time thinking about Stephen Digby.

Digby had soon discovered the way to Fanny's room along the dark corridor, and came regularly rapping on her door with a 'May I come in?' But the relationship was not what it had been at Cheltenham, where she felt she understood him. Now she frequently found herself perplexed, uncertain how to judge behaviour which seemed full of inconsistencies. On the one hand he was constant in his visits, yet sometimes seemed restless and anxious to leave. He resumed reading to her, but once discomposed her by asking a few days after he had read 'with flattering attention' a discourse on friendship, whether it was with her he had read it or 'somebody else'.[24] There was a sense in which Digby seemed to have commandeered her room for his own purposes, bringing official correspondence there to write (he had his own room in the Prince's House – the present Kew Palace – but found it uncomfortable, and perhaps letters to do with the Regency were better not written there). Sometimes Fanny would find Digby in her room in her absence; on some evenings he would sit absorbed in reading or writing while she counted the clock striking the quarters and wished he would *go*. She was very conscious that her room was tucked away at the end of the servants' corridor and that it was just the one room: in effect, she was entertaining Mr Digby in her bedroom.

But with all the reservations, she could not bring herself to turn him away and make her life even emptier, so steadily their relationship intensified. He would come declaring that it was 'an age' since he had last seen her when it had been only the previous day. They conversed on personal subjects; he told her of his children and hoped she would meet them; she talked of Norbury and its people and he said he would like to live in that area; he spoke of her timidity and wished she would defend herself against Cerbera; he played with her fan, discussed her bonnets and her choice of ribbon, and wished he had the 'fattening' of her slight figure. She was conscious of his physical presence, aware of his hands as he toyed with the melting wax of a candle, drew on his white Chamberlain's gloves, took her hand 'apropos of nothing', or grasped the one or two fingers which it was customary to offer as he took his leave.

More intimately, they discussed religion. Fanny was a woman of deep faith, though she kept her thoughts about it out of her daily journals. When Digby discovered that she wrote her own prayers he pressed her to show some to him, returning to the subject again and again. He told her his own favourite prayers and cried, '*Why* may we not wish to go to Heaven the same way?' which startled her into belief that he had become seriously attached to her.[25] Finally she consented to let him see just one prayer. This single sheet of paper was handed over on condition that he return it next day, and she called it 'robbery' when he did not do so though his reason, that he wished to study it further because it had moved him to tears, seemed to confirm his feeling for her.[26]

However, Fanny did become concerned at his obliviousness to the gossip she knew was circulating. No longer was she prepared to excuse blindness to appearances as evidence of lofty superiority to mundane matters. It made her very uneasy that members of the household had come to assume that if Colonel Digby were wanted he would be in her room, and she disliked both the lordly way Digby treated *her* servants, and his use of any servant to fetch her after Columb had become so hostile to him that he would never admit that he knew where she was. Her maid Goter was more compliant; she admired Digby's appearance when she saw him from a window, while reporting that when Columb looked out at the rain he was glad to think that Digby would get wet. Fanny asked Goter why Columb disliked Mr Digby so:

'Because, ma'am, he says he's a villain . . . all the time that he is coming after you in this manner, morning, noon, & night, he pays his addresses to a Lady in town – a very handsome Lady, ma'am, & a Maid of Honour.'
  'Miss Gunning?' cried I.
  'Yes, ma'am, that is the very name.'[27]

Yet Fanny allowed the relationship to continue, sure that Digby could not be paying her such marked attention, and declaring that he would keep her prayer 'to all eternity', if his affections were really engaged elsewhere.[28] No doubt she should have been more cautious, but she

wanted to trust him and there seems no reason to doubt that Digby
believed what he said at the time when he said it. Nevertheless, it was very
disagreeable to hear from Goter both that Miss Planta had told her maid
(with a room on the dark corridor) to report on Miss Burney's visitors,
and that Cerbera had been passing comment; when she discovered that
her maid Mrs Arline had been Digby's messenger to Fanny she had said,
'What, are you turned Cupid's Mercury too, as well as that pert little
Goter?'[29]

Mrs Schwellenberg also resented the hours she was being left on her
own, even though she subjected Fanny to abuse when she did keep her
company. When the Princess Royal began to behave coldly towards her
Fanny realised that Schwelly must have been grumbling about neglect.
The Queen too indicated displeasure. Fanny had always been open about
her entertainment of Digby and the Queen had not seemed to object, but
when the consequence was that Mrs Schwellenberg was left on her own
she intervened, wanting to question Fanny about her Vice-Chamberlain's
movements:

> 'The reason . . . that I asked about Mr. Digby was that the
> Schwellenberg sent to ask Miss Planta to come to her because
> Mr. Digby was – no, not with her – he never goes to her . . . with you,'
> she said, 'Mr. Digby was; and the Schwellenberg was alone.'[30]

Fanny longed to tell her of the 'usage I had endured from this person
thus compassionated', but scrupled to complain of the old favourite. She
did, however, defend herself skilfully, if somewhat disingenuously,
pointing out that since the autumn she had seen no one except
Mr Smelt, Mr Digby and Sir Lucas Pepys, all of whom came on their own
business, not for her. The Queen could not but recognise the deprivation. Indeed, Fanny's present life was not so very different from that of
the prisoners at Gloucester gaol whom the previous year she had pitied
for their confinement and lack of human contact. Kew was a prison, and
Digby and Smelt her 'prison visitors'. Her health was suffering, and at the
end of January 1789 Sir Lucas urged her to take some air and exercise;
apart from one period of ten minutes, she had not been out of doors
since the middle of October. Colonel Greville obtained the key of
Richmond Gardens for her first walk; thereafter she walked daily. On the
second day of February, however, this led to what she called 'the severest
personal terror' she had ever known.

Despite everything his doctors could do to him the King was, by fits
and starts, recovering, and was himself taking exercise in the gardens.

Fanny was always careful to find out where he might be; on this day she was told he would be in Richmond Gardens so she took her walk in Kew. Halfway round her chosen route she observed two or three figures whom at first she took to be workmen; to her horror, when she came closer she saw that it was the King with his doctors. Panic-stricken she turned and ran, only to hear herself pursued, and the hoarse voice of the King calling out 'Miss Burney! Miss Burney!':

> I protest I was ready to die. I knew not in what state he might be at the time; I only knew the orders to keep out of his way were universal; that the Queen would highly disapprove any unauthorised meeting, and that the very action of my running away might deeply, in his present irritable state, offend him. Nevertheless, on I ran, too terrified to stop, and in search of some short passage, for the garden is full of little labyrinths, by which I might escape.
>
> The steps still pursued me, and still the poor hoarse and altered voice rang in my ears: – more and more footsteps resounded frightfully behind me, – the attendants all running, to catch their eager master, and the voices of the two Dr. Willises loudly exhorting him not to heat himself so unmercifully.
>
> Heavens, how I ran! I do not think I should have felt the hot lava from Vesuvius – at least not the hot cinders – had I so run during its eruption. My feet were not sensible that they even touched the ground.[31]

Voices behind her shouted 'Stop! stop! stop!', but she cried out 'I cannot! I cannot!'; only when Dr Willis himself called out that it hurt the King to run, did she stop her flight and turn and face her pursuers:

> When they were within a few yards of me, the King called out, 'Why did you run away?'
>
> Shocked at a question impossible to answer, yet a little assured by the mild tone of his voice, I instantly forced myself forward, to meet him, though . . . I fairly think I may reckon it the greatest effort of personal courage I have ever made.
>
> The effort answered: I looked up, and met all his wonted benignity of countenance, though something still of wildness in his eyes. Think, however, of my surprise, to feel him put both his hands round my two shoulders, and then kiss my cheek![32]

Fanny concluded that the Willises, smiling in pleasure, must have thought that this was the usual way he greeted her.

A long one-sided conversation followed, topics tumbling out one after the other. The King's discourse was coherent but unguarded: suddenly he spoke of Mrs Schwellenberg, laughing, and saying, 'Never mind her! – don't be oppressed – I am your friend! Don't let her cast you down!' He grew increasingly voluble, alarming the doctors, but before she could get away the King returned to Mrs Schwellenberg: 'Never mind her! . . . depend upon me! I will be your friend as long as I live!' And kissed her again.[33] The interview had by no means been normal, yet the King had been so much more in control of himself than when she had seen him last that Fanny was greatly heartened. She hastened to tell the astonished Queen all about it – bar the remarks on 'the Schwellenberg'. Everyone else wanted to know about her adventure including Colonel Greville, who recorded it in his own detailed account of the King's illness:

> [His Majesty] walked out twice this day, & in his Two Walks He continued out about five hours. He accidentally saw in one of these Miss Burney who anxious to avoid Him ran away, but the King having perceived Her, She was called back – Her natural timidity render'd this an unwelcome invitation – She return'd however, & came back much frighten'd. The kindness with which She was received, & the composure which She saw, dissipated Her alarm, & She reported that The King had talked very collectedly, & more so, than She had any idea of – [34]

This is the only instance where Greville mentions Fanny; it not only confirms her story but shows that timidity was what characterised her for one of her tea table 'beaus'.[35]

During the rest of February the King's condition continued to improve and spirits rose. In the middle of the month Fanny rejoiced to see the King and Queen arm in arm in the gardens; conscious of his earlier abuse he was paying her assiduous attention.[36] A day later, with a 'Huzza! Huzza!', Fanny recorded the abandonment of the Regency Bill. Only a few days after that she saw the King again – this time in the Queen's dressing-room:

> On opening the door, there he stood! He smiled at my start, and saying he had waited on purpose to see me, added, 'I am quite well

now, – I was nearly so when I saw you before – but I could overtake you better now!'[37]

Illness had taken its toll, however; the King was very thin, and tired easily. The Queen too had suffered both physically and mentally during this grim time: her hair had turned white, and she had lost so much weight that she could wrap her stays twice around her.[38]

Once the King's recovery had been announced national rejoicing began. London was lit up; in every street, in every window, were placed devices of crowns, stars or initials, created with coloured lamps; the more elaborate illuminated transparencies featured loyal designs.[39] According to Mrs Papendiek, though Fanny does not mention it, the Queen sent her attendants to see the illuminations, Fanny travelling in the company of Lady Charlotte Finch, Miss Goldsworthy and Miss Planta. At Kew the Queen arranged a private celebration for her husband, with a painted transparency showing 'The King – Providence – Health – and Britannia'. Another surprise was a poem, in the Queen's name but written in Fanny's best laureate style, and presented by Princess Amelia:

> Amid a rapt'rous nation's praise
>   That sees Thee to their prayers restor'd,
> Turn gently from the gen'ral blaze, –
>   Thy Charlotte woos her bosom's lord.
>
> Turn and behold where, bright and clear,
>   Depictur'd with transparent art,
> The emblems of her thoughts appear,
>   The tribute of a grateful heart . . .

It had an engaging postscript:

> *P.S.*—The little bearer begs a kiss
>   From dear Papa, for bringing this.[40]

There were also verses on the gateposts, not mentioned by Fanny but quoted by Mrs Papendiek: 'Our prayers are heard, and providence restores/A patriot King to Bless Britannia's shores! . . .'[41] Who else at Kew, if not Fanny, would Queen Charlotte have asked to write such verses?

When on 14 March 1789 the court returned to Windsor, the whole town came out to greet the King; in the evening the battlements of the

Round Tower were the setting for a firework display. 'I could not keep my eyes dry all day long', Fanny wrote. These, however, were tears of joy. She might also have reflected on the irony of this return to Windsor: after Cheltenham she had seemed to be re-entering prison; now, after three and a half months of incarceration at Kew, Windsor's old grey walls represented a kind of liberty.

CHAPTER TEN

Summer by the Sea

*I promised my Esther, I know, to write to her from the main ocean: – And
how I came not to do so, I have scarcely myself any notion. But I'm
rather inclined to suppose that the winds which blow here
Night & Day, seiz'd hold of the thoughts of my Head, & whisk'd them
to sea – far away –* [1]

St George's Day, 23 April 1789, was made a day of thanksgiving for the
King's recovery. The Queen gave Fanny a medal bearing the motto 'Vive
le Roi', and a fan with the words 'Health restored to one, and happiness
to millions'. The great event of the day was a service in St Paul's
Cathedral, undertaken by the King in an ankle-length coat to hide his
emaciated legs. Crowds lining the streets, some of whom had taken seats
in the stands the night before, cheered his coach drawn by eight cream-
coloured horses while hissing that of the Prince of Wales; the Prince
further incensed public opinion by talking in the Cathedral with the
Duke of York. The service lasted three hours and was perhaps most
moving in the singing of the hundredth psalm by 6,000 charity children,
all dressed in white.

A month before, on 26 March, the Queen had held a Grand
Restoration Drawing-room. At it she appeared in richly embroidered
purple and silver, with a diamond-studded miniature of the King, and a
bandeau of purple satin round her cap, pricked out with 'God Save the
King' in more diamonds.[2] Other members of the royal family were also
splendidly arrayed: the Princess Royal in white and gold, Princess
Augusta in green and silver, and Princess Elizabeth in blue and silver. The
Prince of Wales was not yet reconciled with his mother, though he and
his brother had made peace with the King, but he came to the Drawing-
room in a magnificent scarlet suit embroidered with gold. Everyone of
rank or wealth in London was there, including the Locks: to see Fredy
again was for Fanny a further cause of rejoicing. For once Fanny
describes her own costume – 'a suit, in silks upon tiffany, most excessively
delicate and pretty', worked for her by Charlotte Cambridge and much
admired by the Queen. Probably she also wore a fashionable bandeau of
white satin with the words 'God Save the King' in purple and gold.

Next day, Fanny had a visitor: Charlotte Gunning. She called, with other company, 'to inquire after the Queen'. Fanny thought she looked 'serious, sensible, interesting', but took note that the only time she spoke was on the subject of the crowds and confusion at the Drawing-room: 'It was intended to be better regulated,' she said; 'Mr. Digby told me.'[3] She then dropped her eyes and spoke no more. But despite this unexpected appearance, and notwithstanding the rumours and Columb's accusation of black-heartedness, Fanny was certain that it was she who was the object of Digby's attentions. Moreover, contrary to a declaration to Goter that she would no more consider marrying him than 'the Man in the Moon', Fanny was seriously considering what her answer to a proposal of marriage should be.

Fanny wrote lengthily about her feelings; his words, his behaviour, his looks of 'strong, open, undisguised partiality' all led to the conclusion that '*His Heart was Mine*'.[4] The question was, did she want it? At various points in her journals Fanny claimed that *her* heart was not engaged, but had she cared not a jot for him she would hardly have needed to debate an answer, especially since she could find more reasons for rejection than acceptance. In favour of a marriage with Digby was that it would bring release from 'long confinement – incessant labours – & perpetual indignities', a prospect of 'rapture', were it not that she felt '*unworthy*'. Lines in her journal have been deleted, so it is not clear in what way she thought herself unworthy: perhaps of his noble character, but more likely of his noble family, of which she stood in awe. Awareness of Digby's grand family background was an inhibiting factor in Fanny's relationship with him, and she worried at times that they were intervening with him against her. She probably knew of the scandal of 1764 when Lady Susan Fox-Strangways, sister of Digby's former wife, eloped with an actor and was then banished to New York by her unforgiving family.[5] But at forty-seven Stephen could surely marry where he pleased – and Fanny had carefully noted the occasion at Kew when they had discussed the marriage of Leonard Smelt's brother to a woman of low social rank and Digby had asked what that mattered if she was 'a good woman'.[6]

Fanny did not consult Susan, whose advice in favour she could guess, even though there was an occasion when she might have opened her heart to her. On Thanksgiving Day, Susan reminded her sister a month later, 'I hastened to her apartment – & saw Col. D – & then her dear self'. Stephen Digby, there on his own, had introduced himself as her sister's 'especial Friend' with an interest in her health and happiness, and expressed his wish to know Susan too. This brief encounter at least confirms that the relationship was not a product of Fanny's imagination.

But afterwards Fanny said nothing and Susan, who knew only a little of what had been going on, did not probe.[7]

But whether he was to be accepted or not, the potential bridegroom had not yet declared himself and now departed for a nine-week tour to France; after the loyal service he had given he needed and deserved leave of absence. Fanny had given devoted service too, but a Keeper of the Robes did not have the status to be rewarded with time to see her family and to recoup. It is not surprising, therefore, to find that in May she became ill. She had had a tooth removed, and infection must have set in; standard medical treatments were applied to no effect:

> I was grievously ill with a pain in my face. I applied for it a blister, in vain; I had then recourse to leeches, and one of them certainly bit a nerve, for what I suffered surpasses description; it was torture, it was agony! I fully thought myself poisoned . . .[8]

The pain was so severe that Fanny thought she must die.

Digby had said that when he came back he would expect her to tell him '*everything*'. But once again he did not immediately call on her on return. When he did come, wearing 'one of his most flattering smiles', she was therefore cold and distant, answering his enquiries with monosyllables. Eventually he challenged: 'So I see we are *not* to begin where we left off?'[9] Fanny sat silent, continuing her sewing. But afterwards, for reasons unspecified in her journals, she changed her mind and decided his regard was 'irreversible'. This see-sawing between faith and doubt was to continue.

Later that month Digby suffered another attack of gout, and was left behind when the King, Queen, Princesses and attendants left Windsor for Weymouth, where the King had been recommended for his health. Fanny's spirits revived with a change of scene and freedom from Cerberic aggression; she again kept a daily journal and, as at Cheltenham, her accounts of her private thoughts and activities counterpoint the royal progress publicly chronicled in newspapers and magazines. On the journey south the whole route was dense with cheering crowds, and Fanny conveyed the support of all classes in society by listing the medley of vehicles which brought them to see the King: 'chariots, chaises, landaus, carts, waggons, whiskies, gigs, phaëtons'.[10] If his illness had any blessing it was that, on the eve of the French Revolution, it had bound the English people to their monarch, and their affection was manifested in extraordinary displays of loyalty. But crowds are dangerous beasts and there is something sinister in Fanny's description of the behaviour of the country people who crowded up to the windows of the dining-room at Lyndhurst, in the New Forest, where the journey was broken:

> They broke down all the paling, and much of the hedges, and some of the windows, and all by eagerness and multitude, for they were perfectly civil and well-behaved.[11]

In little over three months' time the women of Paris would march on Versailles armed with pikes and pitchforks, massacre the Swiss Guard, and force King Louis XVI's return to Paris. But in England there were cheers not howls, and at Salisbury, on the next stage of the journey to Weymouth, the coaches passed under an arch festooned with flowers; at Dorchester windows had been removed for 'face above face to peep out'; in the villages girls scattered flowers beneath the wheels of the King's coach.

The purpose of the King's stay in Weymouth was sea-bathing, or 'dipping' – no swimming was involved – believed by doctors to be beneficial to health. The theory was that the shock of total immersion in cold salt water (drinking it was also recommended) had a revitalising effect, stimulating the circulation and removing impurities from the blood; for full benefit the dip had to be undertaken very early in the morning. Bathers undressed in horse-drawn bathing-machines which lumbered into the sea; there sturdy 'dippers', usually female, were waiting to push them under. At Weymouth, or Melcombe Regis as the area around the sandy bay was still called, the beach had been used as a rubbish dump until the middle of the century when the shore had been tidied up and bathing-machines installed; there was an assembly room, a circulating library, and a tiny theatre. The Duke of Gloucester, the King's brother, had built a house there, Gloucester Lodge, which the King was borrowing.[12] The Duke's presence had increased the town's popularity, but compared with raffish Brighthelmstone patronised by the Prince of Wales, Weymouth was a staid place, all 'sameness and dullness' and with 'neither wenching, drinking or gaming' according to one traveller who left in disgust.[13] But it was the favoured resort of Mrs Schwellenberg who doubtless recommended it to their Majesties.

For the royal visit the town did its best to avoid dullness. The King was met by the Mayor and council with colours flying, a band of music played the anthem, there was a salute of twenty-one guns, and in the evening fireworks and a display of illuminated boats.[14] The excitement created in consequence of the King's favouring of Weymouth as his resort was such that Fanny wrote to her father:

The loyalty of this place is excessive: they have dressed out every street with labels of 'God save the King': all the shops have it over the doors; all the children wear it in their caps, all the labourers in their hats, and all the sailors *in their voices,* for they never approach the house without shouting it aloud, nor see the King, or his shadow, without beginning to huzza, and going on to three cheers.

The bathing-machines make it their motto over all their windows; and those bathers that belong to the royal dippers wear it in bandeaus on their bonnets, to go into the sea; and have it again, in large letters, round their waists, to encounter the waves.[15]

Fanny thought the bay at Weymouth very beautiful, the sands smooth and pleasant to walk on. But the sea was the only thing worth looking at; her parlour was at the back of Gloucester Lodge with a 'dull' view, while her bedroom was in the attics: 'Nothing like living at a court for exaltation,' she joked.

The King delayed his bathing until he had braved some cold baths in privacy, but on 7 July he was trundled into the sea in a machine adorned with the royal crest.[16] Despite it being a very early hour crowds had assembled to cheer him on. And that was not all:

Think but of the surprise of His Majesty when, the first time of his bathing, he had no sooner popped his royal head under water than a band of music, concealed in a neighbouring machine, struck up 'God save great George our King'.[17]

Men normally bathed naked, but the King had prudently donned an all-enveloping flannel robe such as women wore. Fanny would have worn one for her dips too, though when she took her first bathe at the usual early hour, she was so terrified of being late for the Queen's dressing that she feared she had lost the 'bracing' effect of the water (how did she get her hair dry in time?). Subsequently she adopted the advice of the King's physician, who considered that midday bathing was just as beneficial. Fanny was a keen dipper; she took her first bathe at Teignmouth in 1773 and though she was 'terribly frightened' beforehand, afterwards expressed herself with enthusiasm:

[I] really thought I should never have recovered from the Plunge – I had not Breath enough to speak for a minute or two, the shock was beyond expression great – but after I got back to the machine, I presently felt myself in a Glow that was delightful – it is the finest feeling in the World.[18]

Neptune's embrace was one to which she readily submitted. What the King thought of his first dip is not known, but the Queen with her liking for exactitude noted his every bathe in her diary, on Monday 31 August, for example, recording that 'The King Bathed this Morning for the 14th Time'.[19] Altogether she added up twenty-one dips for the King that summer; he was just outdone by Princess Elizabeth and her twenty-two. In later years the royal family were to take their bathes in privacy in a 'Floating Bathing Machine' moored nearby; it looked like a small Noah's Ark but was designed to let the water in, not keep it out.

There were other maritime activities. The warship *Magnificent* came from Portsmouth, anchored offshore, and became the centrepiece for naval displays. On 14 July 1789, just as the Parisians were tearing down the Bastille, the King inspected the fully-dressed, fully-manned warship, one of those on which the defence of his realm would so soon depend.[20] There must have been talk of events in France at Gloucester Lodge, but Fanny at least seems not to have taken the matter too seriously at first. In the doggerel letter she sent Hetty apologising for not writing before, she makes a joke of what had happened saying that the winds have blown her wits away, but they can't be 'immur'd in th' Bastille' as it no longer exists: 'And this is a Reason, to me, that admits to no cavil or doubt; for how can you poke a thing in to a place that itself is pok'd out?'[21]

Fanny liked to remain on dry land and declined invitations to join the royal party on their sea-cruises, thus avoiding the seasickness which afflicted many who did. But she did attend the theatre, another which soon called itself the Theatre Royal. One day she was walking with Mary Gwynn on the sands when they came on the stately figure of Sarah Siddons. She too had come to Weymouth for her health, but she was soon starring at the theatre, mainly in comedies because of the Queen's dislike of tragedy. Fanny continued to feel that Mrs Siddons was not at her best in comedy; of her Rosalind in *As You Like It* she commented that 'gaiety sits not naturally upon her', and in any case she was too large for her shepherd's costume.[22]

Their Majesties accepted invitations to visit the properties of local landowners, the most important being to Sherborne Castle, childhood home of Stephen Digby and seat of Lord Digby, his brother. Stephen had now joined the Weymouth party where he was greeted by Fanny, as she had determined, 'with the same frank pleasure' as at Cheltenham. He looked better, and he complimented Fanny on her improved looks too. He was anxious that she should see Sherborne Castle, and wondered how it could be arranged, but Fanny 'damped' the idea as much as she could 'without incivility to his kind intentions'. She had once sat next to Lady

Digby at a play, had heard her enquire who she was, and felt herself subjected to supercilious scrutiny for the rest of the evening; she deduced that Lady Digby had heard of her brother-in-law's partiality and disapproved. Lady Digby may have acted offensively, but with her sensitivity on the subject of rank Fanny was predisposed to expect a slight. However, whether the disdain was real or imaginary the result was a determination to avoid a repetition.

Her journal entry for the day, therefore, records only the departure of the royals for Sherborne. But for another diarist, James Woodforde, loyal Tory parson from Norfolk, 4 August 1789, which he spent with family and friends in the Castle park, was a 'Dies Memorabilis'. Fanny frequently wrote of the multitudes of anonymous faces who cheered the King; Parson Woodforde gives identity to just one of the thousands who gathered to see the royal family that day. The weather was good and he had an excellent view as they walked on the terrace: 'We were all very near to them indeed, the King looked very red and is very tall and erect, The Queen and Princesses rather short but very pleasing countenances and fair . . . The King was in his Windsor Uniform, blue coat with red Cape and Cuffs to the Sleeves, with a plain round Hat with a black Ribband round it, The Queen was in a purple Silk, and white Bonnett, The Princesses all in Pink Silk and white Bonnetts.'[23] Afterwards he watched them take coach and ride around the park. Then the King and his party went in to dine with Lord Digby, while Woodforde and *his* party retired to the Antelope in Sherborne to revive themselves on 'cold Ham and Veal, cold boiled Beef, Tarts etc'. His little group, therefore, formed part of 'the Great Assemblage of Gentlemen & People of the Country' who 'Rendered the Scene very animated and Beautiful', as Stephen proudly recorded in the Castle Game-book.[24]

While much of the population of Dorset converged on Sherborne, Fanny enjoyed herself in the quiet way she preferred, and in the company of the beautiful Mrs Gwynn. Taking with them the Queen's little dogs Badine and Phillis, they walked to the ruined Sandsfoot Castle, a relic of Henry VIII's coastal defences; it was built on low cliffs a mile or so west of Gloucester Lodge. The two women clambered around the walls, before climbing down onto the sands and picking up seaweeds and shells. It was the first real country walk Fanny had had since she entered the Queen's service. But there was a price to pay: when Digby next saw her he reproached her for not being of the Sherborne party 'which, he said might *have been perfectly well arranged*'.[25] Fanny commented cryptically, 'I fancy it was proposed – & refused'. Who she thought the proposer and who the refuser is unclear, but it can be inferred that Digby was upset that she would make no effort to see his family home. Fanny does not seem to have recognised cause and effect; she in turn was distressed when two nights later he was at the play with his children and did not introduce them as he had frequently said he wished. Nor did he take his leave when the party left Weymouth on 13 August for the western tour.

Their destination was Saltram House near Plymouth, loaned (with the servants) by its seventeen-year-old owner, Lord Boringdon.[26] The journey followed the established pattern: cheering crowds, triumphal arches, loyal emblems, bells, flower garlands, maidens dressed in white. On the steep hills near Charmouth (triumphal arch of oak boughs crowned with laurel), the King left his coach and walked, chatting to the locals on the way. At Exeter, where they stopped for two nights, he was presented with the keys of the city which he returned saying, 'They are already in very good hands'.[27] At least 40,000 had gathered to acclaim the King, Queen and 'the most beautiful Princesses in the universe'; that night the city blazed with '2,000 variegated lamps'.[28] The party stayed two nights at the Deanery and saw the Cathedral, which Fanny thought 'old and curious' but the city 'close and ugly'. Journeying on, they passed through country 'the most fertile, varied, rural, and delightful in England' (not that Fanny had a very wide experience of English countrysides), until they reached Saltram on the afternoon of 15 August.

Of all the houses in which Fanny lived, if only briefly, Saltram House, standing on a wooded peninsula of land on a tidal reach of the River Plym and now belonging to the National Trust, must be the one which she would most easily find her way around today, for it preserves with little alteration the eighteenth-century interior designed by Robert Adam, and many of the works of art which filled it. These include a number of portraits by Fanny's great admirer Sir Joshua Reynolds, who was born in nearby Plympton. One can still stand where Fanny had her 'parlour' (though the room was later incorporated into the library) and look through the window at a view which she might recognise. Fanny admired Saltram's fine rooms and loved its landscapes, especially a 'beautiful falling wood' which ran down to the water; there she liked to sit, once taking her fountain-pen with her to write to Susan.[29] Her only cavil was the 'uncertainty' of the view, possessed of great beauty at high tide, but at low tide appearing as 'mere swamps'.[30]

Full tides made the river navigable, and the King took some of his journeys to and from the naval port by boat. The Plymouth of today was then three towns, Plymouth itself being largely the area around the Hoe, the Citadel and the old port from which the *Mayflower* sailed, and the towns of Stonehouse and Plymouth Dock, today's Devonport, which had been established as a dockyard by William III. Dock was an orderly place, with wide, well-built streets and handsome buildings – unlike Plymouth, which Fanny dismissed as 'long, dirty, ill built, and wholly unornamented with any edifice worth notice'.[31] In 1789 work was in progress on a fourth dry dock, the biggest in the country, and the King came to see it under construction. He was told that it was being made large enough to take a huge new ship, the *Commerce de Marseille*, being built by the French, and it did indeed become the first ship to enter the dock when it was captured by the British in 1793.[32]

For several consecutive days the King inspected the dockyard and took ship to review the fleet from the sea, his passage accompanied by tremendous noise as cannon answered cannon in salutes fired from ship and shore. As they viewed the great warships, upwards of two hundred small boats attended their Majesties, including a cutter rowed by six young women, with a seventh to steer. They wore 'loose white gowns, with nankeen safeguards, and black bonnets' and sashes of royal purple which, for an attractive variation, were emblazoned with 'God save the Queen'.[33] The women's boat accompanied the King and Queen each day, and they were royally rewarded.[34] Unfortunately, the first of these naval days was marred by tragedy: a sloop loaded with spectators, some of whom had climbed the mast for a better view, was overset, and four adults and a child were drowned. Their Majesties ordered financial assistance to be given to any made needy by the disaster.[35]

Fearful as she was of sea-trips, it was as well that Fanny did not know of this accident when she and Peggy Planta made their own tour to the dockyard, an experience of interest to her because of her brother James. They went on the day when the royals visited the estate of Mount Edgcumbe, which overlooks Plymouth Sound, and the harbour was crowded with shipping. The women entered the masculine world of stores of 'ropes, sails, masts, anchors' and watched an alarming display of anchor-making, aware that if the three men beating out the red-hot iron did not time their swings to perfection they would knock out each other's brains. Then, just as alarmingly for Fanny, they were rowed out to view a 74-gun warship, the *Bombay Castle*, with a Captain Duckworth as their guide. Fanny was delighted to discover that he knew Jem, whom he called 'Burney of the *Bristol*', but she revealed to Captain Duckworth how little of a sea dog she was herself:

'Tell me,' I said, 'and honestly, – should we be overturned in a boat while out at sea, what would prevent our being drowned?'

He would not suppose such an accident possible.

I pressed him, however, upon the possibility it might happen once in a century, and he could not help laughing, and answered, 'Oh, we should pick you all up!'

I desired to know by what means. 'Instruments,' he said. I forced him, after a long and comic resistance, to show me them. Good Heaven! They were three-pronged iron forks, – very tridents of Neptune!

I exclaimed with great horror, 'These! – why, they would tear the body to pieces!'

'Oh,' answered he calmly, 'one must not think of legs and arms when life is in danger.'[36]

Luckily, the day was fine and the sea calm; they cruised close to Mount Edgcumbe and caught glimpses of the royal family driving around the grounds.

Mount Edgcumbe estate is renowned for its unique location, superb views, and landscaped gardens which preserve their eighteenth-century character. Positioned on the Cornish shores of Plymouth Sound, it extends from wooded slopes to craggy headlands. From the house and other vantage points there are spectacular views up the River Tamar and over the water to Devonport, Drake's Island and Plymouth Hoe, with the Plym and the Devon shores in the distance and Dartmoor as backdrop to all; variations of light, season, and shipping create a constantly changing scene. Yet the situation is so sheltered that many exotic species thrive among the native oaks, chestnuts and limes. In 1789 Fanny summed up the attractions of the contrasts:

> The sea, in some places, shows itself in its whole vast and unlimited expanse; at others, the jutting land renders it merely a beautiful basin or canal; the borders down to the sea are in some parts flourishing with the finest evergreens and most vivid verdure, and in others are barren, rocky, and perilous. In one moment you might suppose yourself cast on a desert island, and the next find yourself in the most fertile and luxuriant country.[37]

Just three days before the royal visit to his estate, George, Lord Mount Edgcumbe, had been created 1st Earl.[38]

The new Countess, who described the occasion for her friend Lady Harcourt, was disappointed that the day was not so brilliant as the preceding ones, but at least it did not rain. A special landing-stage had been built and covered with green baize for the royal party, and as their Majesties and the Princesses stepped onto it the Mount Edgcumbe battery fired a 21-gun salute, a band struck up the anthem, and 'twelve little girls, all newly dress'd in white, with garter blue sashes, straw hats bound with the same blue, & the motto round them, & each having a straw basket trimm'd & tyed with blue, strew'd flowers before their Majesties'.[39] The Queen, with her botanical enthusiasm, must have found the gardens of great interest; she picked a slip of myrtle and said, 'I will carry this home, & plant it myself in a pot . . . & have it & always keep it'. The King marvelled at the views, and it was said that the Princess Royal was so affected at one point that an 'involuntary tear of rapture stole down her lovely cheek'.[40] When the royal family took their departure the shores resounded again to the noise of cannon, music, and cheering crowds, and it seemed as if a wood had been created on water when from hundreds of small boats rowers raised their oars in salute. At the end of the day the Countess wondered how they would ever learn to be 'common mortals' again.

Fanny, on the other hand, was very conscious of being a common mortal when she was invited to Mount Edgcumbe and, with her usual companion, had to make the short but sometimes dangerous crossing of the Tamar in the everyday ferry. However, 'a very commodious garden chair' was waiting on the other side to take them up to the house, where they were greeted by the Earl and Countess. But news had just come that the King and Queen planned to sail up the Tamar next day to see their other estate at Cotehele, so they had to set off to superintend arrangements, leaving their less exalted guests to be entertained by the young heir and his wife.[41] The two women were shown over the house and Fanny found in the library a copy of *Cecilia*; knowing that the Countess was an admirer of her own idol, the Italian singer Pacchierotti, she won a wager with herself that the first volume would fall open at the chapter 'An Opera Rehearsal' into which she had introduced him.[42] She and Miss Planta also toured the grounds, but the famous view disappointed: she thought it too flat and lacking any 'striking object to arrest the eye'. Possibly there was no interplay of light and shade that day to animate the scene.

The invitation to Mount Edgcumbe had come directly from the Countess. When the message was delivered to her at Saltram, Colonel Digby who had joined the party demanded, '*Will* that be possible, Miss Burney?'[43] On hearing her answer that she would name the invitation to the Queen, he left the room and did not return. It was 16 August, the second anniversary of his wife's death, and Fanny felt sure that he had gone to spend the evening 'in solemn solitude & tender recollection'. On such an anniversary Fanny herself would certainly have done so, but it seems just as likely that Digby left the room in protest that she was accepting an invitation to Mount Edgcumbe, having refused to contemplate one for Sherborne.

Whatever his reason, Digby's relationship with Fanny was deteriorating in mutual misunderstanding. She claimed not to have changed her behaviour towards him, but her own evidence suggests otherwise. She complained that since reaching Saltram he had only engaged with her in two short conversations, yet when he did attempt to do so he had to force answers from 'an unwilling converser'. Fanny was conscious that he watched her, that he seemed '*not to know how to behave*' to her, and that his behaviour was inconsistent, apparently unconscious that he might have said the same of her. Even as presented through Fanny's eyes and ears, Digby emerges as an unhappy man, uncertain how to treat her, and growing bitter. As a result his social manner changed, Miss Planta lamenting that he had become hard and satirical.

As in Fanny's relationship with George Cambridge, it appears that the longer it lasted the less chance there was that it would end in marriage. The men were very different, but it seems likely that in both cases her habit of daily journalising, of memorising and setting down every word, look and gesture and subjecting them to analysis, tended to interfere with the development of the affair. The way she wrote her journals, in the manner of fictional narrative, was probably also unhelpful. She herself commented when writing out her Kew memoranda that it seemed as if she was copying scenes from *Evelina* and *Cecilia*, with herself as imaginary heroine; though she did not confuse life with art, she did use her writing to define it and give it shape. Consequently, it became difficult for Fanny to act on the basis of present instinct rather than past analysis.

So she continued to scrutinise every incident and to change her assessment of Digby's feelings with weathercock frequency. One day when all the attendants had gathered for tea he spoke to her with 'much softness, much distinction', and carefully prepared a slice of brown bread and 'Clotted Cream' for her, but on another, contrary to all previous habit, he drew his chair *away* from hers when he sat down. A few days later came an incident which seemed especially significant. At the tea table, with Colonel Goldsworthy and Lord Courtown also present, Digby brought out his pocketbook and held it so that it caught her eye. Teasing her a little, he took from it '*The Paper*', the prayer which he had begged and then retained; she recognised the torn-off corner, where she had tried in her room at Kew to snatch it back from him. Having displayed it, he 'very carefully & delicately' put it back saying 'Had you looked at it – you would have found a motto to it'. The motto was 'To *have* & to *hold*'. Hearing this, though not understanding the context, Colonel Goldsworthy began to joke with Lord Courtown about those words which usually come next: *For better for worse – Till Death us do part.* What a scrape they led a man into! Digby, embarrassed, said that he only meant *je tiens*, Lord Harcourt's motto, and quickly turned the subject. The motto, the retention of the paper, and his attitude to it convinced Fanny that 'the old original regard stands'.[44] But next day he was 'silent, sad, & melancholy' again, and she was baffled.

On 27 August the royal party left Saltram for the return to Weymouth.[45] As Fanny and Miss Planta reached Bridport they saw Stephen Digby riding ahead of them. He turned and rode up to Miss Planta's side of the coach, addressing himself entirely to her. Yet as they moved away he kept turning round to look at the carriage and, when only Fanny was visible to him, he 'touched his Hat & pressed his hand to his lips' to her.[46]

The royal holiday continued with another fortnight of cruising and sea-bathing before the return journey to Windsor. Ironically, after all the triumphal arches under which the King and Queen had passed during their two months away, the Windsor arch to greet their homecoming was not ready. The coaches rolled beneath an unadorned framework, the work-men still busy on the scaffolding and running up and down their ladders.[47]

CHAPTER ELEVEN

Resignation

Melancholy was the existence where happiness was excluded, though not a
complaint could be made! where the illustrious personages who were served
possessed almost all human excellence, – yet where those who were their
servants . . . could never, in any part of the livelong day, command liberty,
or social intercourse, or repose![1]

When she reached court again, Fanny heard from Colonel Goldsworthy
that Digby had gone to stay at Sir Robert Gunning's. She had asked his
whereabouts to fulfil a promise that she would let him know of the party's
safe return. The letter was carefully composed, with no salutation or
closure, but in a spirit of 'simple' friendliness. She wrote amusingly of the
tardy preparations for welcome at Windsor, before adding a barbed
postscript, disguised as light-hearted:

> This little Epistle has been written in the hope to cancel some of the
> heavy charges of *intractability, ungovernableness, oddness, queerness,* &c
> &c &c with which its writer has been laden, who, by these presents
> certifies the whole to be calumny, hereby shewing – She can do – *for*
> *once,* – what she is desired.[2]

These words stung him to reply to 'do away the strange accusations' of
which he had been charged:

> I never could have been serious, but yet, I conceive the timidity
> which often makes you hesitate to speak the whole of what you
> intend, may have provoked me to use expressions – less harsh,
> however, than *intractability,* &cc. You know I always thought you very
> good – & I must acknowledge it without reserve.[3]

This letter, copied into Fanny's journals, is the closest it is possible to get
to Digby's feelings about her. It is in the style of the polished courtier,
placatory and a little patronising; the joint correspondence suggests the
tensions which had developed between them and the barriers erected
during the western tour. Digby recognised that Fanny often expressed

less than she thought, which he attributes to 'timidity'; she seems also to have written down less than was said since she does not record any conversations in which Digby accused her of being difficult.

Digby had reason for avoiding any intimacy of tone. One morning in mid-November Fanny was eating her breakfast when Miss Planta came rushing in exclaiming:

> 'Have you heard the news? . . . Mr. Digby is going to be married! I resolved I would tell you.'
>
> 'I heard the rumour,' I replied, 'the other day, from Colonel Gwynn.'
>
> 'Oh, it's true!' she cried; 'he has written to ask leave; but for Heaven's sake don't say so!'
>
> I gave her my ready promise, for I believed not a syllable of the matter; but I would not tell her that.[4]

Two days later Miss Planta was back with 'O! apropôs – it's all declared – & the Princesses wished Miss Gunning joy yesterday in the Drawing Room'.[5] Fanny may have been able to disguise her reaction from Miss Planta, but it was a shock, so much so that she declared that had her heart been engaged she would have dropped down dead from 'an Apoplectick [sic] stroke'. With nobody to confide in, she burst out strongly in her journals: 'He has risked my whole Earthly peace . . . He has committed a breach of all moral ties, & with every semblance of virtue!' Fortunately, her heart was not broken, but her *amour propre* was severely bruised. He had never asked for her hand, but such had been his attentions that '*honourably, & morally*' he should have given her the right of refusal. In page after page of her journals Fanny expressed her indignation, hurt, and incredulity that one who had seemed so open could have proved so duplicitous. Had he had a 'double attachment' throughout, she wondered, or did he take a sudden decision in Miss Gunning's favour?

Stephen Digby never wrote his own version of events, so explanation of his conduct can only be speculation, but perhaps a little light can be cast by looking at the affair from Charlotte Gunning's point of view. Digby's other learned lady was thirty years old, so though younger than Fanny was beyond the normal marriageable age. Her cleverness won her few friends at court – the same Princesses who wished her joy also dubbed her 'Lady Charlotte Hebrew' – but Digby enjoyed her company and did not deny it to himself. For Miss Gunning, who had known him before the death of his wife, Digby must have represented the chance of a like-minded companion. With his four children, some at least of her friends thought him a 'bad match' and did not expect Sir Robert to give his consent, but she said that she could not live without his friendship and 'could not keep that without marrying him'.[6] It is likely that Charlotte was bolder than Fanny and made her own advances, pressing too much in the year following the death of the first Mrs Digby: Fanny remained convinced that Digby had no sentimental attachment to Charlotte during their stay at Cheltenham. It is also evident that Miss Gunning recognised Miss Burney as a deadly rival. Mrs Ord told Fanny that 'Miss Gunning is jealous to Death of you', while another piece of gossip to come her way – from an unnamed informant who had been told by another unnamed informant said to have heard it from Miss Gunning herself – was that when Charlotte heard on Thanksgiving Day that Digby was with her, she called for her smelling salts, waited till he was in the room, and fainted away.[7] Her little visit to Fanny next day, when she murmured 'Mr. Digby told me', must have been another calculated move to stake her claim.

Persistence can pay off, and as Digby's relationship with Fanny grew more difficult it may be that he turned to a woman whose regard for him was more transparent (and a dowry of £10,000 – as Schwelly informed Fanny – has an attraction of its own). Sometime at Saltram he is said to have written his proposal to Miss Gunning.[8] Digby's feelings were almost certainly complicated, and though Fanny now saw unrelieved black where she had once seen purest white she judged him too simply in both cases. As a man who prided himself on being 'fair, open, & explicit' by nature he must have had some scruples about his conduct.[9] Perhaps as she herself suggested, her behaviour at Saltram led him to believe that she would not be hurt. Nevertheless, he ought to have had the courage to tell her personally of the engagement before it became public gossip. Afterwards he did brave her apartment but it was an uncomfortable encounter, even enquiries about her health blocked by 'steady & determined frigidness'. Fanny noted, perhaps with a touch of satisfaction, that he looked 'very ill' himself.[10]

The actual marriage was a strange affair. It did not take place straight away because, as Schwelly reported, 'Mr. has got the Gout . . . so Miss might wait'.[11] But Miss Gunning had only to be patient till the new year. Fanny heard about the wedding, which took place on 6 January 1790, from Dr Fisher, Bishop of Salisbury, who performed the ceremony by special licence in the drawing-room of Sir Robert Gunning's house in Northamptonshire. The guests sat around on sofas, no one even bothering to remove the ladies' workboxes and sewing. Digby asked what they should do, but Dr Fisher had no idea. So they put candles and a prayer-book on a table – the Bishop hoped it was not a card table – and thus Stephen Digby and Charlotte Gunning were made man and wife. Fanny was amazed that someone punctilious about religious forms could marry so casually, but the form of ceremony was said to be the bride's choice (a woman who knew ancient languages was obviously capable of any social enormity). The new Mrs Digby came to call on Fanny, 'quite brilliant in smiles and spirits', but judiciously left Mr Digby behind. Fanny did her the justice to say she believed she had 'long cherished a passionate regard' for her husband, and she wished her well.[12] The King and others kept repeating '*Poor Digby*' – because of his learned wife – but reports came in that he was showering attentions on his bride. Stephen and Charlotte Digby were to have two children, a son and a daughter, but Stephen's innate pessimism must have been confirmed when after only four and a half years of marriage his wife died and he was a widower again.[13]

If Fanny had been more forthcoming, and less prickly and 'intractable' during the summer tour, she might have received the offer which she thought was her right; whether she could have been happy if, contrary to what she now declared, she had accepted him, is another matter. She and Digby had shared interests, she would have been a loyal wife and an affectionate stepmother to his children, and the intimacy at Kew suggests that she was more attracted to him than she would admit. But fear of his grand connections held her back and she did not have the assurance to carry off the position: she would always have been suspecting slights by his relations. Moreover, those aspects of his behaviour which irritated her and put her on her guard – the self-absorption, the thoughtlessness – would not have disappeared in marriage. At Cheltenham, during the halcyon days of their relationship, they once discussed the scene in *Cecilia* where an unknown woman interrupts the heroine's wedding with Delvile, and Cecilia consequently refuses to continue with the ceremony. Digby argued that she should have trusted Delvile and gone on with it, but Fanny knew that Cecilia's action was 'what most precisely and indubitably I could not have resisted doing myself'.[14] In the end Fanny did not trust Digby enough to show him that she wanted to marry him.

After the wedding there were more glacial meetings. In April Fanny wrote that 'There is nothing so painful as meeting with absolute *horrour* any human being; but where it is one so lately met with *every* sentiment of approbation & esteem it is a check to all genial feelings the most frigid and comfortless.'[15] She watched unrelenting as he sought to impress her that he 'suffered much internal disturbance from my lost esteem'. No doubt the doting husband had now convinced himself that friendship was all he had ever sought with Fanny, and found her behaviour unreasonable and disturbing (it *was* disturbing, but she was alone, miserable, and beyond rational judgement). Frustrated in his efforts to make peace, Digby gave Columb a letter for Fanny: he could not 'help thinking', he wrote, that her conduct towards him had radically altered, though he was 'perfectly at a loss' to understand why this might be. 'Feeling – as I do – perfectly innocent', he could not refrain from telling her how her coolness hurt him, and beg for an explanation. Had it not been for those two words 'perfectly innocent' Fanny declared that she might have come to an accommodation, but they were unforgivable. She did not reply.[16]

Susan, though not confided in, had been well aware of the possibilities represented by the man she had nicknamed '*Il Vedovo amabile*' (the amiable widower) when she met Digby on Thanksgiving Day. But Fanny was behind in sending journals and though she had now read of what happened at Cheltenham, Susan had little idea of recent developments. She was shocked when Fanny wrote to tell her of Digby's engagement, and found the news difficult to believe until Fredy Lock showed her the announcement in the paper. Both women were outraged, and desperately disappointed that their hopes for Fanny's escape from court had been dashed. Susan called it a 'catastrophe' and thought Digby's behaviour 'disgraceful to the high idea I had formed of his character', while Fredy quoted her husband, who had called Digby a 'silly fellow' and asked indignantly, 'What did he look for in her that he did not find? Excepting *faults*'.[17] Fredy had paid her annual visit to Queen's Lodge in October and been extremely concerned about Fanny's situation and state of mind. The Digby revelation helped to explain her dejection (and her slowness in sending journals) but increased Susan's and Fredy's anxiety for her.

The year 1790 was a miserable one for Fanny. Apart from feeling humiliated in the eyes of her fellow-courtiers, she had lost the dream of escape with which she had at least toyed. The future stretched blank and drear in front of her unless she herself initiated change. A chance came at the end of May, when the King gave her a ticket for *The Messiah*, performed in Westminster Abbey as part of a Handel commemoration. She went with her father, and the Abbey was so crowded that they could not find seats with other family members. Thus Fanny was able to have 'three hours' conference' with her father (audiences at concerts and plays did not find it necessary to maintain silence). It had been Dr Burney's enthusiasm about the offer of a royal post which had made it impossible to reject and she would not give it up without his consent, but when he introduced the subject she seized the opportunity to explain that despite her 'constant veneration' for her royal mistress, she was very unhappy. She owned that:

I was lost to all private comfort, dead to all domestic endearment;
I was worn with want of rest, and fatigued with laborious
watchfulness and attendance. My time was devoted to official duties;
and all that in life was dearest to me – my friends, my chosen society,
my best affections – lived now in my mind only by recollection, and
rested upon that with nothing but bitter regret.[18]

In her misery she exaggerates her situation, for there were long periods
in the day when she did not have to watch or attend to official duties, but
there had never been any days when she could do exactly as she chose,
and the thought that there never would be was insupportable. As she
spoke to her father, he sat silent. (Could this recital of her miseries have
been to the strains of 'a man of sorrows and acquainted with grief'?)
When Fanny turned to look at him she saw that his head had sunk
dejectedly upon his breast:

We were both perfectly still a few moments; but when he raised his
head I could hardly keep my seat, to see his eyes filled with tears! –
'I have long', he cried, 'been uneasy, though I have not spoken; . . .
but . . . if you wish to resign – my house, my purse, my arms, shall be
open to receive you back!'[19]

It was with a lighter heart that after the concert Fanny returned to court.
But she was still a long way even from hinting to the Queen her wish to
resign. That was a prospect Fanny viewed with horror, so certain was she
that the Queen regarded her as hers for life.

Fanny's feelings for the Queen were always a little equivocal. She had
come straightforwardly to love the King and Princesses, and she would
have claimed to love the 'sweet' Queen too; but the mistress/servant
relationship complicated matters. Fanny was never completely
comfortable about the situation; her dislike of Mrs Schwellenberg almost
certainly included resentment of her dependent position transferred
from the Queen onto her superior's broad back. As she had told Digby
the Queen's moods were not always predictable, and though she said that
she had grown used to it, it is doubtful that she ever did. When the
Queen was all kindness Fanny responded warmly too and was gratified by
the intimacy of her trust, but the silences of displeasure were forbidding
and explain Fanny's terror of being late. Though she now had her
father's sanction to resign, the resolution to do so would be hard to find.

Dejection crept back, and she turned again for relief to the tragedy she
had abandoned during the King's illness. It was 'an almost spontaneous

work', and no sooner had she in some sense finished the play than an
idea for another came unbidden into her mind. In this way she was to
begin four such tragedies, all based on early English history.[20] The
writing 'soothed' her, and since she had long wondered if she would ever
again feel the creative instinct it helped to discover that she had not lost
all contact with it. But it was further evidence of an unhealthy state of
mind; the writing had become almost automatic and the scenes which
filled her thoughts at night deprived her of sleep.[21]

During this summer Fanny faced another distress: the illness and death
of her faithful servant Jacob Columb. After he had grown worse from 'a
swelling upon the liver', Fanny arranged for his admittance to a London
hospital. She tried to pay him arrears of wages, but he would not accept
them, instead giving into her safekeeping the ten guineas which was all
the money he possessed (his action is testimony to the trust and affection
in which he held his mistress). At this, their last meeting, he could
scarcely stand, 'looking already fit for a shroud'.[22] Fanny enquired
constantly after him and heard that he continued hopeful, but in
September he died. She knew he wished his property, such as it was, to go
to his sisters in Switzerland, but a shady-looking character turned up
brandishing a will which appeared to leave everything between him and
Columb's cousin James. Since James worked for Horace Walpole, Fanny
appealed to him for advice. Walpole counselled her to accept the will
since it would cost more in lawyer's fees to dispute it than the sum
concerned. It was all very distasteful, and a sad end to Columb's devoted
service.

In her letter to Walpole Fanny had wondered if he might have
forgotten one who now seemed 'consigned to silence and quiet'. He
answered that being unable to meet her was no reason to suggest he had
forgotten her, and continued:

> But were your talents given to be buried in obscurity? You have
> retired from the world to a closet at Court – where, indeed, you will
> still discover mankind, though not disclose it; for if you could
> penetrate its character in the earliest glimpse of its superficies, will it
> escape your piercing eye when it shrinks from your inspection,
> knowing that you have the mirror of truth in your pocket?[23]

These were flattering words, and they added to a growing chorus of
disapproval of Fanny's seclusion at court. One family friend (the
Reverend Thomas Twining) told her after a brief glimpse that she had
become as much a rarity as 'the Lincolnshire ox, or new American

bird'.[24] Even Mrs Anna Ord had lost her enthusiasm for the court life to which she had so unthinkingly delivered Fanny four years before.

Another voice raised on her behalf was that of James Boswell. Fanny encountered him in October, when he came to Windsor to see the newly refurbished St George's Chapel. She was pleased to see his 'comic-serious' face, but his feelings were mixed:

'I am extremely glad to see you indeed,' he cried, 'but very sorry to see you here. My dear ma'am, why do you stay? – it won't do, ma'am! You must resign! – we can put up with it no longer . . .

If you do not quit, ma'am, very soon, some violent measures, I assure you, will be taken. We shall address Dr. Burney in a body; I am ready to make the harangue myself. We shall fall upon him all at once.'[25]

'We' were the members of the Literary Club, which had been founded by Dr Johnson and of which Dr Burney was a member. Boswell was not so concerned for Fanny's welfare, however, as not to seize an opportunity for himself. He was near completing his *Life of Johnson*, and asked for letters from the great man, saying he wanted to show him 'in a new light':

'Grave Sam, and great Sam, and solemn Sam, and learned Sam, – all these he has appeared over and over. Now I want to show him as gay Sam, agreeable Sam, pleasant Sam; so you must help me with some of his beautiful billets to yourself.'[26]

Whether she had any choice little notes or not, Fanny refused on the grounds of not having any to hand. Boswell then renewed his first theme, pursuing her to the railings of Queen's Lodge and uttering 'stronger and stronger exhortations for my retreat', while Schwelly stared down from her window above.

A campaign for their sister's rescue was launched by Susan and Charlotte, with the encouragement of the Honourable William Windham, the Whig politician who had been meeting Fanny at the trial of Warren Hastings. His family seat was at Felbrigg Hall in Norfolk, not far from where Charlotte lived at Aylsham, and they met at a social occasion. Charlotte afterwards wrote a conspiratorial letter to Fanny about it (*Tatlanthe* is Charlotte, *Captain Ball* Windham, *Rigdumfundus* Susan, and *Bizarre* Fanny):

About 3 Months ago, Tatlanthe met Capt. Ball at Dinner, at a certain L[ds] & he was raving ab[t] Bizarre's situation, s[d] it was 'a profanation of her Talents' – a day or 2 after Tatlanthe wrote to her Father & told him w^t Capt. Ball s^d & added, most openly, *her* opinion of the affair, & concluded wth saying 'If Rigdumfundus & Tatlanthe c^d prevail on Bizarre to come & live with them, in turn, I wonder whether we c^d prevail on you to claim her on the plea of want of Health –'[27]

The group aimed to put pressure on Dr Burney, and they adopted a slogan:

> Heaven free the Encaged –
> And appease the Enraged! – [28]

Windham wrote to Fanny's father saying that her resignation was 'the common cause of every one interested in the concerns of genius & literature'.[29] Dr Burney was guiltily aware that in his daughter's appointment he had been Agamemnon to her Iphigenia, but he was very anxious not to offend royalty and did not like the argument that she must resign because she was too talented to live at court.[30]

Fanny was now becoming worryingly unwell. In October 1790 she had drawn up her 'memorial', her letter of resignation, on the grounds of inadequate strength for her duties, but it then lay in her letter-case while she vainly tried to find the courage to present it. Tension took its toll and in December she wrote to Charlotte asking for her doctor-husband's advice about her symptoms:

> The only actual & continued evil, is *want of sleep* – of which I have early lost the power, even for the turn I can give to it. My Eyes keep wide open, & I rise in the morning as if I had not been to Bed, unrefreshed, heavy, wearied, & listless.
>
> Till within the last 4 months . . . I was the very *reverse* of all this – I could scarcely keep awake – my Eyelids were perpetually dropping, – in my general attendance – at Church – in Company – at all times & all seasons, whenever I was not in *motion*, I found a propensity to sleep creep on me so irresistibly, that I have suffered the severest pain in forcing attention and wakefullness.[31]

She had no appetite and had lost weight, had given up walking, suffered frequent pains in her side and chest, and was sometimes hardly able to stand when she attended the Queen. Clement Francis wrote at once to Dr Burney about Fanny's health; with her father now in a state of alarm Fanny therefore wrote a second memorial, enclosing it with the first. Just before Christmas, with the court at St James's, Dr Burney made her promise that she would not return to Windsor without presenting it. Failing to find an opportunity to hand the paper directly to the Queen, in 'trembling agitation' she passed it to Mrs Schwellenberg for delivery, and waited in dread for the outcome.

What the Queen then read was a long document in appropriately fulsome language, acknowledging Her Majesty's 'goodness . . . condescension . . . sweetness . . . kindness', before making regretful admission of failing health, her father's consequent anxiety and his mortification that his daughter must needs relinquish the high honour of her office. The paper concluded in soliciting 'humbly, earnestly, and fervently' the Queen's continued 'benevolence', and it was signed by Her Majesty's 'ever devoted, ever grateful, most attached, and most dutiful subject and servant, Frances Burney'.[32] The enclosed note explained the two-month delay in presenting the paper as a period when she had, she tactfully claimed, hoped to see an improvement to her health.

The Queen had not been unobservant of the failing health of her Robe-keeper, and had been as sympathetic as it was possible for Majesty to be, wanting to know Mr Francis's diagnosis and urging her to consult with the household's doctor (he prescribed three glasses of wine a day and opium drops, which must have left her stupefied). Now, when Fanny was summoned to Mrs Schwellenberg and entered the room scarcely able to breathe, she was met with smiles: her paper had not offended in the least. Nor had it been taken seriously. It was proposed that she should 'retire & recruit' for four to six weeks; then she might return as usual. It is unlikely that Fanny actually had the courage to say, as she claimed in her letter to her father, that he would 'prefer to see me *well*, with a Crust of Bread, to *ill* – with a coronet'; in her journals she simply notes that she said she would consult her father.[33] Dr Burney's reply sanctioning retreat from court to save her health provoked an angry response from Cerbera: had England a Bastille, Fanny thought, she would have consigned them both to it. Thus ended December, Fanny concluding her journal for the year with with words 'Adieu – and away for ever, most painful 1790!'

But 1791 opened in continued uncertainty. Though the Queen had now accepted the resignation, she had not yet appointed a replacement and Fanny knew she still hoped it would not be necessary. The suspense brought Fanny to complete physical collapse, and for two months she had to be nursed by Susan and Fredy in turn. Illness was Fanny's only effective strategy in her campaign for release; that is not to say that it was a tactic deliberately adopted, but in her deteriorating mental and physical state she would eventually have died if she had not been set free.

The Queen at last accepted the resignation in earnest, though it proved hard to find a successor (so much for the 'thousands of offered candidates' of 1786) and Fanny was left in fear that she had incurred the serious displeasure of her mistress. She was therefore relieved when Mrs de Luc reported a compliment from the Queen which recognised the quality of her devoted service:

> 'Oh, as to character, she is what we call in German "true as gold"; and, in point of heart, there is not, all the world over, one better' – and added something further upon sincerity very forcibly. This makes me very happy; as her fluctuating behaviour, from kind, to grave, from friendly, to severe, has often made me doubtful, of late, if I had the honour to preserve any portion of her good opinion.[34]

In the last few weeks of Fanny's service the Queen became consistently kind, which Fanny found more unnerving than severity, but it is to Queen Charlotte's credit that she set personal pique aside, justly valuing her 'faithful handmaid'.[35]

Before she left court Fanny decided she must make a last effort on behalf of her family, though she found soliciting for favours abhorrent. She had the previous year done what she could for her brother James, who was on half-pay from the navy and wanted a ship, but without success. Now she tried to interest her royal mistress on behalf of her brother Charles, whose scholastic career and hopes of church preferment were still blocked because of the indiscretions of his youth. Fanny nerved herself to make representation, but again to no avail.[36] So ended all the hopes which her father had pinned on her court appointment.

Now, having salved her conscience, she was able to relax, to look outside herself and be amused by what she saw. She treated her friends to a bravura account of the 4 June celebrations of the King's birthday, when Prince William, Duke of Clarence, joined their magnificently provisioned dinner table, presided over by a magnificently attired Mrs Schwellenberg. Among the diners were two sober courtiers: ponderous André de Luc, and pompous Edwyn Francis Stanhope, possessor of an insecure set of false teeth.

The Duke, later William IV, had been sent to sea at the age of thirteen, and had brought his sailor's habits and language back with him (Fanny edited from her account 'certain forcible words'). But he was warm-hearted, and when Schwelly had introduced Fanny to him the Prince had said that it gave him pleasure that the Queen should appoint 'the sister of a sea-officer to so eligible a situation', declaring, 'I look upon her as one of

us. Oh, faith I do! I do indeed!'[37] At the ball to mark this birthday evening
he was to partner the fifteen-year-old Princess Mary, making her court
debut; Fanny thought she had grown up to become 'the first of this truly
beautiful race'. Unfortunately, her brother was already drunk when he
entered the dining-room calling for champagne to drink the King's health.
All rose for the loyal toast, then the Prince called for another. And another:

> 'Hark'ee! Bring another glass of Champagne to Mr. de Luc!'
>
> Mr. de Luc knows these Royal youths too well to venture at so vain
> an experiment as disputing with them; so he only shrugged his
> shoulders and drank the wine. The Duke did the same.
>
> 'And now, poor Stanhope,' cried the Duke; 'give another glass to
> poor Stanhope, d'ye hear?'
>
> 'Is not your Royal Highness afraid,' cried Mr. Stanhope, displaying
> the full circle of his borrowed teeth, 'I shall be apt to be rather up in
> the world, as the folks say, if I tope on at this rate?'
>
> 'Not at all! You can't get drunk in a better cause. I'd get drunk
> myself if it was not for the ball. Here, Champagne! Another glass for
> the philosopher! I keep sober for Mary!'[38]

It then became necessary to drink the Queen's health:

> 'Here are three of us,' cried the Duke, 'all belonging to the Queen:
> the Queen's philosopher, the Queen's gentleman-usher, and the
> Queen's son; but thank Heaven, I'm nearest!'
>
> 'Sir,' cried Mr. Stanhope, a little affronted, 'I am not now the
> Queen's gentleman-usher; I am the Queen's equerry, sir.'
>
> 'A glass more of Champagne here! What are you all so slow for?
> Where are all my rascals gone? . . . Come, a glass of Champagne for
> the Queen's gentleman-usher!' laughing heartily.
>
> 'No, sir,' repeated Mr. Stanhope; 'I am equerry now, sir.'
>
> 'And another glass to the Queen's philosopher!'
>
> Neither gentleman objected; but Mrs. Schwellenberg . . . now grew
> alarmed, and said, 'Your Royal Highness, I am afraid for the ball!'
>
> 'Hold you your potato-jaw, my dear,' cried the Duke, patting her;
> but, recollecting himself, he took her hand and pretty abruptly
> kissed it, and then, flinging it hastily away, laughed aloud, and called
> out, 'There! That will make amends for anything, so now I may say
> what I will. So here! A glass of Champagne for the Queen's
> philosopher and the Queen's gentleman-usher! Hang me if it will
> not do them a monstrous deal of good!'[39]

Fanny worried for the 'pearly ornaments' of the gentleman-usher/ equerry, his mouth agape in perpetual grin. Later she was able to amuse Princess Mary with the tale: 'Oh,' cried she, 'he told me of it himself the next morning, and said, "You may think how far I was gone, for I kissed the Schwellenberg's hand!"'

So Fanny came to the final week of her royal service. Her departure had been kept a secret, but now she had to make her farewells and glad though she was to go she was leaving behind acquaintances of five years' standing. With Digby she had remained 'cold, invincibly cold' despite his continued efforts to please, and she said no goodbye. But most partings were painful and it seems from Fanny's account that those to whom she said farewell were equally sorry to see her go. Her maid Goter did nothing but weep, sorry to lose her mistress and sorry for herself as Fanny had been unable to find her a new place. On her last day at Windsor Miss Planta would not dine with her 'as she felt she should cry all dinner-time'. After her meal Fanny went to say goodbye to the younger Princesses in the Lower Lodge, where she was grieved to find that Princess Amelia was already in bed, but she shook hands 'again and again' with Princesses Mary and Sophia. Then she sought those of her old friends among the equerries who were in attendance, and parted 'most cordially' from Colonels Goldsworthy, Gwynn and Manners.

Her last day, Thursday 7 July, began at Kew, with a farewell meeting with Mrs Schwellenberg. The old tyrant had much softened and with some emotion, though little understanding, she offered Fanny her own place on her retirement or death, before hurrying from the room. From Kew 'Miss Burney's coach' took her on a last journey to St James's for her final attendance on her royal mistress. The Queen had already made known to her that she intended to pay her a pension of half her annual salary, another illustration of the esteem in which Fanny was held. After the Drawing-room Fanny thanked her again, apologising that she could not do so on behalf of her father as she had not yet told him of it. The Queen interrupted her firmly: 'Your father has nothing to do with it; it is solely from *me* to *you*.'[40] There is as usual no account but Fanny's of this meeting, but there seems no reason to doubt her saying that the Queen had her handkerchief in her hand and dabbed her eyes throughout the interview. Then followed a parting so distressing that Fanny abandoned all etiquette:

The King then came into the room. He immediately advanced to the window, where I stood, to speak to me. I was not then able to comport myself steadily. I was forced to turn my head away from him. He stood still and silent for some minutes, waiting to see if I should turn about; but I could not recover myself sufficiently to face him, strange as it was to do otherwise; and perceiving me quite overcome he walked away, and I saw him no more.[41]

For the final time Fanny placed the Queen's cloak on her shoulders, saying as clearly as she was able, 'God Almighty bless your Majesty!':

She turned round, and, putting her hand upon my ungloved arm, pressed it with the greatest kindness, and said, 'May you be happy!'[42]

It was a sign to Fanny of the strength of her feeling that the Queen would touch her 'ungloved' arm in this way.

The very last farewells were with the three elder Princesses. After the Queen's departure they ran into the room; Princess Augusta and Princess Elizabeth each took a hand, and the Princess Royal placed hers over theirs. Fanny was beyond speech, but they each repeated 'I wish you happy! – I wish you health' before they too left to return to Kew. Fanny was alone – and she was free:

Here, therefore, end my Court Annals; after having lived in the service of Her Majesty five years within ten days – from July 17, 1786, to July 7, 1791.[43]

CHAPTER TWELVE

Royal Reporter

*What an awful moment this for such a man! – a man fallen from such height
of power to a situation so humiliating . . . Could even his Prosecutors at that
moment look on – and not shudder at least, if they did not blush?*[1]

When Fanny left court, the trial of Warren Hastings for corruption while
Governor-General of India had already spread over four years. She had
attended it on several occasions and her accounts had proved of such
interest to the King and Queen that after her resignation the Queen
continued to provide her with tickets. This unofficial position as a royal
reporter was far more suited to her talents than that of Robe-keeper;
moreover, it was of benefit to her in arousing her sympathetic interest in
something beyond her own affairs in the narrow court world. It took her
into a very different kind of court, though one which had its own rituals
and, ironically, its own rigidities. Fanny's visits were irregular, her
knowledge of Indian affairs limited and her judgements partisan, yet she
became not only a trusted reporter at the time for the King and Queen,
but a valued observer of a major political event of the eighteenth century
for historians since.

The impeachment of Hastings by the House of Commons has faded
into history now, its details so complex that only specialists seek to
disentangle them. Even at the time the evidence was little understood,
though most people were aware that the trial was an event of great
significance and were proud that England was so scrupulous about the
administration of far-away lands. Support divided along party lines: if
you were a Whig you believed passionately in Hastings' guilt, if a Tory
you were equally certain that he was innocent. In principle Fanny
regarded herself as non-partisan and disapproved of party politics; she
thought that no 'man of principle' should align himself exclusively with
one side or another.[2] Yet like everyone else she had her prejudices,
being generally in agreement with the King and his Tory government led
by William Pitt, while culturally she was closer to the Whig opposition.
Among their leaders were Edmund Burke, friend and admirer of her
writings, and Richard Brinsley Sheridan, who had once wanted her to
write a comedy. Fanny was uncomfortably conscious of these anti-court

connections, but politics played no part in her day-to-day life, indeed the only time she even set eyes on the Prime Minister was at Weymouth (where having seen Pitt she noted that his looks were 'his least recommendation').

English-ruled India consisted of Bengal and other enclaves on the east coast; it was administered not by the Government but by the East India Company, a powerful trading concern with its own army to oppose native uprisings and the territorial ambitions of other European nations.[3] Many people at home wore the imported Indian silks and muslins unthinkingly, but at a time when the anti-slavery movement was beginning to arouse consciences, the treatment of subject peoples in India was also causing concern. There was unease at the way returning Company officials, the 'nabobs', had made fortunes in the east through bribery and intimidation. The very appointment of Warren Hastings as Governor-General in 1773 was part of Government determination to assert some control over the Company's affairs.

Hastings had first sailed to India in 1750 at the age of eighteen. He had spent most of his working life in the Company's service, and had developed a respect for the cultures and languages he encountered.[4] He was no nabob, lining his own purse from Indian coffers, but as Governor-General he sometimes acted controversially – though always, he claimed, in the Company's interest. Hastings' misfortune was that he incurred the enmity of Philip Francis, one of the three-man council appointed with him, who managed to frustrate the Governor on every issue; matters culminated in a duel in which Francis was badly wounded and had to return to England.[5] There he formed an alliance with a man already investigating East Indian corruption – Edmund Burke. When Hastings himself returned to England in 1785 he faced a virulent campaign against him.[6]

Monster or victim? Fanny made no study of the list of the specific accusations presented to the House of Commons, but believed him innocent on the basis of personal knowledge. She had met Hastings three months after his return to England (before her court appointment) at the home of Richard Owen Cambridge in Twickenham, where Hastings 'talked of India, when the subject was led to, with the most unreserved readiness, yet was never the hero of his own tale, but simply the narrator of such anecdotes or descriptions as were called for'.[7] She was powerfully struck by the 'very plain green coat' Hastings wore; for her it indicated the essential modesty of a man who had ruled millions, and it came vividly to her mind during his trial, at a time when she had become familiar with the usual costly adornments of rank and power.

In August 1786 Fanny was granted permission by the Queen to spend an evening as guest of Hastings and his wife Marian at the home they had made at Beaumont Lodge, Old Windsor. There they had recreated something of their Indian past; Fanny's German admirer Sophie von la Roche, who also visited the Lodge, describes the attar of roses which perfumed the whole house, the pictures of Indian landscapes on the walls, the two Indian boys who waited at table, the fine Indian porcelain on which the meal was served, and the steamed Indian rice which accompanied it. Fanny made her visit with her sister Charlotte and her husband Clement Francis; he had been Hastings' doctor in India, and had tended the wounded Philip Francis. Fanny thought it ironic that 'the friend who most loves and the enemy who most hates Mr. Hastings should bear the same name!' She spent 'an agreeable evening with that very intelligent and informing man, whom I pity at my heart, for the persecutions he undergoes, and whom I think the man the most oppressed and injured in modern times'.[8] She also liked his 'lively and very pleasing wife' – though it is unlikely that Marion was dressed with a restraint matching that of her husband. Fanny disliked the kind of showy dressing and ostentatious display of oriental gems with which Marian Hastings was associated, and which had proved a gift to satirists.

After their return from India, Marian was a frequent visitor at court because of her friendship with Mrs Schwellenberg. Nearly twenty years earlier Schwelly had helped her first husband, Baron von Imhoff, to a post in India; by chance the couple travelled out on the same boat as Warren Hastings, then a widower. He fell in love with Marian with her mass of glorious auburn hair, and he persuaded her husband to divorce her.[9] Hastings adored his wife who was fifteen years younger than he was, a devotion which Fanny recognised and admired. Though she was not normally sympathetic to divorce she found herself in partnership with Schwelly against criticism that the Queen should not have received a divorcée, arguing that German divorce was altogether different from the English variety.[10]

The decision by the Commons to impeach Hastings before the bar of the House of Lords was taken in May 1787, causing dismay at court where Burke's name became 'the most obnoxious' in the world.[11] But the King was circumspect: although sympathetic to Hastings, he recognised that 'shocking enormities' had been committed in India and was careful to express no overt support for the former Governor-General. A Board of Managers was appointed to conduct the prosecution, headed by Burke and backed by other leading members of the opposition – Charles James

Fox, Richard Brinsley Sheridan, Charles Grey (the future Prime Minister), and William Windham, MP for Norwich. Westminster Hall, scene of other state trials, was prepared as a setting worthy of the occasion, and proceedings opened on 13 February 1788.

The Queen had given Fanny two tickets for the Grand Chamberlain's box and she invited her brother Charles to accompany her. The Queen even supplied her with cakes from her own breakfast table in case she was hungry. Charles was late, but Fanny left at eight o'clock and would have made her way to Westminster Hall in a chair, through streets lined with horse and foot guards. In her excitement about the occasion she seems not to have noticed the bitter cold which penetrated the Hall that morning. Preparations there had created a scene of very English pageantry and protocol, far removed from the heat, colour and confusion of India. The ancient Hall had been fitted up with tiers of seats, most upholstered in red, but in green for the Commons. A box 'lined with crimson, seats covered with the same' had been provided for the Queen and Princesses, with 'a rich velvet chair, for his MAJESTY, if he comes'.[12] There was another similar box for the Prince of Wales; between them, under 'a rich canopy of state', was a seat for the Lord Chancellor. This was placed directly opposite the small wooden box designed for the accused; on its left was the witness-box and the wooden enclosure for the Managers, on its right an enclosure for defence counsel. Fanny found that the Grand Chamberlain's box was immediately above the dock.

As the Hall filled up, an acquaintance, Lady Claremont, pointed out everyone of consequence and 'all those creatures . . . looking so little like gentlemen, and so much like hair-dressers'. These were members of the Commons. A contemporary painting shows the packed Hall with the 'hair-dressers' looking sober and serious; opposite them are ranks of peeresses in enormous bonnets and plumes, turning, gesticulating, chattering one with the other.[13] While Burke and his associates saw the impeachment as a great example of English justice, for the titled ladies of England it was the social event of the season. The Queen arrived with three of the Princesses; she chose not to occupy the royal box, but to sit 'incognito' in the Duke of Newcastle's gallery, simply attired in fawn-coloured satin and a plain headdress – with just a 'slender sprinkling of diamonds'.[14]

It was as well that Fanny had companions to talk to as nothing happened until midday. Then the doors were flung open and Burke, scroll in hand, led in the Committee. Fanny could not help shuddering as he strode with knitted brow, looking so different from the gay, kindly man she remembered. The other Managers followed, identified for the

short-sighted Fanny by Lady Claremont: recognising the solemnity of the
occasion, they all appeared in full dress, even the normally scruffy Fox
with wig and sword. After them came a procession of heralds, followed by
peers in their coronation robes, then the royal Dukes and the Prince of
Wales (perhaps Lady Claremont pointed out Mrs Fitzherbert in his box).
The Lord Chancellor, with a train borne behind him, brought up the
procession. Fanny heard a Sergeant-at-Arms command:

> 'Warren Hastings, Esquire, come forth! Answer to the charges
> brought against you; save your bail, or forfeit your recognizance!' . . .
>   The moment he came in sight . . . he made a low bow to the
> Chancellor and Court facing him. I saw not his face, as he was
> directly under me. He moved on slowly, and, I think, supported
> between his two bails, to the opening of his own box; there, lower
> still, he bowed again; and then, advancing to the bar, he leant his
> hands upon it, and dropped on his knees, but a voice in the same
> moment proclaiming he had leave to rise, he stood up almost
> instantaneously, and a third time profoundly bowed to the Court.[15]

Fanny does not give details of his costume, but others noticed his plain
suit – variously described as 'poppy-coloured' and 'dark blue' – which
contrasted with the velvets and ermines of state attire.[16]

In writing up her account of the trial, Fanny had to decide how to deal
with the speeches. The Lord Chancellor opened the proceedings with an
exposition of the purposes of the court and of the prisoner's rights,
which she rendered word for word 'to the best of my power from
memory' and in an illustration of her confidence in her retentive powers
she claimed that the 'newspapers have printed it far less accurately than I
have retained it, though I am by no means exact or secure'.[17] She then
heard Hastings reply: 'My Lords – Impressed – deeply impressed – I come
before your Lordships, equally confident in my own integrity, and in the
justice of the Court before which I am to clear it'. In *The History of the
Trial* this is given as 'My Lords, I am come to this high tribunal equally
impressed with a confidence in my own integrity, and in the justice of the
Court before which I stand'.[18] Fanny's version is not quite the same, but
she did not distort the substance, and her repetition of 'impressed' may
represent actual speech which the official publication 'tidied up'. On
subsequent visits to Westminster Hall Fanny heard Burke, Fox and
Sheridan; their speeches were extremely long and it would have been
impossible for her to attempt quotation, though she said that she 'never
more wished to have written shorthand'.[19]

Thus far on the first day everything had seemed worthy of the occasion, but what followed was, for Fanny, an anticlimax. In a 'monotonous chant' one of the lawyers began a reading – which was to last for two days – of both the charges and Hastings' answers from a long parchment roll; Fanny could make out almost nothing. People began to look about for those they knew, including Hastings himself. As he glanced round from beneath her Fanny saw with regret how 'pale, ill, and altered' he looked. She hoped he had not noticed her. Sir Joshua Reynolds did see her, smiled and bowed, gesturing to his ear to show he had not got his ear-trumpet with him. Another man made a deep bow, but 'very ridiculously I was obliged to inquire of Lady Claremont who my own acquaintance might be'. It was Richard Burke, brother of Edmund; he was followed by his son, another Richard who jumped up on a form and called 'How d'ye do, Miss Burney?' Much as she liked him, such recognition was embarrassing in this place and at this time.

She had just finished chatting with young Burke when Charles told her that 'a gentleman' desired to be presented to her:

'Who?' quoth I.
'Mr. Wyndham,' he answered.[20]

Fanny thought he must be joking; when she realised he was serious her embarrassment was acute. To be seen by the Queen conversing with one of the leaders of the prosecuting Committee! But there was no refusing.

Fanny had met William Windham on two previous occasions and thought him 'one of the most agreeable, spirited, well-bred, and brilliant conversers' she had ever spoken with. Two years older than Fanny he had entered politics under the tutelage of Burke, for whom he had a respect amounting to devotion. Despite differing from his political views Windham had also had a close friendship with Dr Johnson, at whose funeral he had been a pallbearer. Fanny took as evidence of a fine nature the 'kindness shown by a young man of fashion towards an old, however dignified, philosopher'. Knowing that she had been Johnson's favourite may have given Windham a reason for approaching Fanny now – there was easy passage between the Committee Box and the Grand Chamberlain's – but he may also have welcomed an excuse to view the scene from her better position, since it was the first thing he commented on:

'What an assembly is this! How striking a *spectacle*! I had not seen half its splendour down there. You have it here to great advantage; you lose some of the Lords, but you gain all the Ladies. You have a very good place here.'

'Yes; and I may safely say I make a very impartial use of it: for since here I have sat, I have never discovered to which side I have been listening!'

He laughed, but told me they were then running through the charges.

'And is it essential,' cried I, 'that they should so run them through that nobody can understand them? Is that a form of law?'[21]

He laughed again when Fanny begged to be told why at the end of the Chancellor's speech there had been cries of 'Hear! Hear! Hear him!' yet no further speech followed.

Looking down on the small figure of the accused, Windham marvelled at the gulf between what he had been and what he had become:

'Wonderful indeed! almost past credibility, is such a reverse! He that, so lately, had the Eastern World nearly at his beck; he, under whose tyrant power princes and potentates sunk and trembled; he, whose authority was without the reach of responsibility! . . . O could those – the thousands, the millions, who have groaned and languished under the iron rod of his oppressions – could they but – whatever region they inhabit – be permitted one dawn of light to look into this Hall, and see him *there*! *There* – where he now stands – it might prove, perhaps, some recompense for their sufferings!'[22]

Possibly Fanny exaggerates the rhetoric, but the language is in keeping with Windham's awed sense of occasion: this is what, from this lofty position, he might have liked to address to the whole Hall rather than just the little woman beside him.

His words made Fanny uncomfortable, however, and she nerved herself to express something of her real feelings, venturing the pertinent observation that in a court of law the ignorant bystander's sympathy will be given to the prisoner in the dock. For the moment she feared going further, but when she realised that Windham merely thought her possessed of a 'weak compassion for the prisoner', she grew more daring:

'May I again, Mr. Wyndham, forget that you are a *Committee-man*, and say something not fit for a *Committee-man* to hear?'

'Oh yes!' cried he, laughing very much, and looking extremely curious.

'I must fairly, then, own myself utterly ignorant upon this subject, and – and – may I go on?'

'I beg you will!'

'Well, then, – and originally prepossessed in favour of the object!'

He quite started, and with a look of surprise from which all pleasure was separated, exclaimed – 'Indeed!'[23]

Windham's answer was that she must come again, to hear Burke and learn the truth about 'That Man', shaped by 'cruelty . . . oppression . . . tyranny . . . arrogance . . . self-confidence'. This Fanny boldly countered with her own personal experience of the prisoner, to her someone 'mild . . . gentle . . . diffident . . . unassuming', the teller of good tales and the wearer of the very plain green coat. Though Windham still urged her to listen to Burke whose irresistible eloquence, 'a torrent that sweeps all before it with the force of a whirlwind', must convert her, Fanny hoped that she was contributing her own 'small mite' towards showing that the prisoner so vilified by the Committee was not formed solely of cruelty and avarice, but a monster of their own devising.

In their debate that afternoon, renewed after an interval, so he had not been offended, Fanny and Windham established a pattern that was to be repeated over many visits, creating a kind of court in miniature with Windham representing the prosecution and herself as defence counsel. She argued Hastings' innocence from personal knowledge and what she saw and heard at the trial; he remained convinced of Hastings' guilt, a conviction based on evidence but even more, it seemed, on his admiration for his mentor Burke, who knew so much about it that he could not be wrong. Their debates centred always on the slight figure they saw below them, to Fanny instancing injustice to an individual, to Windham justice to the Indian 'millions'. They disputed lightly, at times archly if Fanny reports accurately, but with recognition of the seriousness of the situation, and though Fanny does tend to make herself the heroine of her own tale in her reporting for Susan and Fredy, she showed an ability to pick up the weaknesses of the prosecution's case.

The Queen was curious to hear about Fanny's tête-à-têtes with Windham and was even moved by her narration; she soon recognised a reliable witness and furnished her not only with more tickets, but also a transcript of the charges and Hastings' replies, which Fanny now read eagerly. She had become emotionally involved, not one of those motivated solely by what Burke called 'eye-curiosity'.[24] She could not be released on court days, but was able to return to Westminster Hall on

16 February, with her brother James as her escort, for the second day of Burke's four-day introduction of the prosecution's case.

Fanny was thus able to listen to the greatest orator of the day; as it would be impossible to recount a speech which lasted for over three hours (and of which the substance would be printed in newspapers) she contented herself with trying to convey the effect of the oratory:

> All I had heard of his eloquence, and all I had conceived of his great abilities, was more than answered by his performance. Nervous, clear, and striking was almost all that he uttered: the main business, indeed, of his coming forth was frequently neglected, and not seldom wholly lost; but his excursions were so fanciful, so entertaining, and so ingenious, that no miscellaneous hearer, like myself, could blame them . . . When he narrated, he was easy, flowing, and natural; when he declaimed, energetic, warm, and brilliant.[25]

If her assessment is measured rather than adulatory it was because in her sympathy for Hastings Fanny was not to be swayed by rhetoric alone. But she does confess to having been caught up at times in the 'whirlwind' force of Burke's oratory, especially during narratives of some 'dreadful murders'. Mostly, however, she remained detached, helped by the mutterings of James ('When will he come to the point?' – 'These are mere words' – 'This is all sheer detraction!'), and criticised the speech for being general rather than specific, and containing 'more of invective than of justice'. Her comments are borne out by the printed version, which contains much which is not directly connected with Hastings and serves only a rhetorical purpose.[26]

When reporting to the Queen, Fanny must have dwelt rather more on the content of what she heard in the Hall, but in the journals it was the meetings with Windham which formed her principal subject matter. When she offered her criticisms of Burke, Windham told her that she should have heard him on the first day; it was also apparently the wrong day when she came to listen to Fox. The Managers were enraged following the Lords' ruling that judgement would not be given after each individual charge, but only at the end of the trial (Burke knew that the only real chance of a guilty verdict was while opinion was influenced by the Managers' rhetoric). 'It is now all going your way,' Windham told Fanny crossly. Fox's anger, he said, would be directed at the judges, not Hastings, but the five-hour speech shocked her with its ferocity. Yet she perceived an artificiality about Fox's invective compared with Burke's: his anger, she thought, was created not felt.

Fanny also apparently listened to the third of the great orators, Sheridan, though tantalisingly she did not journalise the experience (perhaps Susan and Fredy were there to hear the speech for themselves). Her presence on 13 June 1788, the last day of Sheridan's oration, is revealed only in a letter to Marianne Port where she wrote of having passed Colonels Gwynn and Goldsworthy while on her way to Westminster Hall; as it was not a Drawing-room day she saw them 'lift up their hands and eyes in wonder and amaze' at her full-dressed head and hair.[27] In the Hall she would have heard Sheridan speak with passion about two Indian princesses, the Begums, whom it was claimed that Hastings had robbed and ill-treated. It was the most powerful of the charges against him and Sheridan made the most of it, at the end collapsing stagily into Burke's waiting arms.[28] It is unlikely that Fanny was as affected as Mrs Siddons, said to have been so overwhelmed that she fainted away, but we cannot know.

In Fanny's encounters with Windham she had begged him not to 'betray' her disagreement with him to Burke and he did not. Yet it was very unsettling when during her fourth visit Burke himself, in friendly fashion, came to speak with her, regretting the time since they had last met. 'Yes,' she answered, 'I live in a monastery now.' She made him laugh when she went on to say:

> 'Indeed . . . I had never meant to speak to Mr. Burke again after hearing him in Westminster Hall. I had meant to keep at least that *geographical timidity*.'[29]

Though spoken as a jest, Fanny's words show her recognition of a crucial aspect of the case. Hastings had argued that for administration to be effective in India it was necessary to adapt to the culture of the region. Burke scorned this 'kind of geographical morality' which applied a different set of principles to actions in the East. Hastings and his kind, he argued, considered themselves 'governed not by their relations to the great Governor of the universe, or by their relations to men, but by climates, degrees of longitude and latitude, parallels not of life but of latitudes'.[30] About one thing, however, Fanny agreed with Burke, when he suggested that there was no need to feel sorry for *her* for having to sit so long. It became part of the attraction of the trial that she could have three-hour chats before proceedings began with those who accompanied her there.

It was on this occasion that she encountered Hastings himself as she left the Hall. He called after her and said wryly, 'I must come here to have the pleasure of seeing Miss Burney, for I see her nowhere else'.[31]

In the summer the trial was adjourned – the court never sat outside the parliamentary sessions or when the judges were on circuit – to be reconvened in 1789. In this year the King's illness made attendance impossible, so it was almost two years before Fanny appeared at the trial again. In the interim much had happened to her, but at Westminster Hall nothing seemed changed. Yet the atmosphere was very different. Progress had been so slow – only four of the twenty-two charges had so far been covered – that the public in general had lost interest and, in any case, it was the French Revolution that now occupied people. Fox would have abandoned the trial, but Burke's obsession drove it on. Fanny's attitude too had hardened; following the handling by the opposition of the King's illness and the Regency affair she found it harder than ever to sympathise with Burke.

On her first visit in 1790 Fanny found it all rather humdrum, and Windham seemed to have forgotten her. A month later it was no more lively and she was just 'eating a biscuit to prevent an absolute doze' when he entered her box, apologising once more that it was the wrong day, a 'stupid day'. He told Fanny that the Lords were determined to acquit Hastings and when she asked why answered, 'from the general knavery and villainy of mankind, which always wishes to abet successful guilt'.[32] She recognised the strength of feeling which bound Windham to Burke and which would not allow him to acknowledge any flaws in his hero's arguments.

When James accompanied Fanny on her next visit she was anxious that her notoriously blunt brother would not interrupt if Windham came to talk with her, but the Captain gladly promised 'to leave him to attacks of the little privateer, without falling foul of him with a broadside'.[33] Windham did come, though he was too agitated for dispute as he expected to have to speak. Fanny had previously flattered him that she feared for her side if he did, but in the event she was greatly disappointed. He had a sure grasp of argument but his voice was unpleasant to listen to, with 'a crude accent and expression very disagreeable'. When he finished speaking she saw 'his pale face a fiery red', and he did not come to receive false compliments. On a later visit that year they did spar again and Fanny tried once more to engage Windham's sympathy for Hastings:

'He is so gentle-mannered, so intelligent, so unassuming, yet so full-minded.'

'I have understood that,' he answered; 'yet 'tis amazing how little unison there may be between manners and characters, and how softly gentle a man may appear without, whose nature within is all ferocity and cruelty. This is a part of mankind of which you cannot judge – of which, indeed, you can scarce form an idea . . . villainy, *masked* villainy is a world unknown to you.'[34]

This struck home, not for Hastings but Stephen Digby.

But what of Windham himself? What mask did he wear? It would have perturbed Fanny to discover that whereas he was featuring so importantly in her journals, in *his* diaries she was never mentioned. The editor of these diaries declares that they are a 'muster-roll of his contemporaries, comprehending, probably every individual with whom he associated during a long series of years; but a muster-roll unaccompanied, in almost any instance, by the slightest comment'.[35] It is no surprise, therefore, that he did not discuss the debates he had with Fanny; what is puzzling is that *no* reference to her is made. It is true that there are no diary entries for some of the dates when they talked together, and that his preoccupation at the trial is his self-conscious brooding on his own speaking. Yet a 'Spoke with Miss Burney' would have been natural. Why Fanny is never mentioned is a mystery, especially since that summer he became part of the 'cabal' dedicated to getting her out of the court. He was said then to be in such a 'passion' and 'rage' about Fanny's incarceration that a family friend, Frances Crewe, believed him to be in love with her.[36] But in his diary – nothing.

On 2 June 1791, just before Fanny left court, Hastings opened his defence. Because she had been ill she was reluctant to attend, but the Queen said she 'would give the world' for her to go, adding, 'Surely . . . you may wrap up, so as not to catch cold that once?' So Fanny went to Westminster Hall again, and found it more crowded than she had seen it since the first day. Hastings spoke himself, but was so frequently interrupted by Burke and Fox that at length he protested vehemently. 'Hear, hear, hear!' cried the Lords – this time Fanny knew what they meant – and the Managers were silenced. She was glad not to see Windham in the box, though she met him afterwards in the lobby; her looks were so changed by illness that he did not immediately recognise her. He told her how he had 'raved and raged' about her situation and asked, 'When shall I see you again?'[37]

That evening she gave a detailed report first to the Queen, and then the King, who listened 'with much earnestness and marked compassion' despite having read an official account. Fanny thought she understood why her version was heard with such eagerness:

The words may be given to the eye, but the impression they make can only be conveyed by the ear; and I came back so eagerly interested, that my memory was not more stored with the very words than my voice with the intonations of all that had passed.[38]

It is a pity that the royal couple could not find more ways in which to make use of Fanny's remarkable memory and talent for mimicry. Her analysis also justifies not attempting to convey the substance of the speeches she listened to in her journals: the main speeches of the Managers at the trial were taken down in shorthand and can be read today, but printed oratory is a lifeless thing.

Next year the free Fanny was still favoured with tickets for the trial, afterwards returning to the Queen's House to make report. The audience was diminishing and Fanny thought it 'barbarous' that 'To hear the attack, the people came in Crowds; to hear the defence, they scarcely come in Tête à Têtes!'[39] She resumed her debates with Windham, and they seemed to be on their old footing, but after a while he stopped coming to her box. Fanny wondered if she had pressed her arguments too far, or whether association with a representative of the court was an embarrassment. Perhaps he had heard the rumour that he was in love with Miss Burney, thought she came there to see him and kept away. Fanny had, however, performed a service for him as much as he had for her over her court release, presenting him to the Queen as a man of principle and compassion.

After 1792 Fanny's life changed completely and she went no more to the Hall, but the trial dragged on until 23 April 1795 when Hastings was acquitted on all charges.[40] Reviewing the case since, even those historians like Macaulay, who consider him guilty in spirit if not always in law, have agreed that he did not deserve the long humiliation of the trial.[41] Yet he had survived and was able to retire to the country with Marian, where he lived on until 1818. Burke fared less well. Though Windham never deserted him, he had quarrelled irrevocably with Fox and Sheridan, suffered personal tragedies in the deaths of his brother and his son, and was in ill health himself. After the verdict Fanny wrote to her father that she was 'glad . . . with all my Heart, of Mr. Hastings honourable acquital', but of 'poor Mr. Burke', now the man she pitied, she could only wish for better news; when Burke died in 1797 Fanny wrote to her father, 'That he was upright in Heart, even where he acted wrong, I do truly believe . . . & that he asserted nothing he had not persuaded himself to be true, from Mr. Hastings being the most rapacious of villains, to the King's being incurably insane'.[42] Burke had cared passionately about India and was said to know more about it than anyone who had never been there, so perhaps she should have found the courage to tell *him* of the unassuming man who had talked so sympathetically of 'the people, the customs, habits, cities, and whatever I could name' of his beloved India.

CHAPTER THIRTEEN

Marriage, a Son, and a Daughter

M. d'Arblay is one of the singularly interesting Characters that can ever have been formed. He has a sincerity, a frankness, an ingenuous openness of nature that I had been injust enough to think could not belong to a French Man.[1]

Released prisoners find it difficult to settle back into ordinary life again, and it cannot have been easy for Fanny either. Days of preordained routine now gave way to activities of her own choice, yet she had to adjust to being just an unmarried daughter, no longer with her own suites of rooms in large mansions, but sharing a bedroom with her half-sister Sarah in a small apartment in Chelsea College (where her father was organist). A sign of difficulty in adjustment may be that though a principal reason urged for her resignation had been the wish to see her re-established as a literary figure, Fanny was not to embark on anything more ambitious than tinkering with her tragedies for some time to come. But two weeks after her departure from court, Mrs Ord, who had delivered her to Queen's Lodge five years before, took her for a recuperative tour of the west country which helped her to get used to ordinary life again.

Even so, Fanny carried her memories with her; their route partly retraced the one she had travelled in 1789, and she was strongly conscious of the difference between then and now:

What a contrast this journey to that I took 2 years ago in attendance upon Her Majesty! the Roads now so empty, the Towns so quiet, – & then – what multitudes! what tumults of joy – & how graciously welcomed![2]

She recalled how Salisbury had seemed 'to have neither Houses nor Walls, but to be composed solely of Faces'. Now, a traveller as any other, she could wander the streets at will. After four weeks of sightseeing, the tour ended with a stay in Bath for Fanny to try the waters. She had last been in the city in 1780 with Mrs Thrale, since when it had trebled in size and become a Mecca for fashionable society. Here too court memories were stirred when she had an introduction to one of society's leaders, Georgiana, Duchess of Devonshire. Georgiana belonged to the fast set which revolved round the Prince of Wales, Charles Fox, and the Opposition, and Fanny thought it extraordinary that so soon after leaving the court she should make the acquaintance of the 'head of the *opposition public*' and one of the 'Regency Squadron' in 1789. She made sure to emphasise to the Duchess her distress at the King's illness then and the sufferings of the Queen. Georgiana took it in good part and, as so many others, Fanny was charmed by her; she would have been deeply shocked had she known that the Duchess was carrying the child of her lover, the politician Charles Grey. In happy ignorance Fanny found it pleasant just before she left Bath, to be greeted from the Duchess's sedan chair with blown kisses and a 'How d'y'do? how d'y'do?'[3]

Fanny parted from Mrs Ord much restored in health, but it took rather longer before she felt fully restored to the Queen's favour. In January 1792 she was asked to stand in at a Drawing-room for her successor, Miss Jacobi, who had sprained her ankle. She was glad to be asked but nervous to go, carrying with her a fear of disapproval for having abandoned her post. In the event she was affectionately greeted by all the Princesses, with kisses from Princesses Sophia and Amelia, and the King said he was 'very glad' to see her, making her stand under a lamp so that he could see how well she looked. But the crucial issue was the Queen's attitude; though gracious, Fanny found her 'by no means lively or cordial'. Her own self-consciousness certainly contributed to any strained atmosphere, for the Queen would hardly have asked Fanny to attend her without a wish to see her again. Almost a year after she had left court she attended the King's birthday celebration on 4 June, and this time felt a return to complete cordiality. Once again the Princesses were friendly, and the King came up calling out, 'What! Miss Burney!' and talking gaily:

He said I was grown *quite fat* since he had seen me, . . . he protested my arm was half as big again as heretofore, & then he measured it with his spread thumbs & fore fingers – & the whole of his manner shewed his perfect approbation of the step I had taken of presenting myself in the royal presence on this auspicious Day.[4]

The occasion was the more enjoyable since she could dress 'without Feathers, Flowers, Hoop, or *furbelows*'.

At this time, when Fanny was leading a busy social life in London, caught up in the rituals of card-leaving and visiting, two men from the past made reappearances. At one house she had started up the stairs and begun a smiling 'How do you do' to someone coming down when she recognised in the reciprocal smiles the face of Stephen Digby, who 'in a tone of softness & pleasure in his *first Manner*, began a solicitous enquiry after my Health'.[5] Fanny, unrelenting, replied that she had not the honour to know him, and 'was up the stairs before he could speak or look again'. The other man was George Cambridge, who began to appear at her social engagements and since he had recently obtained preferment there were hints and smiles. However, though 'something keeps him from being wholly at ease about me', Fanny told Susan that she was sure it was not 'regard' (yet she had misread hearts before: perhaps he was looking for encouragement). Gossip spread, and to her annoyance even Mrs Schwellenberg declared, 'Miss Berner, I hear it bin really true you will marry!'[6] But when she reached her fortieth birthday in June 1792 Fanny herself must have seen ahead only a future as an 'old tabby'. Yet in little more than a year her life was to have changed utterly when after a short courtship she married a penniless French refugee.

The French Revolution was not something which could any longer form the subject of a joke. The government of France had fallen into the hands of extremists and at the end of the year King Louis XVI as 'Citizen Capet' faced trial and possible sentence of death. Among the many who were fleeing from the turbulence was a small colony of émigrés who had established themselves at Juniper Hall in Mickleham, near Susan.[7] The liberal-minded Locks had befriended the group because they were Constitutionalists, supporters of the 1791 Constitution drawn up by the Constituent Assembly to create a fairer society. Unfortunately, many in England, including Dr Burney, blamed the Constitutionalists for the present anarchy. Fanny herself warned Susan:

> *All* the *Constituents* are now reviled as authors and originators of all the misfortunes of France, from arrogant self sufficiency in their powers to *stop*, as well as *begin*, when they pleased.[8]

Yet when she went to stay with her sister in January 1793, Fanny was eager to meet the 'Juniperians', especially the two of whom Susan had written most enthusiastically, the former Louis Comte de Narbonne, one-time Minister of War, and his friend Alexandre d'Arblay.

Hard on the heels of her introduction came news of the execution of the French king on 21 January 1793. Fanny expressed her sense of shock and outrage to her father:

> Except the period of illness of our own inestimable King, I have never been so overcome with grief & dismay for any but personal & family calamities. O what a Tragedy! how implacable its villainy, & how severe its sorrows! . . .
>
> M. de Narbonne & M. D'Arblay have been almost annihilated – they are for-ever repining that they are French, &, though two of the most accomplished & elegant Men I ever saw, they break our Hearts for the humiliation they feel for their guiltless *BIRTH* in that guilty Country.[9]

The tragedy bonded her with the men and there were frequent meetings, extended into lessons after d'Arblay proposed that they should exchange teaching in each other's language. Then, precipitately and reluctantly, Fanny left Mickleham after she had received an agitated letter from her father following the arrival at Juniper Hall of the woman who had arranged its rental by the refugees, the writer Germaine de Staël. While Fanny had been dazzled by Madame de Staël's brilliant, forceful personality, Dr Burney was distressed at accusations in London that she had fomented the Revolution in her Paris salon, and by dark rumours that she was engaged in an adulterous union with Narbonne.[10] But before Fanny left, d'Arblay persuaded her to continue the 'Mastering and scholaring' by post, and a month later he sat down to pen not an English essay, but a letter in his own language; though enigmatically phrased it amounted to a proposal of marriage.[11]

Alexandre-Jean-Baptiste Piochard d'Arblay, two years younger than Fanny, came from Joigny, south-east of Paris, and was of the *petite noblesse*, the minor aristocracy. Tall, with a good figure, and a soldier since the age of twelve, he was a cultivated man with a taste for literature. He had served in the same regiment as Choderlos de Laclos, author of the *Les Liaisons Dangereuses*, and that *succès de scandale* of 1782 had inspired him to write some love poetry in the character of the idealistic and open-natured Chevalier Danceny (when Fanny had been told of this novel the very title was enough to determine her not to read it).[12] But if there ever was any French equivalent of Miss Gunning in his past, none has been discovered. Recently d'Arblay had been acting as Adjutant-Général to the

Marquis de Lafayette, commander of the National Guard; he had been on duty at the Tuileries on the night of 20 June 1791 when the King made his abortive attempt to flee from France before being stopped at Varennes. He had also carried news of the massacre of the Swiss Guard at Versailles on 10 August 1792 to Lafayette. This association with the man who had led French troops against the English in the American War of Independence unfortunately did d'Arblay no good at all when he came to England, having lost everything in the Revolution except his life. He arrived in near despair, then he met Fanny, lively, sympathetic, principled, the author of *Evelina* and *Cecilia*, and she awakened hopes for a future. Unlike any other man who had previously seemed to favour her, he did not hesitate.[13]

Answering him was more difficult. Fanny's immediate reaction was to dash off a frantic appeal to Susan for advice, though in the end she did not wait but wrote in his own language a careful reply, saying that if it was her choice whether or not he should find work and stay in England, she did not think that he would leave.[14] It was encouragement enough for a chevalier and next day he set off to walk most of the way to and from London, acquiring a rose-tree in full bloom along the route, and leaving it with a note at Chelsea College. It was a grand romantic gesture, but Fanny was concerned with practicalities. *Could* he find work? If not, how could they live on her annual income of £120? Would she lose most of that if the Queen disapproved of her marriage? He thought she could use her court connections on his behalf, but she knew the difficulties of soliciting for places and the 'prejudice now reigning in the Court against all Constitutionels'.[15]

Her main anxiety was to keep the proposal a secret until she had decided whether marriage was possible: when they met in public there must be nothing said or done to rouse suspicion. She needed her confidante though; as in her other relationships Fanny had immediate recourse to her pen and told Susan of her intention to '*Diarize*' every meeting the instant it had taken place, and to copy out for her their letters to each other. These 'Courtship Journals' with their surreptitiously passed notes, a father to hoodwink, a snatched conversation in a coach, a servant's stares and a younger sister's smiles, read much like an epistolary novel; whatever her expressions of anxiety, Fanny was rather enjoying being the heroine of her own story. The hero, however, became increasingly depressed and frustrated.

Finally, the Locks were let into the secret and William Lock sensibly suggested that £120 a year was more than many a clergyman lived on so they should be able to manage. He also offered them a plot of land on

which to build a house. Fanny did not think she would lose the Queen's favour by her marriage; she also knew that she had a further resource in publishing, or as she phrased it, 'venturing my little Bark on the Ocean of Literature'. Dr Burney could not approve, though more because of d'Arblay's poverty than his politics. So instead of her father James Burney gave his sister away at seven in the morning of 28 July 1793 in Mickleham Church, in the presence of the Locks, the Phillipses, and Narbonne.[16] Nobody recorded what the bride wore.

The transformation of Miss Burney into Madame d'Arblay was a sensation as great as the publication of *Evelina* for those who knew her. All were amazed, but almost all supportive, and Dr Burney was soon reconciled to the marriage.[17] Fanny had prepared the ground at court by telling d'Arblay's story to the Queen and declaring 'That I should cease to think Honour & integrity existed in the World, if ever I lost my opinion of their residing in M. D'Arblay'; she must, nevertheless, have been relieved when she received congratulatory letters first from Miss Planta, then one from Schwelly which offered the good wishes of 'Her Majesty and all the Royal Family' as well as herself.[18]

Until they could build their own house, Fanny and d'Arblay rented a cottage in Great Bookham, a village within walking distance of both Norbury Park and Mickleham. Her life in what she called their 'hermitage' was as socially limited as ever it had been at court but it was by choice, and all she missed was the London theatre. For d'Arblay, however, adjustment was more difficult; he longed for employment in some military capacity in the war against the French Revolutionary government, but his background and the prejudice it aroused made it impossible. Dr Burney urged him to stay unobtrusively in the country and follow Voltaire's advice to 'cultivate his garden'; this he quite literally did, becoming a keen gardener and a familiar local figure in his old green gardening cap (the supply of vegetables for their table proved important as war drove up prices and increased taxes). To their great joy, on 18 December 1794 a son, Alexander Charles Louis, was born. This 'Idol of the World' was to become known as Alex.

Fanny's re-emergence as a published author had already begun, in November 1793, with a pamphlet, *Brief Reflexions relative to the Emigrant French Clergy*, in support of the thousands of destitute priests who had flooded into Britain. She was also slowly building on ideas for a novel which she had first jotted down while at court.[19] But her next immediate venture was a production at Drury Lane Theatre of *Edwy and Elgiva*, one of her blank-verse tragedies. Fanny's brother Charles was a drinking-

partner of John Philip Kemble, actor-manager of the theatre and brother
of Sarah Siddons, and he conducted the negotiations. The play was
endorsed by Sheridan, Drury Lane's proprietor, just before Alex was
born. As ever nervous about the Queen's reaction and no doubt
remembering how the Queen had thought her 'too delicate to suit with
writing for the stage', Fanny asked leave from Mrs Schwellenberg to send
the play for approval.[20] Schwelly replied offering congratulations on
'your dear Littel Babe' and telling her that Her Majesty would 'Peruse
them [sic] with Plasuer'.[21] With Kemble and Mrs Siddons in the leading
roles, *Edwy and Elgiva* was subsequently played on Saturday 21 March
1795. But the performance was a disaster and Fanny's play was, in Mrs
Piozzi's malicious phrase, 'hooted off the Stage'.[22] Readers of its leaden
lines will not be surprised, though it is little worse than other tragedies of
the period and it seems that poor performance was as much to blame as
poor dramatic craftsmanship. Reviewers noted the prominent role taken
by the prompter, the critic of the *Morning Chronicle* commenting, for
example, 'The acting was disgraceful to the Company, and shamefully
injurious to the Author'.[23]

After this humiliation it was important to make no mistakes with the
new novel, for which reason Fanny would not call it by that name,
remembering how 'the Word *Novel* was long in the way of Cecilia', the
Princesses forbidden to read it 'till it was sanctioned by a Bishop's
recommendation'.[24] On 7 July 1795, therefore, the *Morning Chronicle*
simply announced 'a NEW WORK by the author of *Evelina* and *Cecilia*' for
the first day of July the following year. Increasing numbers of popular
novels had brought the form into even greater disrepute, so Fanny was
delighted when she received permission to dedicate her 'little work' to
the Queen. This guaranteed its respectability, though the five substantial
volumes were to make her new novel something more than 'little'.[25]

Fanny took a hard-headed approach to selling: this book represented
Alex's future. Charles again acted as her agent, selling the copyright for
£1,000; Fanny also accepted Edmund Burke's advice to draw up a subscription list at a guinea a head.[26] But she spread herself rather too much
with the writing and it was less than three weeks to publication date before
d'Arblay could tell Susan that '*hier au soir ma femme entre onze heures et
minuit a enfin été heureusement delivrée d'une fille*'.[27] *Camilla* came into the
world with the blessing of over a thousand subscribers countrywide, a
tribute to the esteem in which Madame d'Arblay's writing was held. The
list was headed by the new Duchess of York and included a number of
Fanny's old associates at court: Mrs Schwellenberg, Miss Planta,
Miss Goldsworthy and Mrs de Luc, the promoted Generals Goldsworthy

and Gwynn, Mrs Gwynn, Colonel Greville, Major Price, Leonard Smelt and Sir Lucas Pepys. The Earl and Countess of Harcourt each ordered a sct; thc Honourablc Stephen Digby did not.[28] Other subscribers included Edmund Burke (who had generously ordered fifteen sets but died before he could read it), William Windham who had become Secretary of State for War, Warren Hastings and Marian, the Duchess of Devonshire and numerous other titled persons, Mrs Piozzi and the three Miss Thrales, and many other knowns and unknowns, including a certain 'Miss J. Austen'.[29]

Camilla, or A Picture of Youth is, despite its length, the most Austen-like of Fanny's novels for Camilla is part of a family, the Tyrolds, and the novel recounts the history of all, using one principal setting in Hampshire. There is a moral core founded on drama and distress, but *Camilla* is basically a cheerful and often funny book, its main figures vividly realised. Fanny told her father that in the writing they became for her 'as so many actual acquaintances, whose memoirs & opinions I am committing to *paper*'; for the reader likewise the central characters, especially Camilla herself and her eccentric Uncle Hugh, become old friends. They are ordinary people suffering the ups and downs of (mainly) ordinary provincial life; in a book dedicated to Her Majesty setting and incident are far removed from court life. Indeed, at times Fanny seems to be offering a reverse of her court experiences, as when Camilla and friends sit in a barn watching a grotesque production of *Othello* performed in a variety of rustic accents, or when she is shown over the property of a tradesman which imitates the landed estates of a Harcourt, Edgcumbe or Digby; it has a 'grotto' which is a hole in the ground, a 'labyrinth' inexpertly cut through brushwood, and a muddy pond of a lake with a wooden swan to swim upon it. But there is a moment when Fanny allowed herself to reflect bitter experience at court; Camilla, uncertain of the affections of the man she loves, tells her sister:

> 'Lavinia! If you would avoid deceit and treachery, look at a man as at a picture, which tells you only the present moment! . . . They are not like us, Lavinia. They think themselves free, if they have made no verbal profession; though they may have pledged themselves by looks, by actions, by attentions, and by manners, a thousand, and a thousand times!'[30]

Though undoubtedly Fanny was thinking of Digby when she wrote this, the situation is not a true parallel for Edgar does love Camilla and all is eventually well.

Fanny had two sets of her work bound in red morocco, and on 5 July 1796 she set off with her husband for lodgings in Windsor to lay her work at the Queen's feet, the 'Bambino' being left in Susan's care. She must have been conscious when she entered Queen's Lodge once more that as many years had passed since she had left court as she had served. She was summoned to the Queen's dressing-room, where with considerable emotion she knelt and made her offering. The books were graciously accepted, and a little later the King came in, smilingly received his set, and quizzed Fanny about the writing. When he asked if she was frightened about the critics she told him that they could never cause her pain in proportion to the pleasure the book had given her in the writing.[31]

In her next interview with the Queen, Fanny found that she had already begun to read the novel. She talked excitedly about it, displaying instinctive engagement with the plot and characters despite her supposed dislike of the form:

'I have read', said the Queen, 'but 90 pages yet, – but I am in great uneasiness for that poor little Girl, that I am afraid will get the small pox! – And I am sadly afraid that sweet little other Girl will not keep her fortune! but I won't peep! I read quite fair. But I must tell Mad[e]. d'Arblay I know a Country Gentleman – in Micklenburg, – exactly the very character of that good old Man the Uncle!' She seemed to speak as if delighted to meet him upon Paper.[32]

The King then came in and wanted to know what they had been saying:

'O, your Majesty,' she cried, 'I must not anticipate!' yet told him of her pleasure in finding an old acquaintance. 'Well!' cried the King, archly, '& what other characters have you seized?' – '*None*,' I protested, 'from life'. 'O!' cried he, shaking his head, 'you *must have some*!' 'Indeed your Majesty will find none!' I cried, 'But they may be a little better, – or a little worse, –' he answered, 'but still – – if they are not like *somebody*, how can they play their parts?' 'O, yes, Sir,' I cried, 'as far as *general nature* goes, or as Characters belong to Classes, I have certainly tried to take them. But no individuals!'[33]

Court subscribers were no doubt anxiously waiting to see if they or anyone they knew had been enshrined in her book, but Fanny did not want anyone to point the finger at her for drawing her characters from her court life. Nevertheless, characters were linked with particular people – those who knew him, for example, were sure that Fredy's son William was the model for Edgar Mandlebert, the hero – and it may have crossed say Lady Harcourt's mind that the character of the austere mother Mrs Tyrold, loved yet feared by her children, who obeys her husband even when privately she thinks him wrong, has some resemblance to the Queen herself. And the incorrigible but charming reprobate Lionel Tyrold (modelled it is usually thought on James or Charles in youth) might have reminded a court reader of the scapegrace Princes.

In taking d'Arblay with her to Windsor Fanny wanted to show that her husband was no revolutionary monster. So she was very happy when at the Queen's command both were invited to dine at her old table. The meal was cheerful – Schwelly was absent – and 'all my old friends were curious to see M. d'A. who was in spirits, &, as he could address them in French, & at his ease, did not seem *much disapproved* of by them'. Fanny wanted to take him to the evening promenade on the Terrace where she might have the opportunity to introduce him to the King and Queen, but the weather was poor and it was doubtful if it would take place. They were about to leave Windsor when Princess Sophia sent to say that she, the King, and Princess Amelia, would be on the Terrace. They hurried off, still uncertain that anyone would appear on a raw evening. Very few people were present and after half an hour the musicians packed up; suddenly a messenger arrived, 'helter skelter running after the Horns & Clarinets & Hallooing to them to return'. Back they came, and the King, Duke of York, and all six Princesses appeared:

I have never yet seen M. d'A. agitated as at this Moment. He could scarce keep his steadiness, or even his Ground. The recollections, he has since told me, that rushed upon his mind, of His own King & Royal House, were so violent, & so painful, as almost to disorder him.[34]

The King stopped to speak to one or two people at the further end, then approached them. The Princess Royal said, 'Madame d'Arblay, Sir,'

. . . & instantly he came on a step, & then stopt, & addressed me, – &, after a word or two of the Weather, which, for grateful surprise, I hardly heard, he said 'Is that Monsieur d'Arblay? –' & upon my faint

Yes, sire, faint from encreasing [sic] gratitude & delight, he most graciously bowed to him & entered into a little conversation; demanding how long he had been in England, how long in the Country, &c &c, & with a sweetness, an air of *wishing us* well, that will never, never be erased from our Hearts.[35]

More than thirty years later Fanny remembered this as the 'proudest instant' of her life.[36] Perhaps she hoped that some positive recommendation for a role in English life for her husband might follow. If so, she was to be disappointed, but she did receive a folded packet containing a hundred guineas, with a message that 'it is from us *BOTH*'.

There was someone else on the Terrace that cold evening: Stephen Digby. Fanny wrote the account of her Windsor experiences, *Windsoriana*, for her father not Susan; no doubt she talked to Susan about seeing Digby, but for her father she records only the name. Did she know of the death of his second wife and feel some sympathy? In her own happiness could she now make peace? She did not ever find it easy to forgive and forget; in 1797 not even death could alter her resentment of the five years of misery Mrs Schwellenberg had inflicted on her. This was to be the last time Fanny ever saw Digby, but his story can be ended with warm references to him in the letters of his first wife's sister, Lady Susan Fox-Strangways. In 1799 she underwent a mastectomy without anaesthetic (as Fanny would do in 1811) and she wrote of Colonel Digby's great kindness to her, though he wanted to know no details of the condition from which Lady Lucy had died.[37] He was to die himself the following year, curiously enough while at Cheltenham Spa.

The King had encouraged Fanny to stay on in Windsor so that she could see the Princesses, telling her that she would not recognise Princess Amelia, now fourteen – 'She is taller than you!' Unfortunately, the Princess's growth was almost the only thing which had changed, though Fanny does not comment on the stagnation of life for the Princesses at Queen's Lodge (she would not have written other than positively about the royal family to her father, however). Her account tells of the pleasure of 'chattery' with the young women, who crowded into Princess Elizabeth's apartment to hear all about her house, garden and baby; her hermit existence must have seemed as strange to them as court life had once to her. And enviable – the three elder Princesses were now well over the normal age for marriage but the King could not bear the thought of losing his daughters to continental princes, the only men considered eligible for their hands. Moreover, even as adults they remained subject to the rigid control of their mother, with no money of their own and very little personal freedom (they were not to achieve their own incomes until the Prince of Wales became Regent and, against his mother's wishes, negotiated allowances for them with Parliament). For the Princesses the court was a 'nunnery', matching Fanny's 'monastery'. They hated 'Terracing', so it must have been to give Fanny pleasure – combined with curiosity to see her husband – that they did not take advantage of miserable weather to stay inside on that memorable July evening.[38]

After the Terrace, Princess Elizabeth rushed up to tell Fanny that she had permission to read *Camilla* without waiting for Mama to finish and approve. Fanny presented this to her father as another compliment; it is to be hoped that she herself recognised it as sad that a 26-year-old woman was not trusted to choose her own reading. Yet she seems to have been little aware how constrained the lives of her beloved Princesses were, or to have sensed the frustration beneath their light-hearted charm; in 1794 someone wrote that there was not 'a more unhappy family in England than that of our good King'.[39] Fanny, however, basked in her welcome and made a promise to come to court once every year in future. On her return home she had six sets of *Camilla* bound in white and gold for the Princesses.

It is probably unfair to criticise Fanny for being blind to the problems of the royal family since she saw them only occasionally. When she did next return to court in November 1797 (rather more than the promised year later) she did notice that the Queen 'looked ill – pale & harrassed'.[40] Fanny attributed her state to current problems: the mutiny at the Nore or the separation of the Prince of Wales from his wife Caroline of Brunswick. The Queen probably talked about the latter for she spoke 'upon some subjects & persons that I know she would not for the world should be repeated' and Fanny was proud that her discretion was still trusted. Queen Charlotte, she also mentioned, worried about the King; she was haunted by fears of a repetition of his terrible illness and was anxious about the effect on him of the stress of family and political life. But when the King joined them they spoke cheerfully of their little granddaughter, Princess Charlotte, who could already recognise '*Gan pa*', though only when he was on horseback.

One change since Fanny had last seen the royal family was the marriage and departure from court of the Princess Royal, at the age of thirty-one. No one had envied her the bridegroom, the grossly fat Prince Frederick of Würtemberg, and the King had consented to the marriage only reluctantly, but for the Princess the marriage represented escape and she had argued her way to its acceptance.[41] The Queen spoke happily of the wedding, telling Fanny that she had herself sewn every stitch of the white and silver wedding gown, and Princess Augusta, in her own tête-à-tête with Fanny, paid tribute to the Princess's appearance on the day:

"'T was the Queen dressed her! – You know what a figure she used to make of herself, with her odd manner of dressing herself; but Mama said: "Now really, Princess Royal, this one time is the last; & I cannot suffer you to make such a Quiz of yourself; so I will really have you dressed properly". And indeed the Queen was quite in the right, for everybody said she had never looked so well in her life.'[42]

The word 'Quiz' Fanny assured Susan, to whom this account was written, was never the Queen's. Nor was it Fanny's, who in writing at least never even hinted that any Princess might look a fright.

Princess Augusta chatted while seated at her toilette table, having her head prepared for the theatre and showing no interest in the procedure. When the hairdresser asked to know what ornaments to prepare she answered impatiently:

'O – there! My feathers, – & my Gown is blue – so take what you think right.' And when he begged she would say whether she would have any ribbons, or other things, mixed with the Feathers & Jewels, she said, '*You* understand all that best, Mr. Robinson, I'm sure, – there are the things – so take just what you please.'[43]

After he had gone the Princess called it 'nasty work' and fastened on her long diamond earrings without a glance in her mirror. Fanny saw all this as an object lesson in lack of vanity; given her own loathing of court dressing she might have recognised the wretchedness for the Princess of subjection to a life controlled by the demands of appearance. For her there could be no letter of resignation.

Princess Augusta was also at her looking-glass next time Fanny went to Queen's House, in March 1798, taking three-year-old Alex at the Queen's command. He gazed in astonishment at what was happening to the Princess's head. Fanny had made him a new white muslin frock and was proud of his appearance, though fearful for his behaviour which alternated between silent clinging to his mother and noisy racing round.

But the Princesses were indulgent, admiring his 'beautiful eyes' and loading him with toys and bon-bons, though to Fanny's chagrin the only Princess to whom Alex would allow a kiss was Princess Amelia, perhaps because she had insisted on a kiss from his mother.[44] Princess Elizabeth played peep-bo with him, showing 'a skill and sweetness that made one almost sigh she should have no call for her Maternal propensities' (only 'almost'). Fanny's own maternal propensities were tested to the full when it was time to take Alex to the Queen. She had a Noah's Ark ready for him, and he leant familiarly against the royal lap, naming the animals in delight. But when the Queen wanted some serious conversation with his mother he would not behave, racing off into their Majesties' bedroom where all the jewels were laid out ready for St James's. He was eventually quieted with a cake, for which he was prompted into a 'Sanky Queen'. Fanny left court this time recalling how she had 'struggled for deliverance' from it, and concluding with satisfaction:

> So all is for the best! I have escaped offending lastingly the Royal Mistress I love & honour, & – – I live at West Hamble [sic] with my two precious Alexanders.[45]

The d'Arblays had at last moved into their own home, built on a field belonging to William Lock at West Humble, adjoining Norbury Park. The house was designed and largely built by d'Arblay himself, and paid for with the money which Fanny had earned from *Camilla*. It was therefore named Camilla Cottage. There was one sadness, that Susan was no longer living at Mickleham. Her marriage had turned sour, with Molesworth Phillips grown morose, unpredictable, and violent-tempered. In 1795 he had resigned his commission and gone back to his farm in Ireland, taking their elder son Norbury away from his mother and placing him with a tutor in Dublin. A year later, not long after *Camilla* was published, Phillips returned for his wife and other two children. Reluctantly, Susan agreed to go with him, urged to do so by Fanny who felt strongly the sanctity of the marriage vow of obedience. It was the worst advice she ever gave but she could not know that then; the Burney family trusted Phillips' promise that Susan could return in a year's time, a promise which he did not honour.[46]

So, reversing their situations in the court years, Fanny wrote to her unhappy sister of life in and around Norbury Park, in December 1797 describing the move to Camilla Cottage. When Fanny and Alex arrived by chaise they had found d'Arblay already there with a blazing fire, though the only furniture was a carpenter's bench:

Here we unpacked a small Basket, containing 3 or 4 loaves, & with a Garden knife, *fell to work*; some Eggs had been procured from a neighbouring Farm, & one saucepan had been brought by the Maid. We dined, therefore, exquisitely, & drank to our new possession from a Glass of clear water out of our new Well.[47]

If the King's recognition of d'Arblay was the proudest moment of Fanny's life, this may well have been the happiest.

CHAPTER FOURTEEN

Cruelly Changed

True, she must die at last, but who must not? My Fredy, my Susan, Mr. Locke,
Mrs. Delany, all the world's fairest ornaments must go the same way. Ah! The
survivor of all such – not the departed – will be worthy of pity.[1]

Shortly before Christmas 1817 and between seven and eight o'clock in the
morning, General Alexandre d'Arblay and his wife were set down from
their sedan chairs at the Pump Room in Bath. There, at a morning levée,
d'Arblay was to be presented to Queen Charlotte; for the ceremony the
General (promoted in 1815) wore his military honours, the medals of the
orders of St Louis, la Fidélité, and the Légion d'Honneur.[2] The meeting
was to become for Madame d'Arblay a proud but poignant memory, for
though she did not know it both her husband and her former royal
mistress were mortally ill and were to die in the following year.

Fanny's long life was split almost equally between the eighteenth and
nineteenth centuries, and though it is too much of a generalisation to
say that happiness and success belonged to Miss Burney in the
eighteenth and distress and declining powers to Madame d'Arblay in the
nineteenth, once the century had turned troubles accumulated.[3] The
year 1800 opened with a devastating blow: Susan's death. In 1799 she
had become ill with some bowel complaint and Phillips finally consented
to the family's return. On the last day of the old year they reached
Parkgate in the Wirral, from where Susan wrote in a shaky hand to her
father rejoicing that once again 'I breathe the blessed air you breathe'.[4]
But on 6 January 1800 she died. Three days later d'Arblay heard the
news from the Locks, to whom Phillips had briefly communicated it, and
had to break it to his wife. Fanny was to keep 6 January as a day of
mourning ever afterwards.

For much of the subsequent early part of the nineteenth century Fanny
was in Napoleonic France, in the first instance when she and Alex crossed
the Channel to join the husband and father in 1802. When peace had
been made the previous year d'Arblay went to France hoping both to
recover property lost in the Revolution and to obtain his military
pension. In the first ambition he was unsuccessful and the second was not
achieved until May 1803, just before war broke out again. English

nationals were interned and for the next nine years Fanny was trapped, cut off from family and friends far more decisively than she had been during her five years at court. Correspondence was very limited and dependent on couriers such as Americans who could pass between the two countries; it was from one such rare letter received in 1810 that a casual reference told the d'Arblays that William Lock was dead. In the same year they learned from a newspaper of the tragic early death of Princess Amelia, and of the subsequent descent into permanent derangement, blindness, and deafness of the King.

The family lived very quietly in and around Paris during these years. D'Arblay worked as a clerk in the Buildings section of the Ministry of the Interior, Fanny made friends among the French and lost her John Bullishness, while Alex went to school and won numerous prizes. In September 1811, after much pain and increasing debility, Fanny underwent a mastectomy without anaesthetic conducted by Baron Larrey, Napoleon's foremost surgeon; for her fortitude she earned his undying admiration.[5] A year later Larrey was with Napoleon on his disastrous Moscow campaign; this absence of the Emperor from Paris meant a slackening of regulations and Fanny managed to return to England with Alex, though her husband had to remain behind. They left because husband and wife knew that at sixteen Alex would soon be liable to conscription into the French army; Fanny was also fearful that she might never see her elderly father again. In the event Dr Burney lived till April 1814, dying just hours after the London sky had erupted in fireworks to celebrate Napoleon's defeat and abdication. Sadly, although it had been published in the previous month, he was unable to read his daughter's last novel, *The Wanderer*, which like her first she dedicated to him.[6]

Leaving Alex behind as a student at Cambridge, Fanny returned in the autumn to her husband, but more twists of fate followed. Despite reaching his sixtieth year, d'Arblay had become an artillery officer in Louis XVIII's Garde du Corps; when Napoleon escaped from Elba he rejoined his regiment while Fanny fled from Paris to Brussels. She was there for Waterloo, a witness both to the pre-battle tension and the terrible aftermath when for days on end cartloads of the maimed and dying trundled beneath her windows – even the stench of the 'Hills of Dead' on the battlefield reached her. Then came an urgent summons: her husband was seriously wounded, not in battle, but having been kicked in the leg by a vicious horse. Showing the greatest courage, resourcefulness and determination of her life, Fanny made an epic journey across war-torn northern France and the Rhineland to reach him at Trèves, where he had been stationed.[7] Her worst fears were not realised and eventually, though 'terribly mangled by events of all sorts, public & private' and the General 'cruelly changed', they returned to England.[8]

Unfortunately, they no longer had a home, having been forced to sell Camilla Cottage when the second William Locke (who added the *e* to the surname) decided to dispose of Norbury Park.[9] They chose to settle in Bath, partly in the hope that the waters would help d'Arblay's leg to heal, and partly because it was a cheaper place to live than London.

Bath was no longer the fashionable city that it had been when Fanny stayed there first with Mrs Thrale and later Mrs Ord. Though still drawing invalids for the benefits of its waters, it had been superseded for the social elite by the burgeoning coastal resorts and, now Europe was at peace, the continental spas. It was not any more a city for short-term pleasure-seekers, but for the long-term residence of the genteel poor, such as the d'Arblays.[10] They chose a modest apartment on the first and second floors of 23 Great Stanhope Street, 'GREAT . . . as it is called, not, by any means, from being of a magnitude or magnificence to merit the epithet, but because they have judged proper to name LITTLE Stanhope Street a mere Lane which is by its side'.[11] The house was in the lower part of the city near the river, not one of the better areas, but it had a good view from its rear windows. Fanny liked Bath, to her 'a marvellous City' for its mixture of town and country landscapes:

> Hills rising above Hills, here smiling with verdure, there shadowed by woods, here undulating to catch the Eye to distant prospects, & there striking with noble edifices, terminate almost every street, & spread in broad exilarating views before every Crescent, with a variety of attraction, from local positions or accidents, that are endless in their effects to elevate, or please.[12]

This rather self-conscious attempt at 'fine' writing, representing her feelings nevertheless, comes from a letter to Princess Elizabeth.

Throughout all these years, Fanny had never lost contact with the royal family, and they kept faith with her: even during her exile in France her pension was regularly paid and kept for her by her father. When she first reached France Fanny sent letters to the Queen describing her experiences, addressing her through Miss Planta. The royal family would have had other sources of information about post-Revolutionary France, but they must have read with interest Fanny's accounts of the people she met and the customs she observed. She recalled how 'Miss Rose' had teased her about the flimsy new French fashions, and wrote amusingly of her Parisian maid's horror at her outmoded English wardrobe:

This wont do! – *That* you can never wear! *This* you can never be seen in! *That* would make you stared at as a curiosity! – *THREE* petticoats! No one wears more than one! – STAYS? everybody has left off even corsets! – Shift sleeves? not a soul now wears even a chemise![13]

'Miss Rose' was Fanny's code-name for Princess Augusta. To disguise references to the royal family she employed the pseudonyms which Susan had once used in case prying eyes fell on her letters to her sister: Laurel for the King, Magnolia for the Queen, and various flowers for the Princesses. The code would not have presented Napoleon's spies with a problem, but there were no state secrets being passed across the Channel.

After Fanny returned from her ten years' exile, the Queen and Princesses often sought her company. When at her ease she had always been an engaging companion, but there seems to have been an extra attractiveness when she came back from France – perhaps she had absorbed some Gallic charm. Clement Francis, Charlotte's son, wrote, 'I really think Aunt d'Arblay is the most charming woman I ever saw in my life'.[14] An objective glimpse of her is given by the Scottish poet Thomas Campbell; he met her on an occasion when she had accepted an invitation to wait on the Princess of Wales, the estranged wife of the Prince Regent. Campbell wrote to a friend:

> Her features must once have been excellent; her manners are highly polished, and delicately courteous – just like her Evelina grown old – not bashful, but sensitively anxious to please those about her. I sat next to her, alternately pleased and tormented with the Princess's *naiveté* and Madame D'Arblay's refinement . . . really, you would love her for her communicativeness, and fine tact in conversation.[15]

Such delicacy of manner would have appealed to Queen Charlotte, who did what she could to favour her. It was at the Queen's express desire that Madame d'Arblay had audience with the restored King Louis XVIII, and she was also invited to witness a reception for the Russian Czar Alexander I and the King of Prussia.

The affection in which Fanny was held by the royal family comes across particularly in the letters of Princess Elizabeth, who began the correspondence after Fanny had gone back to France in 1814, hoping to receive 'a few delightful lines from dear Madame d'Arblay' in reply.[16] The Princess, now forty-four and stout, wrote amusingly and unaffectedly as '*Nobody*' but joked that 'when you consider my fat figure you may be inclined to say I think there is some BODY'. Letter-writing was one of her hobbies and she was also a talented artist, known by her sisters as the 'Muse'; still preserved on the walls of the Gallery at Frogmore House in Windsor Great Park are panels of flower garlands which she painted. The Princess had inherited an enthusiasm for farming from her father and, contrary to what she told Fanny at the age of sixteen, a liking for snuff from her mother. Fanny thought her the 'chief life and spirit' of the whole family.

Princess Elizabeth concluded her letter by telling Fanny to 'think of *Nobody* – but recollect that *Somebody* is sincerely attached to you'. Six months later, when Fanny was in Brussels awaiting the outcome of battle, the Princess wrote that she had been 'thought of, pitied & longed for more than words can tell'.[17] Fanny was able to begin her reply 'Oh Madam, what a victory! – how glorious, how stupendous!' when news of the allied success at Waterloo relieved weeks of anxiety. She went on, in a flurry of exclamation marks, to convey the stress felt on that Sunday 18 June 1815, before news of victory was received:

> I remained shut up till about 10 o'clock at night – witnessing from the window – continual, incessant arrivals of wounded, maimed, ill, or dying! on foot, on Horse, on Brancards; on carts, & in waggons! – a sight to break one's heart! – yet upon which the Eye, forever seeking some information, or hoping for some change, while filled with commiseration, was fixed as by Magic! – – at last, an English gentleman, belonging to some army office, came in to tell us he was just returned from the Field of Battle! & he *thought* all was going on well – & that the report that had so dreadfully alarmed the Town of the arrival of Les Français was *TRUE*, though *without* alarm, for Les Français Were indeed, & by hundreds arrived – as Prisoners![18]

Two years later it was from Princess Elizabeth that Fanny had the rumour confirmed that she and the Queen were to visit Bath. The Queen was in poor health, suffering from shortness of breath and a disordered stomach, and it was thought that drinking the waters would benefit her, while the Princess hoped to alleviate her rheumatism by bathing in the hot springs.

The royal visit to Bath, beginning on 3 November 1817, caused great excitement in the city. It was the first by a reigning monarch since Queen Anne, and it opened with the kind of loyal fervour which had attended the royal tours to Cheltenham, Weymouth and Plymouth. Cheering crowds lined the route, and at night there were brilliant illuminations; Fanny and her husband walked out to admire them. The Queen was accompanied not only by Princess Elizabeth but by the Duke of Clarence, and two handsome corner houses in New Sidney Place had been prepared for them. However, the Queen's stay was interrupted by tragedy. At this time Princess Charlotte, the Regent's daughter, was awaiting her confinement, but the Queen's health was of such concern that she had not delayed until after the birth. Her own fifteen pregnancies had been trouble-free and nobody expected problems for the vigorous young Princess. But on 6 November the news came first that she had been delivered of a stillborn child, then, a few hours later, that she herself was dead. There was an abrupt end to festivities, and 'All Bath wore a Face of Mourning'.[19] Ten days later, however, the royal party returned, and though their stay was no longer an occasion for celebration the medical treatments were resumed.

During the visit, which lasted till 22 December, Fanny ignored the cost and took a chair almost every morning to travel the mile and a half between Great Stanhope Street and New Sidney Place to enquire after the health of the Queen and Princess. Sad though the circumstances now were, Fanny at this time enjoyed the longest period of association with the Queen since she had left her service, and she strengthened her friendship with Princess Elizabeth. The good-humoured Princess would not have minded when Fanny later offered her a hint in telling a story she had learnt from her landlord: a countryman had walked seven miles to Bath to look at royalty but had seen little more than their bonnets, ruefully commenting, 'It's a good bit of a way to come, like, only to see a bit of a chin!'[20] There was a tale to be told against herself as well, as she confessed in a letter to Alex. One morning she was greeted at the Queen's residence with a cheerful 'Ah! How do you do Madam?' She tried to recognise the speaker who, seeing her hesitate, said, 'You don't know me?'

> Shocked with the idea it was some one much altered, I answered readily 'Oh yes I do – I only – only – I don't recollect your your!' – I stammered, & he stood stupified. I looked earnestly at him while I spoke, but vainly sought to find out Who he was.
>   'So you don't remember me?' he then cried.
>   'Oh! Yes: I do' I replied; concluding it was Col[el] Greville or G[al] Manners or some ancient Friend of my former cotteries [sic]. 'I know you very well, but I cannot recollect your name.' He was silent a moment & then repeated: 'So you don't know who I am?'
>   'Yes I do – I assure you.'
>   He then solemnly answered: 'No! you do not!'[21]

When he told her 'I am the Duke of Clarence' she was mortified, but he gave her his hand and said he was very glad to see her.

Looking back on this time Fanny was to feel some guilt that she had left her husband every day for her royal pilgrimages, not realising how ill he was. The General was a victim of bowel cancer and had only months to live. Yet he was determined to undertake the presentation to the Queen at the Pump Room, though in his 'suffering, emaciated, enfeebled' condition he found the occasion an ordeal:

> Arrived, he found himself indisposed almost to torture. He could not stand – nor move – nor speak! – some ladies gave up their seats to us – but he could scarcely avail himself of their kindness.[22]

It was only by will power when the Queen arrived and, according to his wife, singled him out for particular attention, that he was able to forget bodily discomfort, to stand erect and reply with animation; afterwards he collapsed and had to be carried home in extreme pain. A few days later there was further distress when news reached them of the death of Fanny's brother Charles following a stroke. D'Arblay never left the house again, enduring with a soldier's courage the last harrowing weeks of his illness. One piece of news cheered his end: Alex had been made 10th Wrangler of his year at Cambridge. General d'Arblay died on 3 May 1818 and was buried at St Swithin's Church, Walcot, in Bath, where there is a plaque to his memory.

In her later account of the scene in the Pump Room, written after both their deaths, Madame d'Arblay paid honest and affecting tribute also to the Queen. She likewise had shown courage and a strong sense of duty in undertaking such public occasions in her poor state of health. When she rose from her chair to make her round of the room, Fanny wrote that it was

> . . . with a Grace indescribable, &, to those who never witnessed it, inconceivable; for it was such as to carry off Age, Infirmity, sickness, diminutive & disproportioned stature, & Ugliness! – & to give to her, in defiance of such disadvantages, a power of charming & delighting that rarely has been equalled.[23]

Fanny wanted to convey the living nature of a woman who had been mocked by satirists and caricaturists throughout her reign, and whose ravaged face was now beyond any portraitist's flattery. Even when so clearly ill, 'Peter Pindar' produced cruel rhymes on the 'pigmy' Queen in the Pump Room:

> Those cheeks were sallow, sunk and lean,
>   Their bones, like *tumuli* did rise;
> The little vales of flesh between,
>   Like parapets to guard the eyes.[24]

Though not published until 1846, Fanny's account of the grace and charm which overcame physical disability helped redress the balance; it was said that in her portrayal of Queen Charlotte, Madame d'Arblay had 'played the Alchemist and turned into gold what was counted lead'.[25]

Such scenes revealed Queen Charlotte at her public best. In private she had a short temper and could show herself less amiable, and she and Princess Elizabeth fell out after their return from Bath when in the new year there was a surprise announcement of the Princess's engagement to the German Prince of Hesse-Homburg; the only other Princess to have married since the Princess Royal was Princess Mary in the previous year to her cousin the Duke of Gloucester.[26] Princess Elizabeth had yearned for marriage and an independent life and there had almost been a match in 1808 with the Duke of Orleans, later King Louis-Philippe, but it had been vetoed by the Queen. Now, gravely ill, it could hardly be expected that she would gladly lose the daughter on whom she most depended and she refused to sanction the marriage, though it had the support of the Prince Regent. The Princess, fearful that yet another of her castles in the air would come crashing down, thought her mother selfish; she wrote to Fanny of her pride in her 'valued and beloved Prince' who had fought and been wounded at the Battle of Leipzig in 1813, but she added with reference to her mother: 'Oh how painful to me, my excellent friend, what I go through! After having slaved to do my duty with affection & zeal.'[27] The Princess expressed a wish to speak face to face with Madame d'Arblay; Fanny would have liked a balloon to fly to Windsor but could not leave her sick husband. She was in any case torn in sympathy, well able to understand the mother's reluctance, and feeling for herself in losing the Princess. She therefore performed her last practical service for her royal mistress with a mediating letter, suggesting that not to feel for the Queen in the situation 'would be inhuman', and concluding:

> For both I shall feel to the bottom of my heart; though for both I shall be consoled in considering that the gayer prospects which will soon enliven the one, will, by Reflexion, & generous sympathy, greatly revivify the other. Heaven bless Both! Amen! Amen![28]

The Princess was married on 7 April, with the Queen reconciled and giving the couple her blessing.[29]

Thereafter Queen Charlotte rapidly declined. When the court learnt of General d'Arblay's death she was not immediately told for fear of the effect upon her, testimony of her attachment to her 'faithful handmaid'. Similar sensibility was shown towards Fanny when, at Princess Mary's command, she was informed in September of the Queen's 'visibly approaching dissolution' so that she might prepare herself for the event. In fact, the Queen lingered on until 17 November, dying not at Windsor near her husband as she wished, but at Kew.[30] The King, lost to all understanding of the world around him, was completely unaware of her funeral in St George's Chapel on 2 December. Fanny mourned 'that venerable & Venerated admirable & virtuous Sovereign – whom I honoured from the bottom of my heart – & from the bottom of it, lament!'[31] She wrote a memorandum of 'Queen Charlotte's Character', paying tribute to her powers of understanding, her kind encouraging manner, lack of the 'pedantry of grandeur', openness, tact and, of course, 'condescension'.[32]

For historians, Fanny's images and anecdotes of the Queen and the royal family through her years of service and beyond have proved a valuable resource, though she has often been found over-deferential. She certainly stood in awe of Majesty and, perhaps as a way to preserve a sense of worth in her appointment, did not look for reasons to devalue either the institution or the individuals who filled it. But she was no bootlicker and it is unfair to describe her attitude as 'artlessly sycophantic' as Dorothy Stuart does in her biography of the Princesses.[33] Fanny wrote without servility and occasionally sharply, though grumbles were mainly left out of the published version of the Court Journals. Her feelings about the Queen were based on real not affected respect, but it is true that as she grew older she sentimentalised the relationship, obliterating from memory the tensions of her period of service, and the fear of the Queen's disapproval which haunted her then.

After the death of her husband Fanny found it difficult to start a new life for herself, but for Alex's sake she left Bath for London, and spent the rest of her life in various houses in Mayfair. One source of brief comfort was a rapprochement with Hester Piozzi before her death in 1821. Fanny had always wanted to heal the breach, but in meetings with the widowed Hester both before and after the General's death she had not effected any thaw in the relationship; Hester acknowledged her charm but declared, 'I will never trust her any more'.[34] Then a final exchange of letters reminiscing about the past re-established friendly relations. Hester must surely have been touched when Fanny wrote that she carried everywhere the locket in which her friend had once woven together strands of her own hair with Susan's. What loss of sympathetic friendship, pleasurable conversation, and correspondence Hester had inflicted upon herself (yet one is reminded of Fanny's unyielding hostility to Stephen Digby after a similar cry of treachery). Hester tried to comfort Fanny about her son Alex, always thin and often ill, telling her to 'Have no fears for the health of your son; a slight frame escapes many ills that beset a robust one; water-gruel and spinach were all you ever wanted'.[35] She was right in this with respect to Fanny, for apart from her half-sister Sarah she was to outlive her brothers and sisters, almost all her contemporaries, and the monarchs George III, George IV and William IV.[36]

Fanny's major work during her last years was the sorting, annotating, censoring and, where she thought necessary, burning of the vast accumulation of her own journals and letters, her sister Susan's, her husband's, and her father's. She was already engaged in the early stages of the *Memoirs of Dr Burney* during the royal visit to Bath, and Princess Elizabeth sent her a present of some silver candlesticks to an ingenious design which she thought would make Fanny's task easier and amuse the General as he was fond of 'clever contrivances'. It took until 1832 for the book to be published, Fanny's eightieth year; it has never been liked for its hagiographic approach to the subject and the ponderous style in which it is written. But there was little other cause for celebration in that year, as it brought the deaths of both her sister Esther and Fredy Lock.

Mrs Piozzi was wrong about Alex, and saddest of all the losses Fanny had to endure was the death three years before her own of her misfit son. Alex, a lively irrepressible boy, grew up to be charming, lovable, and a very clever mathematician, but eccentric, easily distracted, and utterly unreliable. After an erratic career at Cambridge, a source of constant worry to his parents though crowned eventually with success, he was received into the Church and ultimately helped to a curacy by none other than George Cambridge, Archdeacon of Middlesex, the man whom Fanny had once hoped to marry; he took the young man under his wing and helped him in so far as it was possible. Alex had strong faith but was not the sort of whom dependable parish priests are made. His death from flu at the age of forty-two – the age his mother was when she bore him – seems almost to have been self-willed as a release from his own unhappiness.

In 1839 Fanny's youngest sister, Charlotte, died. Her own end came on 6 January 1840, the anniversary of Susan's death forty years before; like

Mrs Delany Fanny was in her eighty-eighth year, and like her too she met death unafraid, firm in faith and confident that the after-life would reunite her with all those she had loved and lost. She was buried with her son and near to her husband in Bath.[37]

Among the papers left by Madame d'Arblay was one sending a 'tenderly posthumous Farewell to my revered and dear Princesses', the four survivors, Augusta, Elizabeth, Mary and Sophia. She had nothing to offer them but her blessing, but wanted them to know that, from first to last, 'They have cheered & soothed still more than they have honoured me –'.[38] The paper was signed 'Frances d'Arblay, otherwise La comtesse Veuve Piochard d'Arblay', the title with which her husband had been honoured by Louis XVIII and which, though not otherwise used, had helped smooth arrangements to visit the Princesses; over 300 notes and invitations from them to their dear Madame d'Arblay in the years of her widowhood still survive. In drawing up a balance sheet of what was gained and lost by Fanny's five years of seclusion at court, their regard, and the friendships which were a comfort to her old age, must be counted one of the principal personal benefits.

Financially also Fanny was the beneficiary of her royal employment. Without her pension her marriage would have been virtually impossible, and though the value of her £100 annual pension was eroded over the years, it was a dependable regular amount and at the time of the d'Arblays' life in Bath represented a quarter of their income.[39] It was continued after the Queen's death to the end of Fanny's life, so five years' work yielded almost fifty years of pension. Another financial gain owed in part to the Queen's support was the Tancred Scholarship awarded to Alex; it was worth about £100 a year and without it the d'Arblays could not have afforded to send him to Cambridge. At the time of application Fanny wrote to the Queen, and with her support Alex was unanimously elected. Though he argued his own case, James Burney's promotion to Admiral in 1821 after being on half-pay as a Captain since 1785 probably owed something to his sister's lobbying of the Princesses. The promotion came just in time: three months later Admiral James Burney was dead.

On the debit side of the royal balance sheet must be counted the unhappiness endured by Fanny during the years of her service. Yet time heals, and as she grew older Madame d'Arblay forgot the misery and recalled only that it had been a privilege to have lived among the royal family. Moreover, when she entered court life she was already rather unhappy, following her disappointment over George Cambridge and the loss of Hester Piozzi's friendship. In any case the kind of social existence she had then and resumed afterwards she often found irksome. How dull those five years would seem in a biography if they amounted to a series of family visits, public breakfasts at Mrs Montagu's, receptions at Mrs Ord's, and so on.

It has often been assumed that if Fanny had not been immured at court she would have written at least one other novel. Her contemporaries thought so, mourning the loss to literature of one 'royally gagged and promoted to fold muslins' as Horace Walpole elegantly expressed it.[40] She herself wondered if she would ever write creatively again. But would she have been any more inspired if she had continued living at home? She had not written anything for four years before she took up her appointment and did not do so afterwards until marriage and the need to earn money spurred her to *Camilla*. Even if she had written another novel it is unlikely that it would today be widely read other than by academics. To put it crudely, a novel between *Cecilia* and *Camilla* would be likely to have shared the characteristics of both: some excellent characters and dialogue, some lively scenes with social interest, but for modern readers too long, too moral and too sentimental, adding only another line or two to the entry under *Burney, Frances*, in literary companions.

On the other hand, had Fanny turned to writing comedies in those years (as opposed to therapeutic tragedies) then, with her ear for dialogue and using her talent for creating distinctive character-types, she might have established herself as the leading woman dramatist of the eighteenth century. After the quashing of *The Witlings*, Fanny left comedy writing alone until the end of the century, when a play *Love and Fashion* was accepted for production at Covent Garden Theatre. It never reached performance, however, because of Susan's death and the renewed hostility of her father to her dramatic writing. But the chance had held out 'golden dreams' and, ignoring her father, she wrote two more comedies, *The Woman-Hater* and *A Busy Day*, each carefully designed for particular theatres and particular performers. Neither is a masterpiece but both have sharp dialogue and good stage moments; *A Busy Day* has received successful production in modern times.[41] It was the exile in France which prevented performance on this occasion. But if Fanny had begun to write such comedies in the late 1780s, and these had been the apprentice pieces from which she learned stagecraft, then her seclusion at court must be seen as a loss. It is, however, a very big *if*.

It is easy to argue that the bird in the hand, the Court Journals, outweighs any putative novel. The journals offer events, characters and dialogue as readable as any to be found in a novel but with the knowledge that these lives, these scenes, are a part of history. Of course, everything is seen from her own perspective and with her prejudices, but what observer is ever wholly objective? Moreover, Fanny interweaves her own compelling personal story with the royal one. If the surface on which the personalities of the court are reflected is not quite Horace Walpole's 'mirror of truth', it is at least a brightly polished one. The King, Queen, and Princesses made their marks in other ways on history, but it is in Fanny's journals that they are not only seen in their domestic circumstances but heard in their everyday conversation. Events also acquire special character through her journals; terrible as it seems from other sources, how much more harrowing the onset of the King's illness appears when presented in Fanny's dramatic day-to-day sequence of events. Princess Amelia's early death seems the more tragic when it is set beside Fanny's portrayal of the engaging child. Who today would have any idea of Colonel Goldsworthy's talent to amuse if Fanny had not recorded his comic flights?

Once, in 1790, Fanny was drinking tea with Thomas Willis and Peggy Planta when Willis spoke of a newspaper paragraph which declared that Miss Burney was writing a new book:

'Oh yes,' cried Miss Planta; 'I have heard of it some time: and Mr. de Guiffardière says we shall all be in it.'

'Why – I have been thinking of that,' said Mr. Willis, in a dry way peculiar to himself, 'and shaking my poor head and shoulders, to feel how I could keep them steady in case of an assault. And, indeed, this thought, all along, has made me, as you may have observed, rather cautious and circumspect, and *very* civil. I hope it has not been thrown away.'

'Well, anybody's welcome to me and my character'; cried Miss Planta; 'and that's always the answer I make them when they tell me of it.'[42]

These and similar remarks show that Fanny's fellow courtiers were always a little wary of what Mrs Thrale called the 'comical girl' with a 'deal of malice' beneath the shy exterior, but they would not have suspected that Miss Burney was storing their words in her phenomenal memory not for a novel but for her journals. As she set down this conversation, however, the diarist herself must have been slyly conscious that she had not waited for an invitation to capture her companions' characters. Neither Thomas Willis nor Peggy Planta lived to read of themselves when the journals were published, nor most other members of the court circle who appear in her pages; had they done so some would have been galled, some gratified, but surely all should have recognised that what they had had conferred upon them by the timid-mannered but tough-minded little Keeper of the Robes was a kind of immortality.

Three Portraits

There are not many portraits of Fanny. The best known, and the one which has come to represent her in the public mind, is the one in the National Portrait Gallery painted sometime between 1784 and 1785 by her cousin, Edward Burney. But is this the best likeness?

After the enthusiastic reception of *Cecilia* in 1782, a portrait of the author by her great admirer Sir Joshua Reynolds might have been expected, to add to his painting a year earlier of her father. But none was ever commissioned. However, in August 1782 Fanny's cousin Edward, student of Reynolds, arrived at Chessington 'loaded with canvasses, pencils, and painting materials' to paint her for Samuel Crisp, and Fanny found that 'remonstrances were unavailing'.[1] The finished portrait embarrassed her by its flattery, so much so that she wrote that if her name were not written beneath 'no one would guess he ever saw me, much less that I sat for the Picture called mine'.[2] In this half-length portrait, three-quarter profile, now at Parham Park in Sussex, Fanny gazes straight ahead in sprightly self-confidence. Of what she wore, Fanny wrote to Susan:

> & as to my Dress, which I have left to himself, he has never been tired of altering & gracing it. It is now the black vandyke Gown, with slashed lilac sleeves, & very elegant.[3]

It is not clear whether it was her own dress, or whether a fashion chosen for the occasion by the portraitist. It was not unusual in portrait painting for the artist to devise appropriate costume for the sitter; Fanny's letter shows that Edward employed at least some imagination in altering it to suit his image of her.[4]

Why did Edward Burney (best known as a book illustrator) choose to present his cousin in black picture hat with ostrich feathers, black dress, white lace ruffle at the cuffs, muslin neckerchief, and black velvet ribbon round her neck? Though diffident, like Fanny, and said to be in love with her for a time, Edward could be a joker in his art, as his painting in the Tate Gallery, *Amateurs of the Tye-Wig Music* ('*Musicians of the Old School*') shows.[5] His portrait of his cousin is in fact almost a mirror image of one by Sir Joshua, exhibited at the Royal Academy in April 1782, of the former actress Mrs Mary Robinson, first mistress of the Prince of Wales and considered one of the most beautiful women in London.[6] The pose (hands gracefully displayed on the lap), the clothes, the hairstyle, even the shape of the face, set against a background of a red curtain draped to reveal a landscape behind, echo each other. If the pictures were to be hung together the two women would appear almost twins. The only striking difference is that Fanny is painted right profile, while Mrs Robinson, disconcertingly swivelling her eyes to the viewer, is left profile. It is inconceivable that Edward Burney was unfamiliar with this portrait, famous in its day and copied by other artists; he is surely having a quiet joke in linking together his moral cousin and the notorious former actress. None the less, there was a connection between the two women of which Edward is unlikely to have been aware: Mary Robinson wrote poetry and was to publish novels in later life so, ironically, Mary and Fanny were literary sisters.[7]

There is no contemporary commentary on Burney's second portrait of Fanny, now in the National Portrait Gallery, painted in 1784 or '85 when the 'Lunardi' hat which she wears, inspired by the balloon exploits of Vincenzo Lunardi, was popular.[8] This portrait is accepted as being a better likeness: the face and nose are longer, and the expression is less self-assured. Even so there are oddities. The eyes are blue though Fanny herself describes her eyes as greenish-grey.[9] The face is very pink though Fanny often refers to her brown complexion and would never have rouged. There is also a curious tideline where pink turns to bluish white; white necks had been fashionable, achieved by using white lead, but after some horrific deaths from lead poisoning this fashion was disappearing. Perhaps Edward wanted to suggest an attribute of beauty for his cousin. Finally there is the question of that hat – did she ever wear it, or is it an example of artist's licence? Fanny was not interested in high fashion, but she wore the clothes of the day which included large bonnets; there are references to the King and Stephen Digby peering under her headgear to see her face, and she told Digby that she needed ten yards of ribbon to trim a bonnet. So she may have sported a Lunardi. On the other hand, it may be another of Edward Burney's jokes. If he knew that Mrs Laetitia Barbauld had said that 'next to ballooning' Miss Burney was 'the object of public curiosity', he may have thought to offer both together.[10]

In 1783 Fanny sat for her portrait to the Scottish miniaturist John Bogle; this was considered the best likeness of her, though she herself still thought it a flattery.[11] Joyce Hemlow has said that the 'identification of this miniature is open to question', and others have doubted that the miniature on ivory which was sold as her portrait by Sotheby's in 1970 does represent her, even though it is signed by John Bogle and dated 1783.[12] If this portrait is compared with the two Burney paintings then the immediate impression may be that it is dissimilar, although it is not easy to make clear comparison between three-quarter and full-face portraits. It is only dissimilar, in any case, if the Edward Burney portraits are accepted as good likenesses, which in the case of the first one we know is not so and may be suspected of the second.

There are many reasons why the Bogle miniature should be accepted, apart from the date and the artist. The pose and the background have been carefully chosen; the picture shows a young woman resting easily on an elbow by a window, looking out onto the world and contemplating it with an amused, quizzical expression. She is of petite figure, with long face and nose, and she has been placed against a background of books. She wears a cream-coloured dress, which suggests a woman who clothes herself carefully but not ostentatiously. She is not a beauty but her face is one which could be described as 'good-humoured' as Dr Willis said, or be the '*marking face*' which made Dr Johnson say Fanny could read a tragedy 'marvellous well'.[13] The mouth is thin in comparison with that of the Lunardi portrait, but if a woman has thin lips a flattering painter may well compensate; what he will not need to do is to alter the eyebrows, a facial feature almost as individual as a fingerprint. If the distinctively shaped, dark, rather heavy eyebrows of the Bogle miniature are compared with those of the Lunardi portrait they appear identical. This is surely the face of Fanny Burney.

Notes

The following abbreviations are used:

Bar.Eg. Barrett Collection of the British Library, Egerton MSS 3690–3708

Camilla Fanny Burney, *Camilla, or A Picture of Youth*, edited with an introduction by Edward A. Bloom and Lillian D. Bloom, World's Classics Edition, Oxford University Press, 1983

Cecilia Fanny Burney, *Cecilia, or Memoirs of an Heiress*, edited by Peter Sabor and Margaret Anne Doody (with an introduction by Margaret Anne Doody), World's Classics Edition, Oxford University Press, 1988

CRO County Record Office

DL *Diary & Letters of Madame D'Arblay*, as edited by her niece Charlotte Barrett, with preface and notes by Austin Dobson, 6 vols, Macmillan and Co. Ltd, 1904–5 (unless otherwise stated, all references to these volumes are to journal-letters addressed to Susan Burney/Phillips)

EJL *The Early Journals and Letters of Fanny Burney*, vols 1 and 2 edited by Lars E. Troide, vol. 3 edited by Lars E. Troide and Stewart J. Cooke, Oxford, Clarendon Press, 1988–94 (and ongoing)

Evelina Frances Burney, *Evelina, or the History of a Young Lady's Entrance into the World*, edited by Stewart J. Cooke, Norton Critical Edition, New York and London, W.W. Norton & Company, 1998

Harcourt Papers Harcourt, Edward William, *The Harcourt Papers*, 8 vols, Oxford, James Parker & Co., 1880

Hedley Hedley, Olwen, *Queen Charlotte*, John Murray, 1975

Hemlow Hemlow, Joyce, *The History of Fanny Burney*, Oxford, Clarendon Press, 1958

JL *The Journals and Letters of Fanny Burney (Madame d'Arblay) 1791–1840*, 12 vols, edited by Joyce Hemlow et al., Oxford, Clarendon Press, 1972–84

Llanover *The Autobiography and Correspondence of Mary Granville, Mrs Delany; with interesting reminiscences of King George III and Queen Charlotte*, edited by Augusta, Lady Llanover, 6 vols, Richard Bentley, 1861–2

Lonsdale Lonsdale, Roger, *Dr. Charles Burney: A Literary Biography*, Oxford, Clarendon Press, 1965

McGill/Berg Transcripts of the original journals of Fanny Burney addressed to Susan Burney/Phillips made at McGill University, Montreal, of

	which the manuscripts are held in the Berg Collection of English and American Literature, New York Public Library, Astor, Lenox and Tilden Foundations
Memoirs	*Memoirs of Doctor Burney arranged from his own manuscripts, from family papers, and from personal recollections, by his daughter, Madame d'Arblay*, 3 vols, Edward Moxon, 1832
Papendick	*Court and Private Life in the Time of Queen Charlotte: being the Journals of Mrs Papendiek, Assistant Keeper of the Wardrobe and Reader to her Majesty*, edited by her granddaughter, Mrs Vernon Delves Broughton, 2 vols, Richard Bentley & Son, 1887
PRO	Public Record Office
RA	Royal Archives
Sermoneta	Sermoneta, Vittoria Duchess of, *The Locks of Norbury: The Story of a remarkable family in the XVIIIth and XIXth centuries*, John Murray, 1940
Thraliana	Thrale, Hester, *Thraliana: The Diary of Mrs Hester Lynch Thrale (Later Mrs Piozzi) 1776–1809*, edited by Katherine C. Balderston, 2 vols, Oxford, Clarendon Press, 1942
Watkins	Watkins, John, *Memoirs of Her Most Excellent Majesty Sophia-Charlotte, Queen of Great Britain*, Henry Colburn, 1819

PREFACE

1. 31 July 1788, McGill/Berg.
2. 31 July 1788, DL, IV, p. 55.
3. For fully detailed accounts of the complex history of the manuscripts and the early editions see Joyce Hemlow's introductions to *A Catalogue of the Burney Family Correspondence*, New York Public Library, 1971, pp. x–xx, and JL, I, pp. xxix–lix.
4. See Chapter Eight.

CHAPTER ONE

1. Samuel Crisp to Fanny Burney (FB), January 1779, quoted DL, I, p. 163.
2. Diary entry, March 1778, EJL, III, p. 1. *Evelina* was published 29 January 1778 in three volumes, for 9s bound, 7s 6d sewn copies. In the second edition, the words '*The History of*' were added to the subtitle. Fanny was paid £20 for the copyright by her publisher, Thomas Lowndes.
3. Diary entry, 26 March 1778, EJL, III, p. 5.
4. Hester Thrale to Dr Charles Burney (CB), 22 July 1778, EJL, III, p. 60; journal-letter to Susan Burney (SB) 23–30 August 1778, EJL, III, p. 109, and *passim*.
5. For full details of Fanny's ancestry and early life see Hemlow, or Kate Chisholm, *Fanny Burney: Her Life 1752–1840*, Chatto & Windus, 1998.
6. Diary entry, 30 May 1768, EJL, I, p. 6.
7. *Memoirs*, II, p. 168.

8. Quoted by Charlotte Barrett, see her introduction in DL, I, p. 9.

9. *Memoirs*, II, p. 124.

10. See Madame d'Arblay's introduction to *The Wanderer*, World's Classics Edition, Oxford University Press, 1991, p. 8.

11. Diary entry, 27 March 1768, EJL, I, p. 2.

12. Perhaps the best advice he gave about her journal writing was not to try too hard: 'Dash Away, whatever comes uppermost; & believe me, You'll succeed better, than by leaning on your Elbows, & studying what to say' (Samuel Crisp to FB, 18 April 1775, EJL, II, p. 108).

13. Samuel Crisp to FB, 17 October 1781, Bar.Eg. 3694, f. 136.

14. FB to Samuel Crisp, 1 December 1774, EJL, II, p. 60.

15. As n. 13. Fanny's and Sir Joshua's 'portraits' can be compared in the case of Omai. Sir Joshua's portrait (which hangs at Parham Park in Sussex) depicts him in native costume, idealising him as the dignified and handsome 'noble savage', while Fanny's pen picture portrays the Polynesian as an exotic curiosity in his English court dress and studied attempt at English manners. Fanny's portrait probably is the closer to the real man: Omai enjoyed being lionised and had a child-like love of attention and display. When he returned home, on Cook's last expedition, he took with him a miscellaneous collection of treasures, including his English finery, a globe, a jack-in-the-box, an illustrated Bible, and a full suit of medieval armour (see Richard Hough, *Captain James Cook: A Biography*, Hodder & Stoughton, 1995, pp. 336–7).

16. FB to Samuel Crisp, 27–8 March 1777, EJL, II, p. 225.

17. See Chisholm, *Fanny Burney*, p. 116.

18. FBA (Madame d'Arblay) to Esther Burney, 21 October 1821, JL, IX, p. 286.

19. Journal-letter to SB, 11 January 1779, EJL, III, p. 228. The speaker was the Earl of Harcourt, later also known to Fanny at court.

20. Journal-letter to SB, 21 August 1778, EJL, III, p. 90.

21. 30 March 1774, EJL, II, p. 14, n. 34.

22. FB to Samuel Crisp, December 1779, DL, I, p. 312.

23. Journal-letter to SB, 21 August 1778, EJL, III, p. 89. Smith, a young man with pretensions to fashion and style, was Johnson's favourite character in *Evelina*. The Branghtons are Evelina's vulgar city cousins.

24. Sarah Harriet Burney to Henry Crabb Robinson, 9 December 1842, in Lorna F. Clark (ed.), *The Letters of Sarah Harriet Burney*, Athens, Georgia University Press, 1997, p. 463.

25. FB to Hester Thrale, undated, Bar.Eg. 3695, f. 26.

26. *Thraliana*, I, p. 400.

27. Journal-letter to SB, 6–9 December 1779, EJL, III, p. 453.

28. *Thraliana*, I, p. 413.

29. Hester Thrale to FB, letters *c.* January 1781, Bar.Eg. 3695, ff. 19, 22b and 32.

30. FB to Samuel Crisp, *c.* 13 August 1779, EJL, III, p. 350.

31. Although the name came to be used as a label for a learned woman, it originally arose because one of the male members, the botanist Benjamin

Stillingfleet, was so poor that he could not afford white silk stockings and appeared at the meetings wearing blue worsted ones.

32. 20 June 1786, McGill/Berg.
33. A different publisher was chosen: Payne & Cadell. They printed an edition of 2,000 and sold it at 12s 6d a volume.
34. Hester Thrale to FB, 28 ?June 1782, Bar.Eg. 3695, f. 72.
35. Mrs Thrale said that James Burney 'brought me some Curiosities from the South seas . . . particularly a Scrap of Cloth torn from the back of the Indian who killed Captn Cook with His Club. This Stuff I thought so pretty, that I got Carr the Mercer to imitate it in Satten . . . It was violently admired to be sure . . .' (*Thraliana*, I, p. 481).
36. SB to FB, 19 January (1781), Bar.Eg. 3691, f. 171b.
37. Hester Thrale to FB, 19 January 1781, Bar.Eg. 3695, f. 31. In an exercise in written French of 1804 Fanny wrote of her first meeting with Mrs Thrale that she was astonished by the ostentation of her dress: '. . . non obstant tout ce qu'elle a fait pour se decorer avec magnificence, il n'y avoit nul apparence du goût, ni d'elegance naturel' – and more to the same effect ['. . . despite all that she did to array herself magnificently, there was neither taste nor natural elegance'] (JL, VI, p. 523).
38. For details see Lonsdale, pp. 297–311.
39. *Memoirs*, III, p. 20.
40. See journal entries and letters, EJL, II, pp. 115–28. Barlow wrote his surprising proposal in a letter; Fanny had no hesitation in rejecting it, but found that both her family and Samuel Crisp thought she should give it serious consideration. She felt under considerable pressure until she had a tearful scene with her father who agreed that she could do as she wished.
41. *Thraliana*, I, p. 439.
42. Ibid, pp. 496 and 505.
43. Those parts of Fanny's journals which relate to the relationships with Crutchley and Cambridge were suppressed in Charlotte Barrett's edition and have not yet been published.
44. FB to Susan Burney/Phillips (SBP), 11 January 1783, DL, II, p. 179.
45. *Thraliana*, I, p. 562.
46. Maria Allen to FB, undated 1768, EJL, I, pp. 331–2.
47. For full details see James L. Clifford, *Hester Lynch Piozzi (Mrs Thrale)*, Oxford, Clarendon Press, corrected edition 1968, pp. 203–31.
48. 17 May 1784, DL, II, p. 258.
49. Edward A. Bloom and Lilian D. Bloom (eds), *The Piozzi Letters*, Vol. I, Newark, University of Delaware Press, 1989, p. 63.
50. Hester Thrale to FB, 13 August 1784, DL, II, p. 262 and *Thraliana*, II, p. 760.
51. 10 January 1788, DL, III, p. 370.
52. For a full account of the Locks and their property see Sermoneta. Fanny wrote the surname both Lock and Locke; following the Duchess the name will be spelt Lock here.

CHAPTER TWO

1. Journal-letter to SBP and CB, 19 December 1785, DL, II, p. 339. All the journal-letters of the period of December 1785 were addressed to Fanny's sister and father jointly.
2. Llanover, 1st Series, I, p. 23. The marriage was supposed to be to the political advantage of Lord Lansdowne.
3. 14 September 1789, DL, IV, p. 325. The quotation is from *Windsor Forest*, which Pope dedicated to Lord Lansdowne.
4. The former Margaret Cavendish Harley, whose mother, Lady Harriet Harley, had been Mrs Delany's friend in earlier years. She is perhaps best known for her purchase of the Portland Vase (now in the British Museum), bought from Sir William Hamilton for 1,800 guineas.
5. 19 January 1783, DL, II, pp. 196–7. Mrs Delany began her paper mosaics in the autumn of 1772 and mainly used ready-stained paper from, for example, wallpaper manufacturers. See Ruth Hayden, *Mrs Delany and her flower collages*, British Museum Press, new edition 1992, pp. 131–58 for an account of the art. The book gives Mrs Delany's full life history and is splendidly illustrated.
6. 19 January 1783, DL, II, pp. 196–7.
7. Ibid., p. 193.
8. Mary Delany to Frances Hamilton, August 1785, quoted in Llanover, 2nd Series, III, p. 279.
9. Llanover, 2nd Series, pp. 271–2. In JL, XII, p. 902, n. 1, Joyce Hemlow notes that the Duchess had purchased Mrs Delany's house in St James's Place for her, a generous gift amounting to a bequest.
10. Quoted in Sophie von la Roche, *Sophie in London 1786, being the Diary of Sophie v. la Roche*, translated from the German with an introductory essay by Clare Williams, Jonathan Cape, 1933, p. 205.
11. Olwen Hedley, 'Mrs Delany's Windsor Home', in *The Berkshire Archaeological Journal*, Vol. 59, 1961, pp. 51–5.
12. Ibid.
13. FB to Frederica Lock, 29 August 1785, DL, II, p. 296.
14. The White House was demolished in 1802; a sundial on the large lawn opposite Kew Palace in Kew Gardens today marks the spot where it once was.
15. Charles Knight, *Passages of a Working Life during Half a Century: with A Prelude of Early Reminiscences*, 3 volumes, Bradbury & Evans, 1864, I, pp. 36 and 47.
16. Ibid., pp. 36 and 37.
17. See Chapter II in Robert Fulke Greville, *The Diaries of Colonel the Hon. Robert Fulke Greville, Equerry to His Majesty King George III*, edited by F. McKno Bladon, John Lane, The Bodley Head Ltd, 1930.
18. 7 April 1780, DL, I, p. 324.
19. See Ernest de Selincourt (ed.), *The Early Letters of William and Dorothy Wordsworth*, Oxford, Clarendon Press, 1935, p. 82.

20. Llanover, 2nd Series, II, p. 379, and Papendiek, I, pp. 163–4.

21. 6 October 1786, DL, III, p. 57.

22. 16 December 1785, DL, II, p. 337.

23. 4 June 1787, DL, III, p. 252. In an article in the *Sunday Telegraph*, 3/10/99, reporting Dr Steve Jones' calculation that 'one in five British people has a direct black ancestor', it is stated that the explanation for Queen Charlotte's 'mulatto' appearance is that she was descended 'from the illegitimate son of an African mistress in the Portuguese royal house'.

24. Princess Elizabeth was often ill at this time, with a problem sometimes described as 'spasms'. It is possible that she was suffering from the porphyria which later afflicted her father so badly; today it is thought it was present in most of the royal children.

25. Philip Yorke (ed.), *Letters of Princess Elizabeth of England, Daughter of King George III, and Landgravine of Hesse-Homburg*, T. Fisher Unwin, 1898, p. 26.

26. Papendiek, I, p. 229.

27. Marianne Port to John Port (her father), 10 September 1786, Llanover, 2nd Series, III, pp. 387–8.

28. Mary Delany to Frances Hamilton, ibid., pp. 308–9. The 'work' they were engaged in would have been sewing.

29. The Prince's marriage, conducted by a compliant priest on 21 December 1785, was contrary to the Royal Marriages Act of 1772 which made it illegal (as it is today) for any member of the royal family to marry without the monarch's consent. The Act was in response to the secret marriage of George III's brother, the Duke of Cumberland, to a widow, Mrs Anne Horton, in 1771, which the King refused ever to recognise.

30. 3 December 1785, DL, II, p. 314.

31. 16 December 1785, DL, II, p. 316. The star was the sign of the Order of the Garter, founded by Edward III in 1348. The diamond-encrusted badge was always worn by the King on his left breast.

32. Ibid., pp. 319–20.

33. The volatile Giuseppe Baretti (1719–89) came to London as a teacher of Italian in 1751. He made the acquaintance of Dr Johnson, Reynolds, Burke and Garrick, as well as Dr Burney, and tutored Queeney Thrale in Italian.

34. 16 December 1785, DL, II, pp. 331–2.

35. 19 December 1785, DL, II, p. 344.

36. See Chapter Ten. For the Lancelot Gobbo letter see FBA to Esther Burney, 3 April 1797, JL, III, p. 296.

37. FB to Esther Burney, 17 December 1785, DL, II, pp. 352–3. Black pins were used to fasten extra hairpieces to the head.

38. Journal-letter to SB, September 1774, EJL, II, p. 51.

39. The full title of Swift's work of 1738 is *A Complete Collection of Genteel and Ingenious Conversation, according to the Most Polite Model and Method now used at Court, and in the Best Companies of England.*

CHAPTER THREE

1. 17 July 1786, DL, II, p. 382.
2. FB to SBP, 21 May 1786, DL, II, p. 356. Leonard Smelt (*c.* 1719–1800) fought at the Battle of Fontenoy and against the Jacobites in 1745, and was responsible for a number of engineering projects, including the construction of the military road from Carlisle to Newcastle. He was a cultured man and despite his political support for the Whigs, the King took a liking to him. Smelt later accepted the position of Deputy Ranger of Richmond Park.
3. De Selincourt, *The Early Letters of William and Dorothy Wordsworth*, p. 82. Dorothy's uncle by marriage had been made a Canon of Windsor which required a three-months residence, and they were staying in the Horseshoe Cloister of the Castle.
4. Knight, *Passages of a Working Life*, I, p. 42.
5. CB to FBA, 22 July 1799, DL, V, p. 439.
6. For details see Lonsdale, pp. 319–23.
7. FB to SBP, 21 May 1786, DL, II, p. 359.
8. Mary Wollstonecraft, 'Thoughts on the Education of Women', in *The Works of Mary Wollstonecraft*, edited by Janet Todd and Marilyn Butler, 7 Vols, London, William Pickering, 1989, Vol. 4, p. 25.
9. FB to Charlotte Cambridge, June 1786, DL, II, p. 365.
10. Mary Delany to Frances Hamilton, 3 July 1786, and Hester Chapone to Mary Delany, 11 July 1786, Llanover, 2nd Series, III, pp. 365 and 368.
11. *Memoirs*, III, p. 93.
12. *Thraliana*, II, p. 662.
13. FB to Charlotte (Burney) Francis, 27 June 1786, DL, II, p. 373.
14. *Memoirs*, III, pp. 94–6.
15. 17 July 1786, DL, II, p. 381.
16. FB to SBP and Frederica Lock, 19 July 1786, Bar.Eg. 3690, f. 166. In the crabbed handwriting of her old age Fanny endorsed the letter 'after a Heart-rending separation from the loved Friends with whom she was no longer to live'.
17. Lord Chamberlain's accounts for 1786, PRO LC/9/334, where the details given later also appear.
18. They were identified by Constance Hill as 'very pleasant' rooms on the second floor of the Palace, and were drawn by Ellen Hill, *Fanny Burney at the Court of Queen Charlotte*, John Lane, The Bodley Head Ltd, 1926, pp. 40–3.
19. Major William Price (1749–1817) was Equerry to the King from 1782 to 1787. He afterwards became the Queen's Vice-Chamberlain, then her Secretary and Comptroller; he helped Queen Charlotte to design the gardens which can still be seen at Frogmore in the private grounds of Windsor Castle.
20. 11 September 1786, DL, III, p. 33.
21. This is the view accepted by Lonsdale, p. 323, following Llanover, 2nd Series, III, pp. 361–2. Lady Llanover was prejudiced against the view that Fanny could have won anything on her own merit.

22. FB to CB, 19 June 1786, DL, II, p. 368.

23. McGill/Berg, from the opening of Fanny's Court Journals.

24. Ibid.

25. From a letter of Frederica Lock, November 1790, quoted in Sermoneta, p. 58.

26. April 1788, DL, III, p. 496. Fanny made the remark to William Windham during the trial of Warren Hastings.

27. Llanover, 2nd Series, III, p. 361.

28. Princess Sophia was later the first member of the royal family to wear spectacles in public.

29. For the Queen's liking for snuff and the manner of its preparation see Hedley, pp. 57–8 and p. 335, n. 17.

30. 6 August 1786, DL, II, p. 427.

31. *Thraliana*, II, p. 821, n. 4.

32. *Evelina*, p. 58. Aprons were decorative adornments to dress rather than protections of it; lutestring was a lightweight silk with a crisp finish.

33. *Camilla*, p. 721.

34. 24 July 1786, DL, II, p. 396.

35. Mrs Thielcke demonstrated her devotion to duty when on the night of her confinement she stayed at Windsor to prepare the Queen for bed, only afterwards leaving for London and the delivery of the child (Papendiek, I, p. 305). RA GEO/Add 36901b shows her salary as £30.

36. 3 November 1786, DL, III, pp. 95–6.

37. *Evelina*, p. 22.

38. Papendiek, I, p. 308.

39. Ibid., p. 247.

40. 29 September 1786, DL, III, p. 45.

41. 8 August 1786, DL, II, pp. 436–7.

42. *Thraliana*, I, p. 367. As an animal Fanny was designated a 'Doe or Antelope'; she might have taken notice that Mrs Thrale put herself down as a 'Rattlesnake' (p. 414).

43. October 1786, DL, III, p. 77.

CHAPTER FOUR

1. FB to CB, 3 August 1786, Bar.Eg. 3690, f. 26.

2. 2 August 1786, DL, II, pp. 415–16.

3. The information comes from *Gentleman's Magazine* 56, pp. 708–10, and *The New Lady's Magazine* for 1786, p. 397. When Margaret Nicholson reached Bedlam she was entertained to a meal, then taken to a cell which had been new-furnished. There a chain was fastened round her leg and attached to the floor. She was asked if it hurt her leg as 'it should be altered if it did; she replied, "No, not at all".' (*Gentleman's Magazine* 56, p. 710).

4. As n. 1 above, f. 27.

5. The King had also visited the University in 1785.

6. 12 August 1786, DL., II, p. 445.
7. Lord Harcourt could not ride, but the Master of the Horse was in charge of travel arrangements for the royal family as well as responsible for the royal stables.
8. *Harcourt Papers*, VI, p. 79.
9. 12 August 1786, DL., II, p. 447. See *Harcourt Papers*, III, pp. 187–289 for a full description of the house, now owned by Oxford University but leased to the Brahma Kumaris World Spiritual University. They welcome visitors to the gardens which, if not as Fanny saw them, are still impressive.
10. On a visit to the house I noticed that maps of the layout of the rooms are frequent: my young guide said it had taken him five days to learn his way around and he could understand the difficulties which Fanny encountered.
11. Chamberry was a fine muslin with a silk warp and cotton weft. Muslins were becoming increasingly popular.
12. *Harcourt Papers*, VI, p. 15.
13. 12 August 1786, DL., II, p. 462.
14. *Jackson's Oxford Journal* for 19 August 1786.
15. Ibid.
16. Both speeches are printed in *Gentleman's Magazine* 56, p. 711.
17. 12 August 1786, DL., II, p. 466.
18. Ibid., p. 473.
19. 8 August 1788, DL., IV, p. 78.
20. *Oxford Journal* for 19 August. Fanny gives the college where the meal was served as Christ Church, but she admitted that she got muddled between the different colleges and the *Journal* places it at Trinity. Other colleges visited were New College, Wadham, Lincoln and Brasenose.
21. 12 August 1786, DL., II, p. 469, where the pseudonym 'Fairly' is used for Digby, as it is throughout the *Diaries & Letters*.
22. Ibid., p. 475.
23. *The Journeys of Celia Fiennes*, with an introduction by John Hillaby, Macdonald & Co (Publishers) Ltd, 1983, p. 399.
24. Quoted in Mark Girouard, *A Country House Companion*, Leicester, Magna Books, 1987, p. 114.
25. See Anne Somerset, *Ladies in Waiting: From the Tudors to the Present Day*, London, Weidenfeld & Nicolson, 1984, p. 203.
26. FB to CB, 29 August 1786, Bar.Eg. 3690, f. 28.
27. Watkins, p. 311.
28. General Harcourt succeeded to his brother's title in 1809, and his wife then became Countess.

CHAPTER FIVE

1. 16 January 1787, DL., III, pp. 161–2.
2. 13 December 1786, DL., III, pp. 131–2.

3. Part of an undated 'Sketch of Queen Charlotte's Character' quoted from a memorandum book of Madame d'Arblay, DL, VI, p. 379.

4. 18 March 1789, McGill/Berg.

5. 2 January 1787, DL, III, pp. 155–6.

6. *Thraliana*, II, p. 821.

7. February 1792, JL, I, p. 126.

8. 11 January 1788, DL, III, p. 374.

9. 29 September 1788, DL, IV, p. 107.

10. 28 November 1786, DL, III, p. 121.

11. The diary begins on 24 August and just a few days earlier, on 17 August (DL, IV, p. 312), the Queen asked Fanny to listen to extracts and 'tell her if it was English'; Fanny commented that 'indeed there was scarce an expression that was foreign' (these entries were written during the Western Tour when the Queen was making more effort to write in descriptive detail). The destruction of the Queen's papers is explained by Robin Mackworth-Young in 'The Royal Archives, Windsor Castle', *Archives*, Vol. XIII, No. 59, Spring 1978.

12. RA GEO/Add 43/2. Charles Frederick Horn, from Saxony, was the Princesses' Music Master. Mary, Countess of Holdernesse was a Lady of the Bedchamber, Lady Charlotte Finch was Governess to the younger Princesses, and General Budé an equerry. Mary, Countess of Courtown was so much liked by the Queen that she created a special position for her equivalent to a Lady of the Bedchamber (RHI).

In France the women's march on Versailles and brutal slaughter of the King's Swiss Guards had recently taken place, and he had been forced to move to Paris.

13. Watkins, p. 236.

14. They are also known to have played 'whisk' (whist).

15. 4 June 1787, DL, III, p. 254.

16. 2 August 1786, DL, II, p. 411.

17. 7 August 1786, DL, II, p. 431.

18. 4 November 1786, DL, III, p. 95.

19. Not recorded by Fanny, but Constance Hill saw the box and the slip of paper on which Fanny had written 'Gift to F.B. with a sponge of sweet odour, of the lovely Princess Amelia, then 3 years old': Hill, *Fanny Burney at the Court of Queen Charlotte*, p. 65.

20. The Queen's actual birthday was 19 May, too close to 4 June, the King's birthday, to be celebrated then.

21. RA GEO/Add 36905. The exact sum, which also included payment of £3 6s 0d to an 'umbrella maker', was £4,479 1s 0d. A milliner supplying the trimmings received the largest amount, £1,870 18s 9½d, and the silk mercer £1,326 11s 5d. By contrast the mantua-maker who made up the robes earned only £116 19s 0d.

22. Hedley, p. 16.

23. 3 November 1786, DL, III, p. 88.

24. *The Morning Chronicle and London Advertiser*, 19 January 1787. Enquiries to experts at the Museum of Costume & Fashion Research Centre at Bath, and

on my behalf by Catherine Dolman to the Victoria and Albert Museum, have failed to identify what is meant by 'puissé'.

25. The immediate circumstances of the break was a crisis in the Prince's financial affairs and his sacking of his Treasurer, Colonel George Hotham, who would not do his bidding (see A. Aspinall (ed.), *The Later Correspondence of George III*, 5 vols, Cambridge University Press, 1966, I, pp. 261–9). The Prince did send a letter of congratulation to his mother on her celebratory day.

26. It is surprising to find the Duke of Cumberland at the ball, since he was on bad terms with the King. The quarrel began over the Duke's unauthorised marriage and continued because of the bad influence he exerted over the Prince of Wales. But Christopher Hibbert says that the King and Duke 'sometimes appeared in each other's company . . . because the King, anxious to break the influence the Duke had over the impressionable Prince of Wales . . . wished to keep an eye on them' (*George III*, p. 172).

27. 18 January 1787, DL, III, p. 167.

28. Undated journal fragment, Bar.Eg. 3696, f. 15 (3691 f. 4b for Susan's comment, May 1789).

29. 27 February 1787, DL, III, p. 226.

30. 6 October 1786, DL, III, pp. 64–5.

31. Ibid., p. 67.

32. Ibid., pp. 67–8.

33. From Canto II. 'Peter Pindar' was the pseudonym of John Wolcot.

34. 10 August 1786, DL, II, pp. 441–2.

35. 22 September 1786, DL, III, p. 35

36. Frederica Lock to FB, 22 October 1786, Bar.Eg. 3697, f. 156. The passage is also quoted in Sermoneta, p. 57, but using 'her' and attributing the thoughts to Fredy's young son.

37. *Sophie in London*, p. 271.

38. RA GEO/Add 36901b. The accounts also place Fanny's name above Mrs Schwellenberg's, making her appear to be the superior.

39. 25 September 1786, DL, III, p. 43.

40. FB to SBP, 20 August 1786, DL, III, p. 9.

41. 10 July 1787, DL, III, p. 278.

42. 30 September 1788, DL, IV, p. 111.

43. 2 July 1787, DL, III, pp. 274–5.

44. 4 January 1788, DL, III, p. 362.

CHAPTER SIX

1. September 1787, DL, III, p. 322. Following the departure after a visit of Susan Phillips and the Locks, Fanny had been to see the astronomer William Herschel and his sister.

2. *The History of Lady Sophia Sternheim*, Joseph Collyer, 1776, p. 93.

3. 11 September 1786, DL, III, p. 25.

4. *Sophie in London*, p. 179.

5. Ibid., p. 277. When the Hawaiians attacked, most of the marines fled over the rocks, but Phillips stood his ground. Though stabbed in the shoulder he managed to reload his musket and shoot his assailant before swimming out to a boat. He then noticed a badly wounded companion floundering in the water and went back to rescue him. When the man had been dragged on board, Phillips, despite his own wound, made for another, less crowded, boat. See Richard Hough, *Captain Cook: A Biography*, London, Hodder & Stoughton, 1995 paperback edition, pp. 425–7.

6. Sophie was impressed with Bedlam, a converted monastery building, where the occupants lived in 'spacious and bright' rooms, had access to gardens for fresh air, and were humanely treated if straitjackets and chains are ignored (Sophie does not mention Margaret Nicholson's chain). She writes of her 'horrible grey eyes wildly upon us', probably sure that a would-be assassin's eyes must be horrible, but noted that she was tidily dressed, wearing hat and gloves while reading (*Sophie in London*, pp. 166–70). Margaret Nicholson died in Bedlam in 1828.

7. Fanny's account of her encounters with Sophie are found in DL, III, pp. 23–34.

8. *Sophie in London*, p. 186.

9. Stéphanie Félicité de Genlis was author of *Adèle et Théodore*, 1782, a book of stories illustrating educational precepts, which Fanny had in general admired. They had met in 1785, and Fanny received a courteous and friendly letter from her (DL, II, pp. 288–9). The rumours of the relationship with the Duke of Orleans were true. Her later novels acquired a reputation for their 'indelicacies'.

10. 21 August 1786, DL, III, p. 12.

11. 22 January 1787, DL, III, pp. 182–3.

12. They are all clerics: Evelina has her godfather, the Reverend Mr Villars; Cecilia suffers because her guide and uncle, the Dean, is dead; Camilla has her father, while Juliet's guardian is a French Bishop.

13. March 1787, DL, III, p. 92.

14. The watercolour by John Nixon is reproduced as frontispiece to Harry William Pedicord, *'By Their Majesties Command': The House of Hanover at the London Theatres, 1714–1800*, The Society for Theatre Research, 1991. The book reveals that between these dates the King and Queen attended 297 comedies but only 32 tragedies. If farces (210) and pantomimes (157) are counted as comedies the disproportion becomes even more noticeable (see table on p. 36).

15. March 1787, DL, III, p. 238. *Such Things Are* is set in the East Indies and is a rather ponderous mixture of comedy and melodrama *Seduction* is a more sophisticated comedy attacking the follies of fashion; its moral condemnation of vice ought to have satisfied Fanny.

16. Ibid., p. 239. Plays traditionally ended with an epilogue, a moralising speech in rhyming couplets. This one was concerned with women writers and Fanny heard the lines: 'And oft let sweet *Cecilia* win your praise/While Reason guides the clue in Fancy's maze.'

17. January 1783, DL, II, p. 175.

18. 15 August 1787, DL, III, p. 306.
19. Quoted in Carola Oman, *David Garrick*, Hodder & Stoughton, 1958, p. 351.
20. 2 March 1790, DL, IV, p. 359.
21. Ibid., p. 360.
22. See Hedley, pp. 113–14, and *passim*.
23. March 1788, DL, III, p. 481.
24. 1 December 1787, DL, III, p. 351.
25. September 1787, DL, III, p. 322.
26. Quoted in Constance A. Lubbock (ed.), *The Herschel Chronicle: The Life-Story of William Herschel and his Sister Caroline Herschel*, Cambridge University Press, 1933, p. 133.
27. Ibid., p. 157. Despite high hopes, the 40-foot telescope did not prove as successful as the old 20-foot one.
28. 30 December 1786, DL, III, p. 148.
29. 21 August 1786, DL, III, p. 18. Caroline Herschel was to discover another seven comets; in recognition of her work the King awarded her a salary of £50 a year.
30. September 1797, DL, III, p. 322.
31. In 1788 the French astronomer Lalande suggested that Herschel was seeing a brilliant reflection of the light of the earth on the face of the mountain which he had identified as a volcano (Lubbock, *The Herschel Chronicle*, p. 218).
32. 8 June 1787, DL, III, pp. 263–4.
33. The best-known work of Jacob Bryant (1715–1804) was his three-volume study of ancient mythology, *A New System or an Analysis of Ancient Mythology*, 1774–6. At this time he was working on *A Treatise on the Authenticity of the Scriptures*, which was published in 1791.
34. 26 November 1786, DL, III, p. 115. James Hutton's *A Theory of the Earth*, which showed that geological processes were continuous, thus contradicting the notion of a single-day creation, was published in 1785.
35. 13 July 1787, DL, III, p. 284.
36. 8 June 1787, DL, III, p. 259.
37. SBP to CB, 24 April 1787, DL, III, pp. 507–9.
38. 2 August 1787, DL, III, p. 297.
39. 14 August 1787, DL, III, p. 304.
40. See Diana Donald, *The Age of Caricature: Satirical Prints in the Reign of George III*, New Haven and London, Yale University Press, 1996, p. 2.
41. See Dorothy George, *Catalogue of Political and Personal Satires preserved in the department of prints and drawings in the British Museum, Vol. VI, 1784–1792*, British Museum Publications Ltd, 1978, p. 445.
42. 23 August 1787, DL, III, p. 316.
43. 27 November 1787, DL, III, pp. 338–9.
44. *Horace Walpole's Correspondence with Hannah More et al*, Vol. 31 of The Yale Edition of Horace Walpole's Correspondence, edited by W.S. Lewis et al., Oxford and New Haven, Oxford University Press and Yale University Press, 1961, letter of 15 June 1787, p. 247.
45. 31 January 1788, DL, III, p. 395.

CHAPTER SEVEN

1. 8 January 1788, DL, III, p. 368. These words were written after Fanny had been reading Mrs Delany's memoirs.
2. FB to Charlotte Burney Francis, 31 July 1787, Bar.Eg. 3693, f. 25b.
3. Quoted in R. Brimley Johnson (ed.), *Fanny Burney and the Burneys*, Stanley Paul & Co. Ltd, 1926, p. 134.
4. Mary Delany to Frances Hamilton, 17 May 1787, Llanover, 2nd Series, III, p. 438.
5. October 1786, DL, III, pp. 79–80.
6. They were published in Llanover, 1st Series, I.
7. October 1786, DL, III, pp. 69–70.
8. Quoted in Llanover, 2nd Series, III, pp. 316–17.
9. 26 July 1797, DL, III, p. 295.
10. Mary Delany to Mary Port, 21 December 1785, Llanover, 2nd Series, III, p. 325.
11. 8 June 1787, DL, III, pp. 257–8.
12. Ibid., pp. 265–6.
13. June 1787, McGill/Berg.
14. Llanover, 2nd Series, III, p. 361.
15. Ibid.
16. 2 February 1787, DL, III, p. 200. The Honourable Colonel Robert Fulke Greville (1751–1824) had been made an equerry in 1781, and later became a Groom of the Bedchamber. He kept a diary of the early days of his service as an equerry, and wrote a detailed account of the day-to-day fluctuations in the King's condition during his period of 'madness'.
17. 9 January 1788, McGill/Berg.
18. Quoted in Sermoneta, p. 36.
19. Quoted in Hemlow, who tells the whole story, pp. 256–9. Hemlow believes that Fanny created the plot of *Camilla* from the characters of Marianne Port and William Lock.
20. Quoted in Sermoneta, p. 38.
21. Quoted in Hemlow, p. 258.
22. April 1788, DL, III, p. 484.
23. In 1832 Mrs Agnew wrote that she could not recall this message, though she did not deny that there might have been such a one and admitted that her memory was poor (Llanover, 2nd Series, III, p. 480).
24. April 1788, DL, III, p. 488.
25. George Paston, 'A Burney Friendship', in *Sidelights on the Georgian Period*, Methuen and Co. Ltd, 1902, pp. 1–56, p. 12.
26. Ibid., where it is also said that 'there is a suspicion that her friend Miss Burney aided her [Miss Goldsworthy] in nipping the little romance in the bud'. Fanny's journals show that while she was not enthusiastic for the match, because of the inequalities of age and situation, she thought it should take place.

27. May 1788, McGill/Berg.
28. Quoted in 'A Burney Friendship', p. 13.
29. Ibid., pp. 14–15.
30. 11 August 1788, McGill/Berg.
31. Bar.Eg. 3696, f. 19b.
32. 14 May 1790, McGill/Berg.
33. February 1790, DL, IV, p. 350.
34. Joyce Hemlow records that in 1812, when Fanny returned from her exile in France, she was approached by Marianne's two elder daughters seeking information about what had happened in the past to make their mother always so sad (Hemlow, pp. 258–9). Goldsworthy died in 1801, following a series of strokes.
35. *Memoirs*, III, p. 50.
36. Llanover, 2nd Series, III, p. 125.
37. Ibid., p. 125, and FBA to Frances Waddington (Augusta's sister), *c.* 17 February 1816, JL, IX, p. 62.
38. 17 July 1788, DL, IV, p. 32.

CHAPTER EIGHT

1. 13 July 1788, DL, IV, p. 2.
2. Fanny calls the house Fauconberg Hall, but it was locally known as Fauconberg Lodge (preferred here), Fauconberg House, just Lord Fauconberg's or Bays Hill Lodge. It was demolished in the mid-nineteenth century (information kindly supplied by Steven Blake of Cheltenham Museum).
3. 13 July 1788, DL, IV, pp. 2–3. All unsourced quotations in this chapter can be found in DL, IV, pp. 1–89.
4. Ibid., p. 4.
5. Letter of Judith Milbanke to her aunt, Mary Noel, 11 July 1788, quoted in Malcolm Elwin, *The Noels and the Milbankes: Their Letters for Twenty-Five Years 1767–1792*, Macdonald, 1967, p. 332. Judith Milbanke (who became mother of Annabella, Byron's future wife), was piqued to find herself turned out of Lord Fauconberg's house for the King and Queen.
6. Fanny names the hills as the Malverns, but it seems more likely that she means the Cotswolds. The Malverns are visible from Cheltenham, but in the distance. From the position of Fauconberg Lodge, which faced north-east, the nearer Cotswolds dominate the view.
7. A chemical analysis printed in J.K. Griffith, *A General Cheltenham Guide*, 1818, claims that in a wine gallon of the spring water are to be found 480 grains of sulphate of soda and magnesia (Glauber and Epsom salts), 5 of oxyde of iron, 5 of muriate of soda (sea salt), 40 of sulphate of lime, and 25 of carbonate and muriate of magnesia (p. 85).
8. *Gentleman's Magazine* 58, p. 758.
9. *Harcourt Papers*, V, p. 4.

10. 13 July 1788, DL, IV, p. 21. Margaret Planta (1754–1834) was the daughter of a Swiss minister who had given Queen Charlotte Italian lessons. She succeeded her sister Frederica as English teacher to the Royal Nursery in 1778 at a salary of £100 a year; by this date she seems to have become more of an attendant to the older Princesses.

11. Penelope Hatfield, College Archivist, has kindly searched but been unable to find any reference to Digby at Eton: entry books signed by every boy on arrival do not begin until 1791, the same year as the annual printed school lists. Nor is there any record in the Sherborne Castle archives. However, Mrs Hatfield reports a letter from an Admiral Digby in 1907 enquiring about Stephen, so it must have been a family tradition that he went to Eton; Stephen's own son Charles was at the school while Fanny was at court.

12. Stephen Digby entered the army in 1761 as a Captain and served with the 24th Regiment of Foot, being promoted to Major in 1771. In 1774 he transferred, with the rank of Lieutenant-Colonel, to the 1st Regiment of Foot (PRO/355.3 WOD). His desire to leave the army ('having lost by my profession [£]1900') is revealed in letters dated 22 November 1778 and 17 December 1778 to his brother, Henry, Lord Digby, preserved in the Sherborne Castle archives.

13. Information from Ann Smith, Archivist of Sherborne Castle.

14. 13 January 1789, DL, IV, p. 223, where Digby speaks of his mother 'with a very tender sigh', and letters in the Sherborne archives of 22 and 28 November 1778.

15. The exact date of the portrait is unknown.

16. Fanny does not specify what type of cancer it was, but later letters between Digby and his sister-in-law, Susan Fox-Strangways, identify it as breast cancer. See Susan Rand, 'A Successful Operation for Cancer, 1799', in *Somerset and Dorset Notes and Queries*, 1999, pp. 321–7, pp. 325 (thanks to Ann Smith for drawing my attention to this article).

17. 11 January 1788, DL, III, p. 379.

18. 21 July 1788, DL, IV, p. 30.

19. 26 July 1788, DL, IV, p. 41.

20. *Gentleman's Magazine* 58, pp. 978–9.

21. The author of this anonymously published novel of 1784 has been identified as William Combe (1742–1823), best known for his later comic verses, *Doctor Syntax*. Digby was of an age with Combe and could have known him at Eton. See Harlan W. Hamilton, *Dr Syntax: A Silhouette of William Combe, Esq.*, Chatto & Windus, 1969.

22. 26 July 1788, DL, IV, p. 45.

23. Ibid., p. 46.

24. 26 July 1788, McGill/Berg.

25. SBP to FB, October 1789, Bar.Eg. 3692, f. 128b. The date indicates how far behind Susan was at this time in reading Fanny's journals. Fanny's slowness in sending them was at first because of the King's illness which followed the return from Cheltenham; after his recovery her own troubled feelings about Digby held her back.

26. In Chapter 18 of Jane Austen's *Persuasion*.
27. Sir Robert Gunning (1731–1816) made his reputation in Russia in negotiations with Catherine the Great. He was created Knight of the Bath in 1773.
28. 24 July 1788, DL, IV, p. 33, and the last sentence McGill/Berg (the name given to Miss Gunning in the *Diary & Letters* was Miss Fuzilier). Charlotte Gunning was appointed Maid of Honour in 1780, one of six unmarried girls, paid £300 a year each. In earlier reigns the position had been dubiously regarded: they were identified as 'those maidens six without one virgin' in the reign of George I (quoted in Somerset, *Ladies in Waiting*, p. 209).
29. 27 July 1788, DL, IV, pp. 47–8.
30. 9 August 1788, McGill/Berg.
31. *Gentleman's Magazine* 58, p. 884.
32. See Claire Tomalin, *Mrs Jordan's Profession: The story of a great actress and a future King*, Viking, 1994, pp. 79–87. Dora Jordan was to become the long-term mistress of Prince William, Duke of Clarence.
33. Quoted from the *Morning Post*, in Gwen Hart, *A History of Cheltenham*, Gloucester, Alan Sutton, 1981, p. 170.
34. 19 July 1788, DL, IV, p. 26. Howard had inspected the gaol in 1777 and criticised the lack of single cells. See the *Victoria County History of Gloucestershire*, IV, Oxford University Press, 1988, pp. 246–7. *Such Things Are* by Elizabeth Inchbald, which Fanny had seen the previous year, has a character based on John Howard.
35. *Gentleman's Magazine* 58, p. 884.
36. Ibid.
37. 1 August 1788, DL, IV, p. 61.
38. 3 August 1788, DL, IV, pp. 67–8.
39. *Gentleman's Magazine* 58, p. 1075.
40. Joseph Taylor, *Relics of Royalty: or Remarks, Anecdotes, and Amusements, of His Late Most Gracious Majesty, George III*, A.K. Newman, 1820, p. 20.
41. 9 August 1788, DL, IV, pp. 82–3.
42. 10 August 1788, DL, IV, pp. 84–5.
43. St Katharine at Tower is a charitable church foundation first established by Queen Matilda, wife of Henry I, on land by the Tower of London. Successive Queens supported the foundation and it was so highly valued that local people intervened during the Gordon Riots of 1780 to protect the hospital (see Lady Jocelyn, *St Katharine at Tower: an Historical Summary*, R.K. Harrison & Co. Ltd, World Trade Centre, undated). Today in the gift of the Queen Mother, St Katharine's is based in Poplar, on the site of the old parish church of St James Ratcliffe, and is a valued resource for the local community.
44. Before he left, the King ordered a well to be sunk at Fauconberg Lodge to provide fresh water. However, the water struck proved to have a mineral content similar to the existing well, and became the Royal Well of Cheltenham.

CHAPTER NINE

1. 5 November 1788, DL, IV, p. 131.
2. 17 October 1788, DL, IV, p. 117.
3. 19 October 1788, DL, IV, p. 118. The play is not named, but was probably *Edwy and Elgiva* (see pp. 167–8).
4. 25 October 1788, DL, IV, p. 120.
5. 1 November 1788, DL, IV, p. 121.
6. 5 November 1788, DL, IV, p. 129.
7. Ibid., DL, IV, p. 131.
8. 6 November 1788, DL, IV, p. 135.
9. Ibid., p. 136.
10. This diagnosis was first proposed by Ida Macalpine and Richard Hunter in *George III and the Mad Business*, Harmondsworth, Allen Lane, The Penguin Press, 1969, especially pp. 172–5. Biographers were soon ready to accept the theory, but medical experts were initially more sceptical: see John C.G. Röhl, Martin Warren and David Hunt, *Purple Secret: Genes, 'Madness' and the Royal Houses of Europe*, Bantam Press, 1998.
11. Battiscombe served the royal household from 1782 to 1835. Dorset CRO holds his memorandum book (D.239/F3) with short notes of treatments given to patients. The events of this night were so extraordinary that he squeezed into the bottom of the page in tiny writing: 'Nov 5 Miss Goldsworthy sate up wth the Queen – who was in ye utmost consternation all night'.

    The most painful treatment endured by the King was the blistering, especially those blisters later used on his legs, which suppurated and were extremely slow to heal.
12. *Harcourt Papers*, IV, p. 60.
13. Ibid., p. 66.
14. 6 November 1788, DL, IV, p. 147. Greville writes: 'Colonel Digby then fixing his Eyes stedfastly on H. M^y took Him by both hands, & earnestly pressed his return. The King looked at the Duke of York and exclaimed, "Oh My Boy" & soon after he was persuaded to return to his bed' (Greville, *Diaries*, p. 80).
15. 28 November 1788, DL, IV, p. 187.
16. 20 November 1788, DL, IV, pp. 167–71.
17. Greville, *Diaries*, pp. 94–8.
18. 29 November 1788, DL, IV, p. 188.
19. Ibid., p. 189. Sending the King to Kew against his will was such a delicate matter that the whole Cabinet met at Windsor, and all ministers signed the document authorising the move.
20. Dr Willis is supposed at this point to have reminded the King that Christ healed the sick, whereupon the King rejoined 'Yes, yes, but he had not £700 for it'. Greville, who was present, records the King saying more prosaically but just as rationally, 'You have quitted a profession I have always loved, & You have Embraced one I most heartily detest – Alter your line of Life, ask what preferment You wish & make Me your Friend' (Greville, *Diaries*, p. 119).

21. Ibid., p. 189.
22. *Harcourt Papers*, IV, pp. 33–4.
23. 4 December 1788, DL, IV, p. 204.
24. 20 December 1788 McGill/Berg.
25. 18 December 1788, McGill/Berg.
26. 22 January 1789, McGill/Berg.
27. 9 March 1789 McGill/Berg (and quoted in Hemlow, p. 210). The foregoing incidents concerned with Digby are mainly drawn from the unpublished journal transcripts at McGill.
28. 24 February 1789, McGill/Berg.
29. 9 March 1789, McGill/Berg.
30. 22 January 1789, DL, IV, pp. 236–7.
31. 2 February 1789, DL, IV, pp. 243–4.
32. Ibid., p. 245.
33. The King seems to have kissed most people when he saw them again after recovery, including Digby who wrote to Mrs Harcourt on 19 February that when he had found the King in the library 'he quitted his papers, leaned himself back, extending his arms & came forward with great glee & said, Ah Digby! Took me by the hands & kissed me . . .' (quoted in Elizabeth, Countess of Harcourt, 'Mrs Harcourt's Journals', in *Miscellanies of the Philobiblon Society*, Vol. XIII, Whittingham & Wilkins, 1871–2, p. 4).
34. Greville, *Diaries*, p. 203.
35. Columb believed that given Digby's assurance Greville would have sought Fanny's room in the same way. In this he was wrong: Greville had already given his heart to the woman he was later to marry.
36. Lady Charlotte Finch told Mrs Harcourt on 22 February that the King was showing the Queen the 'attention of a lover. He seemed to delight in making her presents – kissed her hand & showd every mark of tenderness' ('Mrs Harcourt's Journals', p. 8).
37. 23 February 1789, DL, IV, p. 263. There were minor relapses: on 27 February Robert Battiscombe was told by Colonel Greville that he need attend no more at Kew as the King was cured, yet at the beginning of March the entries, with underlinings expressing the apothecary's sense of their significance, read:
    1 Went to Kew (express)
    2 Bled the King returnd to Windsor – & back again to Kew in the Eveng: –
    3 Illuminations, & Fireworks at Windsor in honour of His Majesty's recovery
    (Dorset CRO D.239/F3).
38. See Papendiek, II, p. 16, and 'Mrs Harcourt's Journals', p. 10.
39. Mrs Papendiek gives a vivid description of the illuminations, Papendiek, II, pp. 69–72.
40. 10 March 1789, DL, IV, pp. 269–70.
41. Papendiek, II, pp. 73–4.

CHAPTER TEN

1. Opening of a rhyming letter sent to Esther Burney from Gloucester Lodge, Weymouth, 9 September 1789. Bar.Eg. 3690, f. 112.
2. *London Chronicle* for 24–6 March 1789.
3. March 1789, DL, IV, p. 279.
4. 19 March 1789, McGill/Berg (and the subsequent quotation). Most references to events related to Digby in this chapter come from the McGill transcripts of Fanny's unpublished journals.
5. See Stella Tillyard, *Aristocrats: Caroline, Emily, Lousia and Sarah Lennox 1740–1832*, Vintage, 1995, pp. 183–8. The errant pair had been brought back into the family circle by 1789.
6. 22 January 1789, McGill/Berg.
7. SBP to FB, 22 May 1789, Bar.Eg. 3691, f. 12 and Fanny's journal written for April 1789, McGill/Berg. At this time Susan had not yet read even the Cheltenham journals.
8. May 1789, DL, IV, p. 288.
9. 1 June 1789, McGill/Berg.
10. 25 June 1789, DL, IV, p. 290.
11. Ibid., p. 291.
12. The King subsequently bought Gloucester Lodge and had it enlarged. Today it is a hotel.
13. John Byng, Viscount Torrington, on his visit to Weymouth, reported the views of 'a gentleman' who left the place in disgust (*The Torrington Diaries*, edited by C. Bruyn Andrews and abridged by Fanny Andrews, Eyre & Spottiswoode, 1954, p. 77). Byng was not much more impressed, though he enjoyed the fresh fish of the market.
14. *Gentleman's Magazine* 59, p. 855. Weymouth was right to be ecstatic since the King's presence did for the town what it had done the year before for Cheltenham; grateful inhabitants were to erect a statue of the King in 1809 which still stands on the esplanade.
15. 30 June 1789, DL, IV, pp. 297–8.
16. The King's eight-sided machine is preserved in Weymouth.
17. 8 July 1789, DL, IV, p. 298.
18. 27 August 1773 (from the 'Teignmouth Journal'), EJL, I, p. 302.
19. RA GEO/Add 43/1.
20. *Gentleman's Magazine* 59, p. 952, gives the date as 14 July; Fanny writes about the occasion under 15 July, but may not be suggesting that the event took place that day (DL, IV, p. 299).
21. FB to Esther Burney, 9 September 1789, Bar.Eg. 3690, f. 112.
22. 29 July 1789, DL, IV, p. 303.
23. James Woodforde, *The Diary of a Country Parson 1758–1802*, selected and edited by John Beresford, Oxford University Press, 1978, p. 356.
24. A copy of Digby's game-book account can be seen in the Castle kitchens today.

25. 6 August 1789, McGill/Berg.
26. John Parker, 2nd Lord Boringdon (1772–1840), had inherited the property only the previous year. It was his father who employed Robert Adam in 1768 to transform the interior of the house with a series of neo-classical rooms, and who was the first patron of Sir Joshua Reynolds.
27. *Gentleman's Magazine* 59, p. 1047.
28. *Exeter Flying Post*, 27 and 20 August 1789.
29. Dr Geoff Roe kindly explains 'fountain pens' of that time: 'Strictly, these early devices were "reservoir pens" in that they held a quantity of ink and did not need dipping in an ink pot. They usually ceased to flow after a couple of written lines and needed priming – a shake or pushing down a plunger.' The nib would be a push-in quill one, with a metal reservoir; Fanny's pen was probably the gold one given to her by the Queen in 1787 (10 July 1787, DL, III, p. 279). See also Geoff Roe, *Writing Instruments: A Technical History and How They Work*, Stockport, G.E. Roe, 1996.
30. 17 August 1789, McGill/Berg.
31. 21 August 1789, DL, IV, p. 314.
32. See Crispin Gill, *Plymouth: A New History: 1603 to the present day*, Newton Abbott, David & Charles, 1979, p. 79.
33. Quotation from *Gentleman's Magazine* 59, p. 1142, which gives 'Long live their Majesties' as the message on the sash. The feminist alternative comes in a letter from Countess Mount Edgcumbe to Lady Harcourt, *Harcourt Papers*, VIII, p. 283. Since the Countess would have learnt it from the King and Queen, her version is more likely to be correct.
34. The amount is variously reported: the *Exeter Flying Post*, 3 September 1789, reports that 'The women who rowed before the King were handsomely rewarded by a present from the Queen of £50'.
35. *Gentleman's Magazine* 59, p. 1143, and the *Exeter Flying Post* for 20 August 1789.
36. 21 August 1789, DL, IV, pp. 317–18.
37. 24 August 1789, DL, IV, p. 320.
38. George, Earl Mount Edgcumbe (1721–95) had pursued a career in the navy rising to Admiral. In 1779, during a French invasion scare, he ordered the felling of a hundred ancient oaks on the estate to allow fortifications to be built, and for this sacrifice was created Viscount.
39. *Harcourt Papers*, VIII, p. 284.
40. *Gentleman's Magazine* 59, p. 1144.
41. Cotehele, on the banks of the Tamar near Callington, is now owned by the National Trust.
42. *Cecilia*, I, Chapter 8. Gasparo Pacchierotti (1740–1821) was a castrato who made his debut in London in 1778, the year of *Evelina*. He became a friend of the Burney family, and was admired to adoration by Fanny and Susan. Lady Mount Edgcumbe makes appearances at musical evenings in Fanny's early journals.
43. 16 August 1789, McGill/Berg.
44. 25 August 1789, McGill/Berg.

45. Anne Robinson, Lord Boringdon's aunt, wrote to her brother that after their Majesties' visit the servants were all well pleased except that 'Old Anthony grumbles that there was not wine left in the pantry'. Her own complaint was that 'the Lawn has not been fed or Mowed for Hay which is a great Loss, & I believe the King did not pay for the Hay he used which I understand was a very absurd piece of Magnificence of the Serj^ts' (Parker Correspondence 1259/1/37, West Devon Area Record Office).
46. 28 August 1789, McGill/Berg.
47. 16 September 1789, McGill/Berg.

CHAPTER ELEVEN

1. 28 May 1790, DL, IV, p. 392. Part of Fanny's reported account of her court life to her father.
2. 16 September 1789, McGill/Berg.
3. Ibid.
4. 18 November 1789, DL, IV, pp. 333–4.
5. 20 November 1789, McGill/Berg, as are the four following quotations.
6. Letters from Mary Noel to her niece Judith Milbanke (Charlotte Gunning's friend), 12 October 1789, and November/December 1789 (quoted in Elwin, *The Noels and the Milbankes*, pp. 358 and 364). In a further letter to Judith, her brother, Viscount Wentworth, asked her if she had not 'lost a Bet' by the match (26 November 1789, p. 362), so she cannot have been expecting it to come about.
7. 28 November 1789, McGill/Berg.
8. Ibid.
9. Stephen Digby to FB, letter quoted in her journals for 17 May 1790, McGill/Berg.
10. 28 November 1789, McGill/Berg.
11. 20 November 1789, McGill/Berg.
12. January 1790, DL, IV, p. 349. Charlotte Gunning's ten-page wedding settlement is being conserved by Northamptonshire CRO [G (H) 803]. She would also have received from the Queen the customary £1,000 for retiring Maids of Honour.
13. *Gentleman's Magazine* 64 reports her death on 9 June 1794. No cause is given, but it could have been the result of pregnancy or childbirth.
14. 26 July 1788, DL, IV, pp. 43–4. The scene is found in *Cecilia*, VIII, Chapter 2.
15. Unpublished journal fragment, Bar.Eg. 3696, f. 20b, dated conjecturally April 1789, but clearly belonging to 1790.
16. 17 May 1790, McGill/Berg.
17. SBP to FB, 30 November 1789, Bar.Eg. 3692, ff. 144 and 173, and Frederica Lock to FB, 28 November 1789, Bar.Eg. 3697, f. 162b.
18. 28 May 1790, DL, IV, p. 392.
19. Ibid.

20. The titles are *Edwy and Elgiva, Hubert de Vere: A Pastoral Tragedy, The Siege of Pevensey*, and the incomplete *Elberta*. After Fanny left court she continued to work on them, so the versions which can be read in Peter Sabor's edition of the complete plays (William Pickering, 1995) are not as they were at first.

21. Margaret Anne Doody has studied the manuscripts and discusses their psychological implications in *Frances Burney: The Life in the Works*, New Brunswick, Rutgers University Press, 1988, pp. 178–98.

22. August 1790, DL, IV, p. 417.

23. October 1790, DL, IV, p. 424.

24. 6 May 1790, DL, IV, p. 374.

25. October 1790, DL, IV, pp. 431–2.

26. Ibid.

27. Charlotte Burney Francis to FB, 14 November 1790, Bar.Eg. 3693, f. 36. The names Tatlanthe and Rigdumfundus (actually Rigdum Funnidos) come from Henry Carey's 1734 burlesque *The Tragedy of Chrononhotonthologos*. For Windham's meetings with Fanny at the trial of Warren Hastings see the following chapter.

28. McGill/Berg, quoted by Fanny July 1791 (also quoted in Hemlow, p. 216).

29. Letter copied by Fanny into her journals, July 1791, JL, I, p. 4.

30. See Lonsdale, pp. 356–7.

31. Bar.Eg. 3693, f. 38. Undated, but Fanny refers to her letter under December in her journals.

32. 4 June 1791, DL, IV, p. 442.

33. FB to CB, 26 December 1790, Bar.Eg. 3690, f. 41b.

34. 4 June 1791, DL, IV, p. 452, but from the word 'happy' McGill/Berg (a good example of Barrett's censorship).

35. The phrase is found in Fanny's 'Narrative of the Last Illness and Death of General D'Arblay', written between 17 November 1819 and 20 March 1820, JL, X, p. 851.

36. See Hemlow, pp. 213–15 for more particulars.

37. May 1789, DL, IV, p. 287.

38. 4 June 1791, DL, IV, p. 472.

39. Ibid., p. 473.

40. 7 July 1791, DL, IV, p. 490.

41. Ibid., p. 491.

42. Ibid.

43. Ibid.

CHAPTER TWELVE

1. 13 February 1788, DL, III, p. 413. Fanny comments on the arrival of Warren Hastings at the bar of Westminster Hall.

2. Ibid., p. 416.

3. The East India Company was granted its first Charter by Queen Elizabeth I in 1600, thereafter building up its fortunes by importing goods from all over Asia, notably spices, and China teas and porcelain. It was only in India that the Company had administrative power. For a history of the Company, see Anthony Wild, *The East India Company: Trade and Conquest from 1600*, HarperCollins*Illustrated*, 1999.

4. Warren Hastings (1732–1818) was proficient in Urdu and Persian and encouraged translations from oriental languages into English. He studied and collected Islamic art, and commissioned a study of Hindu cosmogony. See J.L. Brockington, 'Warren Hastings and Orientalism', in Geoffrey Carnell and Colin Nicholson (eds), *The Impeachment of Warren Hastings: Papers from a Bicentenary Commemoration*, Edinburgh University Press, 1989, pp. 91–108.

5. Philip Francis (1740–1818) had proved himself an able administrator in the war-office, but was not an old India hand (he has been identified as 'Junius', the anonymous author of venomous personal attacks on the King and other leaders). Hastings took the desperate decision to kill or be killed by him, provoking the duel by accusing his antagonist of being 'devoid of truth and honour'. See Keith Feeling, *Warren Hastings*, Macmillan and Co., 1954, pp. 225–30.

6. For a full account of Burke's involvement in Indian affairs, and the growth of his antagonism to Hastings, see P.J. Marshall, *The Impeachment of Warren Hastings*, Oxford University Press, 1965, pp. 1–21.

7. FB to CB, 24 September 1785, DL, II, p. 297.

8. 25 August 1786, DL, III, p. 19.

9. Feeling, *Warren Hastings*, pp. 62–3.

10. '. . . the mode of a second marriage from a divorce was precisely the contrary here of what it was in Germany; since here it could only take place upon misconduct, and there, I had been told, a divorce from misconduct prohibited a second marriage, which could only be permitted where the divorce was the mere effect of disagreement from dissimilar tempers' (10 August 1787, DL, II, p. 442).

11. When Pitt voted against Hastings on one of the charges put before Parliament, impeachment became inevitable. This charge was one of the two most significant made against Hastings, but whether he acted illegally depends on interpretation of the laws by which Indian landholders were governed. Chait Singh was a subject prince with a large fortune, bound to pay a certain sum annually to the Company and, according to Hastings, to make extra payments when the Company was in need as it was in 1780. When the Prince did not pay, Hastings went to his palace at Benares to enforce his order and fine the Indian. Chait Singh was arrested, whereupon some of his people burst into the palace and murdered 200 sepoys. He fled and his property was seized. Pitt did not dispute Hastings' right to make the financial demands but declared the amount of the fine oppressive.

12. Anon., *The History of the Trial of Warren Hastings Esq.*, J. Debrett, 1796, p. 1. The King did not attend the trial, nor did Pitt.

13. This picture can be seen in Wild, *The East India Company*, pp. 100–1. A black and white copy is also reproduced in DL, III, p. 413, where the original is credited to Edward Dayes.

14. *The History of the Trial*, p. 1

15. 13 February 1788, DL, III, pp. 412–13.

16. 'Poppy-coloured', *The History of the Trial*, p. 1; 'dark blue', *Public Advertiser* for 18 February 1788. Fanny was asked by William Windham if she thought it a blue or purple suit; he thought the prisoner should have worn black.

17. 13 February 1788, DL, III, p. 414.

18. Ibid., p. 415 and *The History of the Trial*, p. 3.

19. 13 February 1788, DL, III, p. 451.

20. Ibid., pp. 418–19. The following quotations about Windham are found on pp. 419–20.

21. Ibid., p. 421.

22. Ibid., p. 424.

23. Ibid., p. 428.

24. *The Correspondence of Edmund Burke*, ed. by Thomas W. Copeland et al., 10 vols, Cambridge and Chicago, Cambridge University Press and The University of Cambridge Press, 1958–78, Vol. V, p. 378.

25. 13 February but referring to 16 February 1788, DL, III, p. 448.

26. Ibid., p. 472. For Burke's speech see E.A. Bond, *The Speeches of the Managers and Counsel in the Trial of Warren Hastings*, 4 volumes, Longman, Brown, Green, Longmans & Roberts, 1859–61, I, pp. 45–100.

27. Quoted in Paston, 'A Burney Friendship', p. 15.

28. The Begums, or Princesses of Oudh were a mother and grandmother in possession of great wealth following the death of the younger woman's husband. Hastings knew he could get access to the money if certain treasures which the man's son had ceded to the women were reclaimed. He therefore encouraged the son to demand his 'rights' and did not object when the women's two eunuchs were put in irons and starved until they revealed where the treasures were, which they soon did. Sheridan made the most of the mistreatment, though it was pointed out that even after the treasures were yielded up the women were still wealthy, and the eunuchs suffered no lasting harm either. For more details of Sheridan's speech, and the comment on Mrs Siddons, see Linda Kelly, *Richard Brinsley Sheridan, A Life*, Sinclair-Stevenson, 1997, pp. 147–50.

29. 13 February for 16 February 1788, DL, III, p. 467.

30. Bond, *The Speeches of the Managers and Counsel*, I, p. 69.

31. April 1788, DL, III, p. 498. Hastings was not merely polite, but ironically reflecting on his current exclusion from the court.

32. 27 April 1790, DL, IV, p. 370.

33. 11 May 1790, DL, IV, p. 377.

34. Ibid., p. 389, except for the last part about 'masked villainy', which is quoted in Hemlow, p. 212.

35. Mrs Henry Baring (ed.), *The Diary of the Right Hon. William Windham, 1784–1810*, Longmans, Green, & Co., 1866, p. xix.

36. She reportedly said 'O, he [Windham] was in a passion – a rage! – *I* believe . . . he is in love with Miss Burney!' (April 1791, McGill/Berg).
37. 2 June 1791, DL, IV, p. 467.
38. Ibid., p. 469.
39. Journal-letter to SBP and the Locks, February 1792, JL, I, p. 116.
40. Only 29 out of the 230 peers considered that they had been often enough to vote (the court had been in session for 149 days over the seven years). On both the Benares and Begums charges six peers cast their votes against Hastings, the highest number of votes against on any charge. See Marshall, *The Impeachment of Warren Hastings*, p. 85.
41. In 1841 Macaulay wrote an essay, 'Warren Hastings' (ostensibly a review of a hagiographic biography), which for a long time was a favourite school text on account of its lucid and colourful prose.
42. FBA to CB, 18 June 1795, and 27 July 1797, JL, III, pp. 120 and 332.

CHAPTER THIRTEEN

1. FB to CB, 16–19 February 1793, JL, II, p. 19.
2. Journal-letter to SBP and the Locks, August 1791, JL, I, p. 21. The principal places they visited were Winchester, Southampton, Salisbury, Blandford, Lyme Regis, Sidmouth, Exmouth, Exeter, and Wells.
3. Ibid., pp. 41–52, or see Amanda Foreman, *Georgiana Duchess of Devonshire*, HarperCollins, 1998, pp. 256–65, for more details of the meeting.
4. Journal-letter to SBP and the Locks, June 1792, JL, I, p. 188.
5. Ibid., April 1792, JL, I, p. 137.
6. George Cambridge married Cornelia Mierop, but not till 1795, the year following Fanny's own marriage.
7. The Hall, much altered, is now an environmental centre owned by the National Trust. Outside the gates a board, erected by the English School in Brussels in 1994, reads: 'This house gave shelter in 1792 to a group of progressive French aristocrats who had fled to England to escape the worst excesses of the French Revolution.' See Linda Kelly, *Juniper Hall: An English Refuge from the French Revolution*, Weidenfeld & Nicolson, 1991.
8. FB to SBP, post-4 October 1792, JL, II, p. 2.
9. FB to CB, 28 January 1793, JL, II, pp. 8–9.
10. For more detailed understanding of the complex situation and personalities at Juniper Hall see Kelly, *Juniper Hall*. For Madame de Staël's history see J. Christopher Herold, *Mistress to an Age: A Life of Madame de Staël*, Hamish Hamilton Ltd, 1959. While the charge of aiding and abetting the Revolution was rightly seen by Fanny as malicious, she discovered that Narbonne *had* been Madame de Staël's lover.
11. D'Arblay had been hoping for employment as agent for one of a proposed corps of émigrés, but had found that the pay would be too poor for him to live on in London. After explaining this he went on in a convoluted sentence: 'Ce que vous ne savez pas non plus c'est que j'ai regretté d'autant

plus cette place dans le cas où elle m'eut donné quelque chose que je savais très bien avec qui je desirais le partager . . .', roughly: 'What you don't know either is that I've been the more sorry about this employment in case it would have given me something which I knew very well with whom I wanted to share it' (Alexandre d'Arblay to FB, 31 March 1793, JL, II, p. 39).

12. January 1783, DL, II, pp. 178–9.

13. Apart of course from the precipitate Thomas Barlow in 1775.

14. '. . . ainsi – s'il tient à moi – le moindre du monde – que vous travailliez pour rester en angleterre – je ne crois pas que vous partira . . .' (FB to Alexandre d'Arblay, 31 March 1793, JL, II, p. 43).

15. FB to SBP and the Locks, 31 May 1793, JL, II, p. 135.

16. A plaque in the church commemorates the marriage. Because d'Arblay was a Roman Catholic, and in the hope that he might one day be able to reclaim property in France, he was anxious that his marriage would be recognised there, so the ceremony was repeated two days later at the Sardinian Chapel in Lincoln's Inn Fields, with other family members present.

17. Fanny was especially grateful to Edmund Burke whose support helped to reconcile her father to the match. But the ultra-Tory Mrs Ord renounced her friendship with Fanny in disgust at her marriage with a Roman Catholic and a Constitutional.

18. FBA to Marianne Waddington, 19 September 1793, JL, III, p. 11.

19. For the genesis of the novel see the introduction by Edward A. Bloom and Lillian D. Bloom to *Camilla*, pp. ix–xiv, and Doody, *Frances Burney*, pp. 205–15.

20. 1 December 1785, DL, II, p. 309.

21. Quoted in Hedley, p. 194.

22. *Thraliana*, II, p. 916. Mrs Piozzi got her information from Sarah Siddons, who described the failure with more sympathy.

23. 23 March 1795, British Library, Burney 885.

24. FBA to CB, 18 June 1795, JL, III, p. 117.

25. Fanny was later told by the Princesses that their father had liked the Dedication because it was not 'fulsome', though modern readers will find it fulsome enough. She combines in it her sense of the honour, and her devotion, etc., with a claim for the book's serious moral content.

26. Three women acted as Fanny's 'Book-keepers': Frederica Lock, Frances Crewe (for whom Fanny had written the pamphlet urging charity for the French priests), and the Blue Stocking hostess the Honourable Mrs Frances Boscawen. To them must be given much of the credit for the huge list of subscribers.

27. 'Yesterday evening between eleven o'clock and midnight my wife was at last happily delivered of a daughter' (Alexandre d'Arblay to SBP, *c.* 12 June 1794, JL, III, p. 165).

28. His niece, Lady Charlotte Digby, ordered a set.

29. The cousin of Jane Austen's mother, Cassandra Cooke, was wife of the vicar of Great Bookham and had become a friend of Madame d'Arblay. References in Jane's letters show her liking for *Camilla*, and it is cited in Chapter 5 of

Northanger Abbey, along with *Cecilia* and Maria Edgeworth's *Belinda*, in her famous defence of the novel.

30. *Camilla*, p. 538.
31. The critics were generally favourable, though not as enthusiastic as Dr Burney would have liked. Fanny took all criticisms seriously and for the 1802 edition made many changes, much reducing the book's length.
32. 'Windsoriana' (written for CB), Part IV, for 6 July 1796, JL, III, p. 192. The characters referred to by the Queen are Eugenia (who *did* get the smallpox), Camilla (who *did* lose her fortune), and their uncle, Sir Hugh Tyrold, the most engaging character in the novel but a man whose inability to foresee consequences leads to various disasters.
33. Ibid.
34. Ibid., p. 190.
35. Ibid.
36. *Memoirs*, III, p. 214.
37. Susan Rands, 'A Successful Operation for Cancer, 1799', in *Somerset and Dorset Notes and Queries*, 1999, pp. 321–7. Lady Susan was to live on for another twenty-six years.
38. For the story of the later lives of the Princesses see Dorothy Margaret Stuart, *The Daughters of George III*, Macmillan and Co., 1939, and Morris Marples, *Six Royal Sisters: Daughters of George III*, Michael Joseph Ltd, 1969. A biography of the sisters by Flora Fraser is forthcoming.
39. Sir James Bland Burges, politician and writer, quoted in Marples, *Six Royal Sisters*, p. 86.
40. Court Journal for SBP, for 3 November 1797, JL, IV, p. 12.
41. The Prince of Würtemberg was a widower of forty. Apart from his size there were misgivings about the Prince's character in England, but the Princess seems to have been happy in her marriage, though her only child was stillborn. In time she became Queen of Würtemberg.
42. Court Journal, JL, IV, p. 7.
43. Ibid., pp. 11–12.
44. Court Journal for SBP, *c.* 26 February–8 March 1798, JL, IV, p. 95.
45. Ibid., p. 102.
46. Had she not agreed to go to Ireland the law would have allowed Phillips to take the children, a powerful consideration for Susan.
47. FBA to SBP, December 1797, JL, IV, p. 51.

CHAPTER FOURTEEN

1. 1 February 1788, DL, III, p. 401. Fanny was writing in February 1788, at a time when Mrs Schwellenberg was very ill, 'so ill as to fill me with compassion'.
2. D'Arblay had been promoted to Lieutenant-Général by the restored King Louis XVIII in 1815, after Waterloo.

3. There are many events of this second half of Fanny's life that are necessarily ignored or only touched briefly upon in this chapter. For more details see JL, V–XII or a general biography.

4. SBP to CB, 30 December 1799, Bar.Eg. 3700A, f. 58. The letter is also printed in JL, IV, p. 376, n. 2.

5. For Fanny's graphic account of the horrors of the operation (supposedly for removal of a cancerous growth) see FBA to Esther Burney, for September 1811, JL, VI, pp. 598–615.

6. *The Wanderer* was Fanny's least successful book, though it was eagerly anticipated and sold well at first. Her readers expected a novel based on her years in France but discovered a story set in the 1790s; its heroine is a refugee from French Revolutionary terror, but the wandering takes place over southern England, particularly around Brighton, Lewes and the New Forest. *The Wanderer* has interested feminists in recent years.

7. JL, VIII, pp. 339–456 for 'The Waterloo Journal', and pp. 474–541 for 'Journey to Trèves, 1815', written between 1823 and 1825.

8. FBA to Charlotte Broome, 20 October 1815, JL, IX, p. 2. After her first husband's death in 1792 Charlotte Francis had married Ralph Broome in 1798. 'Cruelly changed' comes from a letter to James Burney, ibid., p. 1.

9. The business of the sale threatened Fanny's friendship with Fredy, since the d'Arblays believed that they had been given a 99-year lease on the land by William Locke's father. But there was no legal documentation to support the d'Arblays, and they had to accept an offer from William of £700 for the property, which Fredy thought generous though it was less than the building cost of the cottage.

10. See Graham Davis and Penny Bonsall, *Bath: a New History*, Keele, University Press, 1996, pp. 63–73.

11. FBA to James Burney, 22–9 November 1815, JL, IX, p. 24.

12. FBA to HRH Princess Elizabeth, pre-29 November 1815, JL, IX, p. 12.

13. FBA to Margaret Planta, 27 April 1802, JL, V, p. 290. Though these fashions were also being adopted in England, hoops continued *de rigueur* at court.

14. Quoted in a letter from Charlotte Barrett to her sister Marianne Francis, 26 August 1812, Bar.Eg. 3702A, f. 162.

15. William Beattie (ed.), *The Life and Letters of Thomas Campbell*, 3 vols, Edward Moxon 1849, II, p. 225.

16. HRH Princess Elizabeth to FBA, 28 December 1814, quoted JL, VIII, p. 7, n. 1.

17. HRH Princess Elizabeth to FBA, 2–3 June 1815, quoted in JL, VIII, p. 201, n. 13.

18. FBA to HRH Princess Elizabeth, 20 June 1815, JL, VIII, pp. 222–3.

19. FBA to Alexander d'Arblay, 9 November 1817, JL, X, p. 748.

20. FBA to HRH Princess Elizabeth, 27 December 1817, JL, X, p. 763.

21. FBA to Alexander d'Arblay, *c.* 30 November 1817, JL, X, p. 755.

22. JL, X, pp. 847–8. Between November 1818 and March 1820 Fanny wrote her 'Narrative of the Last Illness and Death of General d'Arblay' to exemplify his father's courage for Alex and as a 'relief' and 'solace' to herself.

23. Ibid., p. 850.
24. From 'The Bath Pump Room'. The attack was made on the Queen for her perceived insensitivity to the death of Princess Charlotte by returning so rapidly to Bath after her death.
25. Quoted from a letter in 1842 of a Dr Jones to Charlotte Barrett, Fanny's niece and editor of her journals, in JL, XII, p. 968, n. 4.
26. Rumours about Princesses making secret marriages (Elizabeth, Augusta) or giving birth to unacknowledged offspring (Elizabeth, Sophia) are accepted in Marples, *Six Royal Sisters*, but treated with a little more caution in Stuart, *The Daughters of George III*; a union between Princess Augusta and the Irish Major-General Sir Brent Spencer seems more plausible than the others.
27. HRH Princess Elizabeth to FBA, 17 March 1818, quoted JL, X, pp. 824–5, n. 1.
28. FBA to HRH Princess Elizabeth, 23–4 March 1818, JL, X, pp. 826–7.
29. For details see Stuart, *The Daughters of George III*, pp. 178–84, and Marples, *Six Royal Sisters*, pp. 155–60. Despite many chauvinist jokes about the Prince's size, his smoking, and his alleged uncleanliness, the Princess, who became Landgravine of Hesse-Homburg, adored her husband and her marriage was a happy one. When he died in 1829 she did not return to England.
30. See Hedley, pp. 293–8.
31. FBA to Esther Burney, December 1818, JL, XI, p. 32.
32. DL, VI, pp. 378–80.
33. *The Daughters of George III*, p. 10.
34. Hester Piozzi to James Fellowes, 15 October 1818, quoted JL, X, p. 918, n. 2.
35. Hester Piozzi to FBA, DL, VI, p. 392.
36. George III lingered on till 1820; George IV died in 1830, and William IV in 1837. He was succeeded by Queen Victoria, daughter of the 4th son, Edward Duke of Kent. Princesses Sophia (d. 1846) and Mary, Duchess of Gloucester (d. 1857), could both have read of themselves in Fanny's journals, though they would have had to be read to the blind Princess Sophia. Sheila de Bellaigue, Registrar of the Royal Archives, kindly informs me that in letters of Princess Mary to Queen Victoria no references to Fanny have been identified.

    Fanny was also outlived by George Cambridge (d. 1841) who is said to have come to the house as she was on her death bed.
37. For the controversy surrounding the d'Arblay graves and monuments see 'D'Arblay Gravestones in Bath', JL, XII, pp. 982–9, and Maggie Lane, *A City of Palaces: Bath through the Eyes of Fanny Burney*, Bath, Millstream Books, 1999, pp. 85–90.
38. JL, XII, pp. 974–5.
39. See JL, IX, pp. 8–9, n. 12.
40. Lewis et al., *Horace Walpole's Correspondence with Hannah More et al*, letter to Hannah More of 12 July 1788, p. 271.
41. In 1993 Alan Coveney directed a performance of *A Busy Day* in Bristol that was so successful that it was revived in 1994 at the King's Head Theatre in Islington. Critics were generally enthusiastic: 'robust, well-plotted piece',

wrote Michael Billington in the *Guardian*, while Irving Wardle in the
Independent on Sunday called it an 'uproarious and warm-hearted comedy'.
There has been a new production at the Old Bristol Vic in April 2000. See
Peter Sabor (ed.), *The Complete Plays of Frances Burney*, 2 vols, William
Pickering, 1995, pp. xi–xii, and 290–1.
42. 16 February 1790, DL, IV, pp. 353–4.

APPENDIX

1. 12 August 1792, DL, II, p. 94.
2. Letter to Molesworth Phillips quoted in Richard Walker, *Regency Portraits*,
   National Portrait Gallery, 1985, I, p. 146.
3. Quoted in Hemlow, p. 156.
4. Ibid. Aileen Ribeiro discusses contemporary theories of painting dress in
   portraits, including 'Painters imaginary dress' (Reynolds' phrase), in *The Art
   of Dress: Fashion in England and France 1750–1820*, New Haven and London,
   Yale University Press, 1997, pp. 6–28.
5. This painting is an oil version of one of four watercolours in which he
   'satirizes contemporary musical and social life', the theme being 'the battle
   between "traditional" and "modern taste" in the musical world', possibly
   influenced by Dr Burney's opinions (Robin Hamlyn, The National Art
   Collection Fund, 1997 Review, pp. 100–1). A sketch called *The Practical Joker* is
   figure 10 in Doody's *Frances Burney*.
6. For details of the affair see M.J. Levy, *The Mistresses of King George IV*, Peter
   Owen Publishers, 1996, pp. 13–29. The Reynolds portrait can be seen at
   Waddesdon Manor in Buckinghamshire (National Trust). The many portraits
   of Mrs Robinson are illustrated and discussed in John Ingamells,
   Mrs Robinson and her Portraits, The Trustees of the Wallace Collection, 1978.
7. Mary Robinson published collections of poems in 1775 and 1777 (with the
   support of Georgiana, Duchess of Devonshire) but these were little known;
   her later verse was admired by Coleridge. Her novels are out of print but her
   poetry can be read in Judith Pascoe (ed.), *Mary Robinson: Selected Poems*,
   Ontario, Canada, Broadview Press Ltd, 2000.
8. Vincenzo Lunardi (1759–1806), secretary to the Neapolitan Embassy in
   London, made the first ascent by hydrogen balloon in England on
   15 September 1784. His red and blue balloon (with oars) lifted off from the
   Artillery ground at Moorfields, and he was seen waving a flag as he flew over
   London. He touched down at North Mimms and finally landed at Standon in
   Hertfordshire. A pigeon, which flew away, and a cat and dog went with him.

   Dr Burney watched the take-off, Charlotte Burney saw the balloon sail over
   her head while walking in a garden with friends, George Cambridge followed
   it on horseback '& at Ware conversed with the Aerial Traveller' (Alvaro
   Ribeiro (ed.), *The Letters of Dr Charles Burney Vol. 1 1751–1784*, Oxford,
   Clarendon Press, 1991, p. 442).

9. Journal-letter to SBP, 12 October 1779, EJL, III, p. 370.

10. Quoted in Hemlow, p. 157. Anna Laetitia Barbauld (1743–1825) was an influential children's writer, a poet, anthologist and editor of Richardson's correspondence.

11. Ibid., p. 156, n. 1. Margaret Anne Doody quotes for 28 June 1783: 'I sat for the last Time to Mr Bogle, & my miniature is now improved into a flattered Picture' (*Frances Burney*, p. 153).

12. Daphne Foskett, *Collecting Miniatures*, Woodbridge, Baron Publishing, 1979, p. 204.

13. May 1791, DL, IV, p. 460, and journal-letter to SBP, September 1778, EJL, III, p. 137.

Select Bibliography

Unless otherwise stated, the place of publication is London.

WORKS OF FRANCES BURNEY, MADAME D'ARBLAY

Novels

Camilla or A Picture of Youth, edited with an introduction by Edward A. Bloom and Lillian D. Bloom, World's Classics Edition, Oxford University Press, 1972

Cecilia, or Memoirs of an Heiress, edited by Peter Sabor and Margaret Anne Doody with an introduction by Margaret Anne Doody, World's Classics Edition, Oxford University Press, 1988

Evelina, or, the History of a Young Lady's Entrance into the World, edited by Stewart J. Cooke, Norton Critical Edition, New York and London, W.W. Norton & Company, 1998

The Wanderer; or Female Difficulties, edited by Margaret Anne Doody, Robert L. Mack, and Peter Sabor with an introduction by Margaret Anne Doody, World's Classics Edition, Oxford University Press, 1991

Plays

A Busy Day, edited by Tara Ghoshal Wallace, New Brunswick, Rutgers University Press, 1984

The Complete Plays of Frances Burney, edited by Peter Sabor, 2 vols, William Pickering, 1995

Edwy and Elgiva, edited with an introduction by Miriam J. Benkowitz, Skidmore College, Hamden, Shoestring Press, 1957

Memoirs

Memoirs of Dr Burney arranged from his own manuscripts, from family papers, and from personal recollections, by his daughter, Madame d'Arblay, 3 vols, Edward Moxon, 1832

Letters and Journals

The Diary & Letters of Madame d'Arblay (1778–1840), edited by Charlotte Barrett, 7 vols, Henry Colburn, 1842–6

—— with preface and notes by Austin Dobson, 6 vols, Macmillan and Co. Ltd, 1904–5

The Early Diary of Frances Burney 1768–1778, edited by Annie Raine Ellis, 2 vols, G. Bell & Sons Ltd, 1913 (first published 1889)

The Early Journals and Letters of Fanny Burney 1768–1791, vols 1 and 2 edited by Lars E. Troide, vol. 3 edited by Lars E. Troide and Stewart J. Cooke, Oxford, Clarendon Press, 1988–94 (and ongoing)

Fanny Burney and the Burneys, edited by R. Brimley Johnson, Stanley Paul & Co. Ltd, 1926

The Journals and Letters of Fanny Burney (Madame d'Arblay) 1791–1840, edited by Joyce Hemlow et al., 12 vols, Oxford, Clarendon Press, 1972–84

BIOGRAPHY AND CRITICISM

Adelstein, Michael E., *Fanny Burney*, New York, Twayne Publishers Inc., 1968

Baldwin, Louis, *One Woman's Liberation: The Story of Fanny Burney*, Wakefield, New Hampshire, Longwood Academic, 1990

Chisholm, Kate, *Fanny Burney: Her Life 1752–1840*, Chatto & Windus, 1998

Doody, Margaret Anne, *Frances Burney: The Life in the Works*, New Brunswick, Rutgers University Press, 1988

Epstein, Julia, *The Iron Pen: Frances Burney and the Politics of Women's Writing*, Bristol Classical Press, 1989

Farr, Evelyn, *The World of Fanny Burney*, Peter Owen, 1993

Gerin, Winifred, *The Young Fanny Burney*, Thomas Nelson and Sons, 1961

Hahn, Emily, *A Degree of Prudery*, Arthur Barker Ltd, 1951

Hemlow, Joyce, *The History of Fanny Burney*, Oxford, Clarendon Press, 1958

—— (edited with Jeanne M. Burgess and Althea Douglas), *A Catalogue of the Burney Family Correspondence 1749–1878*, New York Public Library, 1971

——, 'Fanny Burney: Playwright', in *University of Toronto Quarterly*, 19 (1950), 170–89

Hill, Constance, *Juniper Hall: A Rendez-Vous of Certain Illustrious Personages during the French Revolution including Alexandre d'Arblay and Fanny Burney*, John Lane, The Bodley Head Ltd, 1904

——, *The House in St Martin's Street: being Chronicles of the Burney Family*, John Lane, The Bodley Head Ltd, 1907

——, *Fanny Burney at the Court of Queen Charlotte*, John Lane, The Bodley Head Ltd, 1914

Howells, Coral Ann, '"The proper education of a female . . . is still to seek": Childhood and Girls' Education in Fanny Burney's *Camilla; or, A Picture of Youth*', in *The British Journal for Eighteenth-Century Studies* 7 (1984), 191–8.

Keener, Frederick M., and Lorsch, Susan E. (eds), *Eighteenth-Century Women and the Arts*, Westport, Connecticut, Greenwood Press, 1988

Lane, Maggie, *A City of Palaces: Bath through the Eyes of Fanny Burney*, Bath, Millstream Books, 1999

Lonsdale, Roger, *Dr. Charles Burney: A Literary Biography*, Oxford, Clarendon Press, 1965

Rogers, Katherine M., *Frances Burney: The World of Female Difficulties*, Hemel Hempstead, Harvester Wheatsheaf, 1990

Simons, Judy, *Women Writers: Fanny Burney*, Basingstoke, Macmillan Ltd, 1987

Spencer, Jane, *The Rise of the Woman Novelist: From Aphra Behn to Jane Austen*, Oxford, Basil Blackwell Ltd, 1986

Spender, Dale, *Mothers of the Novel: 100 good women writers before Jane Austen*, London and New York, Routledge & Kegan Paul, 1986

Wiltshire, John, 'Fanny Burney's face, Madame D'Arblay's veil', in Marie Mulvey Roberts and Roy Porter (eds), *Literature & Medicine during the Eighteenth Century*, Routledge, 1993, 245–65

THE ROYAL FAMILY AND THE COURT

Arch, Nigel, and Marschner, Joanna, *Splendour at Court: Dressing for Royal Occasions since 1700*, Unwin Hyman, 1987

Aspinall, A. (ed.), *The Correspondence of George, Prince of Wales 1770–1812*, 8 vols, especially vol. I 1770–89, Cassell & Company Ltd, 1963

——, *The Later Correspondence of George III*, 5 vols, especially vol. I December 1783–January 1793, Cambridge University Press, 1966

Ayling, Stanley, *George the Third*, Collins, 1972

Brooke, John, *King George III*, Constable, 1972

Clarke, John, *The Life and Times of George III*, Weidenfeld & Nicolson Ltd, 1972

Colvin, H.M. (gen. ed.), *The History of the King's Works: The Royal Palaces 1660–1782*, HMSO, 1976

Glasheen, Joan, *The Secret People of the Palaces: The Royal Household from the Plantagenets to Queen Victoria*, B.T. Batsford Ltd, 1998

Greville, Robert Fulke, *The Diaries of Colonel the Hon. Robert Fulke Greville, Equerry to His Majesty King George III*, edited by F. McKno Bladon, John Lane, The Bodley Head Ltd, 1930

Harcourt, Edward William, *The Harcourt Papers*, 8 vols, Oxford, James Parker & Co., 1880

Harcourt, Elizabeth Countess of, 'Mrs Harcourt's Journals', in *Miscellanies of the Philobiblon Society*, XIII, Whittingham & Wilkins, 1871–2

Hedley, Olwen, *Queen Charlotte*, John Murray, 1975

——, *Windsor Castle*, revised paperback edition, Harmondsworth, Allen Lane, 1977

——, 'Mrs Delany's Windsor Home', in *The Berkshire Archaeological Journal*, 59 (1961), 51–5

Hibbert, Christopher, *George IV*, Harmondsworth, Penguin Books Ltd, 1976

——, *The Court at Windsor: A Domestic History* (revised edition), Harmondsworth, Allen Lane, 1977

——, *George III: A Personal History*, Viking, 1998

Llewellyn, Sacha, 'George III and the Windsor Uniform', in *The Court Historian*, Newsletter of the Society for Court Studies 2 (1996), 12–16

Macalpine, Ida, and Hunter, Richard, *George III and the Mad Business*, Harmondsworth, Allen Lane, The Penguin Press, 1969

MacDonogh, Katharine, *Reigning Cats and Dogs: A History of Pets at Court since the Renaissance*, Fourth Estate Ltd, 1999

Marples, Morris, *Six Royal Sisters: Daughters of George III*, Michael Joseph, 1969

Moreau, Simon, *A Tour to the Royal Spa at Cheltenham*, Bath, R. Crutwell, 1789

Morris, Marilyn, *The British Monarchy and the French Revolution*, New Haven and London, Yale University Press, 1998

Morshead, Sir Owen, *Windsor Castle*, Phaidon Press, 1957

Pedicord, Harry William, *'By Their Majesties' Command': The House of Hanover at the London Theatres, 1714–1800*, The Society for Theatre Research, 1991

Pyne, W.H., *History of the Royal Residences*, 3 vols, A. Dry, 1819

Reese, M.M., *The Royal Office of Master of the Horse*, Threshold Books Ltd, 1976

Roberts, Jane, *Views of Windsor: Watercolours by Thomas and Paul Sandby from the Collection of Her Majesty the Queen*, Merrell Holberton, 1995

Röhl, John C.G., Warren, Martin, and Hunt, David, *Purple Secret: Genes, 'Madness' and the Royal Houses of Europe*, London, New York, Toronto, Sydney, Auckland, Bantam Press, Transworld Publishers Ltd, 1998

Somerset, Anne, *The Life and Times of William IV*, Weidenfeld & Nicolson, 1980

——, *Ladies in Waiting: From the Tudors to the Present Day*, Weidenfeld & Nicolson, 1984

Stuart, Dorothy Margaret, *The Daughters of George III*, Macmillan and Co., 1939

Taylor, Joseph, *Relics of Royalty: or Remarks, Anecdotes, and Amusements, of His Late Most Gracious Majesty, George III*, A.K. Newman & Co., 1820

Tomalin, Claire, *Mrs Jordan's Profession: The story of a great actress and a future King*, Viking, 1994

Trench, Charles Chenevix, *The Royal Malady*, Longmans, 1964

Van der Kiste, John, *George III's Children*, Stroud, Sutton Publishing Ltd, 1999

Walker, Richard, *Regency Portraits*, 2 vols, National Portrait Gallery, 1985

—— (ed.), *Miniatures in the Collection of Her Majesty the Queen: The Eighteenth and Early Nineteenth Centuries*, Cambridge University Press, 1992

Watkins, John, *Memoirs of Her Most Excellent Majesty Sophia-Charlotte, Queen of Great Britain*, Henry Colburn, 1819

Yorke, Philip (ed.), *Letters of Princess Elizabeth of England, Daughter of King George III, and Landgravine of Hesse-Homburg*, T. Fisher Unwin, 1898

Ziegler, Philip, *King William IV*, Collins, 1971

SOCIAL, CULTURAL AND HISTORICAL BACKGROUND

Anon, *The History of the Trial of Warren Hastings Esq.*, J. Debrett, 1796

Ashelford, Jane, *The Art of Dress: Clothes and Society 1500–1914*, The National Trust, 1996

Attwooll, Maureen, and West, Jack, *Seaside Weymouth: A Celebration in Pictures*, Wimborne, The Dovecote Press Ltd, 1989

Barker, Hannah, and Chalus, Elaine (eds), *Gender in Eighteenth-Century England: Roles, Representations and Responsibilities*, Harlow, Longman Ltd, 1997

Blake, Steven, and Beacham, Roger, *The Book of Cheltenham*, Buckingham, Barracuda Books Ltd, 1982

Blomfield, David, *Kew Past*, Chichester, Phillimore & Co. Ltd, 1994

Bond, E.A., *The Speeches of the Managers and Counsel in the Trial of Warren Hastings*, 4 vols, Longman, 1859–61

Boswell, James, *The Life of Samuel Johnson, LL.D.* (with an introduction by Angus Calder), Ware, Wordsworth Editions Ltd, 1999

Brewer, John, *The Pleasures of the Imagination: English Culture in the Eighteenth Century*, HarperCollins, 1997

Buck, Anne, *Dress in Eighteenth-Century England*, B.T. Batsford Ltd, 1979

Burney, Charles, *Memoirs of Dr. Charles Burney 1726–1769*, edited by Slava Klima, Garry Baers, and Kerry S. Grant, Lincoln and London, University of Nebraska Press, 1988

——, *The Letters of Dr Charles Burney, Vol. 1 1751–1784*, edited by Alvaro Ribeiro, Oxford, Clarendon Press, 1991

Burney, Sarah Harriet, *The Letters of Sarah Harriet Burney*, edited by Lorna F. Clark, Athens, Georgia University Press, 1997

Byng, John Viscount Torrington, *The Torrington Diaries*, edited by C. Bruyn Andrews and abridged by Fanny Andrews, Eyre & Spottiswoode, 1954

Clifford, James L., *Hester Lynch Piozzi (Mrs Thrale)*, Oxford, Clarendon Press, 1968.

Cunnington, C. Willett, and Cunnington, Phillis, *Handbook of English Costume in the 18th Century*, Faber & Faber Ltd, 1957

Donald, Diana, *The Age of Caricature: Satirical Prints in the Reign of George III*, New Haven and London, Yale University Press, 1996

Donkin, Ellen, *Getting into the Act: Women Playwrights in London 1776–1829*, Routledge, 1995

Draper, Jo, *Discover Dorset: The Georgians*, Wimborne, The Dovecote Press Ltd, 1998

Ellis, George Alfred, *Ellis's History of Antiquities of the Borough and Town of Weymouth and Melcombe Regis*, Weymouth, B. Benson, 1829

Elwin, Malcolm, *The Noels and the Milbankes: Their Letters for Twenty-Five Years 1767–1824*, Macdonald, 1967

Feeling, Keith, *Warren Hastings*, Macmillan and Co., 1954

Fergus, Jan, and Thaddeus, Janice Farrar, 'Women, Publishers, and Money, 1790–1820', in *Studies in Eighteenth-Century Culture* 17 (1988), 191–208

Ford, Boris (ed.), *The Cambridge Cultural History of Britain, Vol. 5: Eighteenth-Century Britain*, Cambridge University Press, 1992

Foreman, Amanda, *Georgiana Duchess of Devonshire*, HarperCollins, 1998

Granville, Mary (Mrs Delany), *The Autobiography and Correspondence of Mary Granville, Mrs Delany; with interesting reminiscences of King George III and Queen Charlotte*, edited by Augusta, Lady Llanover, 6 vols, Richard Bentley, 1861–2

——, *Mrs Delany at Court and among the Wits*, edited with an introduction by R. Brimley Johnson, Stanley Paul & Co., 1925

Girouard, Mark, *Life in the English Country House: A Social and Architectural History*, New Haven and London, Yale University Press, 1978

Harcourt, Amédée and Sophia, *The Harcourt Journals and St Leonard's Hill, Windsor: The Memoirs and Diaries of General Amédée and Sophia d'Harcourt*, translated and edited by Sheila and Pat Rooney, Windsor Local History Publications Group, 1998

Hart, Gwen, *A History of Cheltenham*, Gloucester, Alan Sutton, 1981

Hayden, Ruth, *Mrs Delany and her flower collages*, British Museum Press, new edition, 1992

Hibbert, Christopher, *The French Revolution*, Harmondsworth, Penguin Books Ltd, 1982

Hogan, Charles Beecher (edited with a critical introduction), *The London Stage 1660–1800: A Calendar of Plays, Entertainments & Afterpieces together with Casts, Box-Receipts and Contemporary Comment, Part 5: 1776–1800*, 3 vols, Carbondale, Illinois, Southern Illinois University Press, 1968

Hyde, Mary, *The Thrales of Streatham Park*, Cambridge, Massachusetts, Harvard University Press, 1977

Jackson, Alan A., *Dorking: a Surrey Market Town through twenty centuries*, Dorking, Local History Group of the Dorking and District Preservation Society, 1991

Johnson, Samuel, *The Letters of Samuel Johnson 1731–1772*, 5 vols, edited by Bruce Redford, Oxford, Clarendon Press, 1992–4

Jones, M.G., *Hannah More*, Cambridge University Press, 1952

Kelly, Linda, *The Kemble Era: John Philip Kemble, Sarah Siddons and the London Stage*, The Bodley Head, 1980

——, *Juniper Hall: An English Refuge from the French Revolution*, Weidenfeld & Nicolson, 1991

——, *Richard Brinsley Sheridan: A Life*, Sinclair-Stevenson, 1997

Knight, Charles (senior), *The Windsor Guide; containing a Description of the Town and Castle etc.*, Windsor, C. Knight, 1793

Knight, Charles, *Passages of a Working Life during Half a Century: with A Prelude of Early Reminiscences*, 3 vols, Bradbury & Evans, 1864

Lane, Margaret, *Samuel Johnson & his World*, New York and London, Harper & Row, 1975

Lubbock, Constance A. (ed.), *The Herschel Chronicle: The Life-Story of William Herschel and his Sister Caroline Herschel*, Cambridge University Press, 1933

Manvell, Roger, *Elizabeth Inchbald: England's Principal Woman Dramatist and Independent Woman of Letters in 18th Century London: A Biographical Study*, Lanham, Maryland, University Press of America, 1987

Marshall, Dorothy, *Eighteenth Century England*, Longman Group Ltd, 1962

Marshall, P.J., *The Impeachment of Warren Hastings*, Oxford University Press, 1965

Moon, Penderel, *Warren Hastings and British India*, Hodder & Stoughton Ltd, 1947

Murray, Venetia, *High Society: A Social History of the Regency Period, 1788–1830*, Viking, 1998

Paston, George, *Sidelights on the Georgian Period*, Methuen and Co. Ltd, 1902

Porter, Agnes, *A Governess in the Age of Jane Austen: The Journals and Letters of Agnes Porter*, edited by Joanna Martin, The Hambledon Press, 1998

Porter, Roy, *English Society in the Eighteenth Century* (The Penguin Social History of Britain), Harmondsworth, Penguin Books Ltd, 1990 (revised edition)

——, *The Greatest Benefit to Mankind: A Medical History of Humanity from Antiquity to the Present*, HarperCollins, 1997

Reeby, Margot, *Taking the Waters at Weymouth*, Weymouth, Spa Publications, 1995

Ribeiro, Aileen, *The Art of Dress: Fashion in England and France 1750–1820*, New Haven and London, Yale University Press, 1995

Rivers, Isabel (ed.), *Books and their Readers in Eighteenth-Century England*, Leicester, Leicester University Press, 1982

Roche, Sophie von la, *Sophie in London 1786, being the Diary of Sophie v. la Roche*, translated and with an introduction by Clare Williams, Jonathan Cape, 1933

Sermoneta, Vittoria Duchess of, *The Locks of Norbury: The Story of a remarkable family in the XVIIIth and XIXth centuries*, John Murray, 1940

Shepperd, Ronald, *Micklam: The Story of a Parish*, Mickleham Publications, 1991

Swann, June, *Shoes*, B.T. Batsford, 1982

Thrale, Hester, *Thraliana: The Diary of Mrs Hester Lynch Thrale (Later Mrs Piozzi) 1776–1809*, edited by Katharine C. Balderston, 2 vols, Oxford, Clarendon Press, 1942

Thrale, Hester Maria, *The Queeney Letters, Being letters addressed to Hester Maria Thrale by Doctor Johnson, Fanny Burney and Mrs Thrale-Piozzi*, edited by the Marquis of Lansdowne, Cassell & Co., 1934

Tillyard, Stella, *Aristocrats: Caroline, Emily, Louisa and Sarah Lennox 1740–1832*, Vintage, 1995

Todd, Janet, *Sensibility: An Introduction*, Methuen and Co. Ltd, 1986

Vickery, Amanda, *The Gentleman's Daughter: Women's Lives in Georgian England*, New Haven and London, Yale University Press, 1998

Vulliamy, C.E., *Aspasia: The Life and Letters of Mary Granville, Mrs Delany, 1700–1788*, Geoffrey Bles, 1925

Wild, Anthony, *The East India Company: Trade and Conquest from 1600*, HarperCollins*Illustrated*, 1999

Windham, William, *The Windham Papers: The Life and Correspondence of the Rt. Hon. William Windham 1750–1810*, with an introduction by the Rt. Hon. The Earl of Rosebery, Herbert Jenkins Ltd, 1913

——, *The Diary of the Right Hon. William Windham, 1784–1810*, edited by Mrs Henry Baring, Longmans, Green, & Co., 1860

Woodforde, James, *The Diary of a Country Parson 1758–1802*, selected and edited by John Beresford, Oxford University Press, 1978

Index

Alexander I, Czar of Russia, 180

Allen, Elizabeth, step-sister, 3

Allen, Maria, later Rishton, step-sister, 3, 12

Allen, Stephen, step-brother, 3

Amelia, Princess (1783–1810), 21, 119, 178, 189, 203 n.19; with FB: 40–1, 54–5, 82, 146, 163, 171, 175; *see also* Princesses

Ancaster, Mary Duchess of, 42, 47–8

Anne, Queen, 18

d'Arblay, Alexander (1794–1837), son, 6, 88–9, 99, 167, 170, 174–5, 177–8, 182–3, 185–7

d'Arblay, Alexandre (1754–1818), husband, 12, 165–8, 170–2, 175–9, 181, 183, 186, 219–20 n.11, 220 n.16, 221 n.2

d'Arblay, Frances, *see* Burney

Astley, Anne, later Agnew, 17, 81, 86, 207 n.23

Augusta Sophia, Princess (1768–1840), 20, 57, 59, 121, 223 n.26; with FB: 36, 54, 56, 71, 74, 101, 147, 174, 180, 187; *see also* Princesses

Austen, Jane, 98 (*Persuasion*), 169, 220–1 n.29

Badine, Queen's spaniel, 35, 54, 127

Baker, Sir George, 91

Banks, Sir Joseph, 16, 70

Barbauld, Mrs Anna Laetitia, 192, 225 n.10

Baretti, Giuseppe, 24, 90, 199 n.33

Barlow, Thomas, 11, 197 n.40

Barrett, Charlotte, née Francis, niece, xii–xiv, 78, 89

Bath, 11, 19, 163, 177, 179, 181–5, 187

Battiscombe, Robert, 73, 108–9, 211 n.11, 212 n.37

Bedlam, 43, 66–7, 205 n.6

Begums, Indian princesses, 157, 218 n.28

Bertie, Charlotte, Lady, 42, 47

Blenheim Palace, 50

'Blue Stockings', 9, 16, 76, 196–7 n.31

Bogle, John, 192–3

Boringdon, John Parker, Lord, 128, 214 n.26

Boscawen, Honourable Mrs Frances, 76, 220 n.26

Boswell, James, 141

Brown, 'Capability', 50

Brussels, 178, 181

Bryant, Jacob, 72–3, 206 n.33

Budé, General, 53, 107, 203 n.12

Bunbury, Henry, 74–5

Burke, Edmund, admirer of FB: 2, 31, 168–9, 220 n.17; politician: 148–9, 150–2, 155–61

Burke, Richard (Edmund's brother), 152, 160

Burke, Richard (Edmund's son), 152, 160

Burney, Ann and Rebecca, aunts, 68

Burney, Dr Charles (1726–1814), father, 1–7, 10–11, 29–30, 33, 47, 162, 178; FB's writing: 2, 9, 69, 178; her court appointment: 30–2, 73, 138–9, 141–3, 146; French Revolution: 164–5; FB's marriage: 167; letters to and from FB: 15, 22, 44, 50, 172

Burney, Charles (1757–1817), brother,
   1, 3, 144, 151, 153, 167–8, 183
Burney, Charles Rousseau, cousin, 3
Burney, Charlotte Ann, later Francis
   then Broome (1761–1838), sister, 1,
   3, 31, 78, 114, 141–2, 186, 222 n.8
Burney, Edward Francesco (1760–1848),
   cousin, ix, 1, 191–3, 224 n.5
Burney, Elizabeth, formerly Mrs Allen
   (1725–96), step-mother, 1, 3
Burney, Esther (1723–62), née Sleepe,
   mother, 3
Burney, Esther, 'Hetty' (1749–1832),
   sister, 1, 3, 6, 13, 26–7, 73, 121, 126,
   186
Burney, Frances, Madame d'Arblay
   (1752–1840), appearance: 3, 33,
   192–3; personality: 3–4, 6–9, 17, 22,
   25, 62, 66, 76–7, 111, 137, 172, 180,
   189–90; personal qualities:
   abstemiousness: 34–5, 65, 75–6, 186,
   compassion: 3, 17, 62, 86, 100,
   106–7, 140, 165, 167, 181, 184, lack
   of penetration: 9, 159, 173–4, moral
   delicacy: 52–3, 68–9, 100, 163, 165,
   religious faith: 72, 86, 95, 115, 187,
   social uncertainty: 8, 35, 40–1, 44–6,
   51, 67–8, 89, 122, 127, witness
   reliability: 6–7, 81, 89, 152, 160;
   men and marriage: 11–13, 132; for
   relationships with family, friends,
   royals and courtiers see entries
   under individuals
At court: accommodation: 32–3, 92,
   112, 125, 128; duties: 34–9, 56–8;
   terms of employment: 30; thoughts
   on dress: 10, 36–40, 57, 66, 174;
   equerries: 59, 62, 82–4, etiquette:
   23, 26–8, 47–9, 57, 70; reading to
   royalty: 69–70; 'servitude': 35, 51,
   134, 139; discretion: 33, 52, 173;
   illnesses: 52, 73, 101–2, 116, 123,
   116, 123, 142–3; secret journal
   writing: 33–4; theatre visits: 68–9,
   100, 126

Works: *Evelina*: 1–3, 7, 9–11, 24, 36, 39,
   65, 72, 132, 166–7, 195 n.2, 196
   n.23, 201 n.32, 205 n.12; *Cecilia*:
   10–12, 59, 69, 72, 131–2, 137, 166,
   168, 188, 1919, 205 nn.12, 16, 214
   n.42, 221 n.29; *Camilla*: 36, 41, 89,
   168–73, 175, 188, 205 n.12, 207
   n.19, 220 n.25, 29, 221 nn.31, 32;
   The Wanderer: 30, 178, 205 n.12, 222
   n.6; plays: *The Witlings*: 9, 188, *Edwy
   and Elgiva*: 167–8, 211 n.3,
   tragedies: 105, 110, 188, 216 n.20,
   comedies: *A Busy Day*: 188, 223–4
   n.41, *Love and Fashion*: 188, *The
   Woman-Hater*: 188; *Brief Reflexions*:
   167; *Memoirs*: 11, 80–1, 89, 186;
   Diary & Letters: xii–xiii, 89
Observed by others: Barlow: 11,
   Burke: 31, Dr Burney: 4, Esther
   Burney's suitor: 6, Sarah Burney: 8,
   Susan Burney: 4, Campbell: 180,
   Chapone: 31, 77, Queen Charlotte:
   11, 33, 52, 144, Delany: 17, 82, 86,
   Digby: 134, Francis: 180, Greville:
   118, Johnson: 7, Llanover: 83,
   89–90, von la Roche: 66–7, Thrale:
   7–11, 13, 31, 185, Walpole: 76–7,
   140, 188, Windham: 141–2
Burney, James, 'Jem' (1750–1821),
   brother, 3, 5, 10–11, 129, 144, 156,
   158, 167, 187
Burney, Richard Gustavus, cousin, 100–1
Burney, Richard, half-brother, 3
Burney, Sarah Harriet (1772–1844),
   half-sister, 3, 8, 162, 166, 186
Burney, Susanna Elizabeth, 'Susan',
   later Phillips (1755–1800), sister:
   1–4, 6, 8, 73, 75, 138, 141–3, 166–7,
   170, 177, 186; correspondence with
   FB: 8, 10, 12, 15, 26, 32–4, 37, 52,
   84–5, 155, 164, 175–6, 209 n.25;
   marriage: 11, 14, 25, 175, 177; on
   Digby: 98, 122–3, 138; court
   nicknames: 59–60, 85, 93, 138, 180
Brighton (Brighthelmstone), 74, 124

Cambridge, Charlotte, 12, 31, 121
Cambridge, George Owen, 12–13, 31, 132, 164, 186, 219 n.6, 223 n.36
Cambridge, Richard Owen, 12, 40, 76, 149
Cambridge University, 3, 144, 178, 183
Camilla Cottage, West Humble, 175–6, 179, 222 n.9
Campbell, Thomas, 180
Caroline, Princess of Wales, mother of George III, 50
Caroline of Brunswick, Princess of Wales, 173, 180
Chapone, Hester, 16–17, 31, 76–7
Charlotte Sophia, Queen
  (1744–1818), 19–20; appearance, speech and dress: 20, 29, 33, 37–41, 63, 102, 127, 199 n.23, 203 n.11; daily routine: 34–9, 53; official duties: 10, 25, 56–7, 121–2; interests: books: 25, 52, botany and science: 16, 54, 70, 131, card-games: 54, dogs: 35, 72–3, jewelry: 56, needlework: 19, 40, 174, snuff: 35–6, theatre: 9, 68–70; satirised: ix–x, 183–4, 223 n.24; relationship with King: 19–20, 44, 46, 111–13, 118–19, 173, 185; response to King's illness: 106, 108–10, 119; relationships with children: 20–1, 172–4, 121, 184–5; opinion of FB: 11, 24–5, 35–6, 52, 57, 144, 147, 155–6, 159, 168, 173, 180, 185; treatment of FB: 32–3, 40–1, 51–3, 68–70, 73, 92, 100, 102–4, 116, 121, 139, 143–4, 146–8, 151, 163, 166–7, 170, 175, 187; friendship with Mrs Delany: 16–18, 21–2 (and see George III); with Lady Harcourt: 45–6; hostility to Marianne Port: 87–8; visits to Oxford: 46, Cheltenham: 92–3, 99, Weymouth: 126, Plymouth: 129 (and see George III); Bath visit: 181–4; death: 185; and *passim*

Charlotte Augusta Matilda
  (1766–1828), Princess Royal, 20, 56, 106, 121, 131, 173–4, 221 n.41; with FB: 35–7, 40–1, 52, 54, 101–2, 116, 147, 171; *see also* Princesses
Charlotte, daughter of Prince of Wales (1796–1817), 173, 182
Cheltenham, 87, 91–3, 99–104, 172
Chessington, 2, 4, 27, 68, 191
Clarence, William Duke of
  (1765–1837), later William IV, 21; with FB: 144–6, 182–3
Columb, Jacob, 92–3, 97, 99, 115, 138, 140, 212 n.35
Combe, Thomas, 97 (*Love Letters. . .*), 209 n.21
Cook, Captain James, 3, 5, 11, 66, 70, 205 n.5
Coombe, seat of Earl of Coventry, 96
costume, 5, 10, 36–41, 44, 47, 56–7, 121, 127, 129, 131, 164, 179–80, 191–3, 197 n.35, 201 n.32, 202 n.11, 222 n.13
Courtown, Lord, 93, 132–3
Courtown, Mary, Lady, 53, 70, 203 n.12
Crewe, Frances, 159, 219 n.36, 220 n.26
Crisp, Samuel, 2, 4–5, 7–9, 13, 27, 68, 191, 196 n.12
Crutchley, Jeremiah, 12
Cumberland, Henry Frederick Duke of, brother of George III, 57, 199 n.29, 204 n.26

Delany, Mrs Mary, née Granville
  (1700–88), 15–18, artistry: x, 16–17, 19, 36, 198 n.5; royal favourite: 16–18, 21–4, 41, 44, 79, 81–2; friendship with FB: 14, 16–18, 21–28, 31, 42, 68, 71–2, 80–1, 90; care of Marianne Port: 18, 82, 84–6; health: 21–2, 44, 78–80; death: 86, 89; and *passim*
Delany, Dr Patrick, 15–16

Devonshire, Georgiana Duchess of, 37,
   163, 169
Devonport ('Dock'), 128–30
Dewes, Bernard, and daughter Anne,
   22
Dewes, Court, 86
Digby, Charles, son of Stephen, 99,
   209 n.11
Digby, Charlotte, second wife of
   Stephen, *see* Gunning
Digby, Lord Henry, brother of
   Stephen, 94, 126–7
Digby, Lady Lucy (née
   Fox–Strangways), first wife of
   Stephen, 94–5, 122, 136, 172
Digby, Lady Mary, wife of Lord Digby,
   126–7
Digby, Colonel the Honourable
   Stephen (1742–1800), Queen's
   Vice-Chamberlain, 93–5, 209 nn.11,
   12, 14; royal service: 48–9, 61–2,
   101–4, 107, 110, 112–14, 122, 211
   n.14, 212 n.33; ill health: 95–7, 110,
   125, attentions to FB: 10, 05–0,
   102–3, 105, 107–8, 110–11, 114–6,
   122–3, 126–7, deteriorating
   relationship: 127–8, 131–5;
   marriage: 135–7; FB's hostility:
   136–8, 164; last meeting: 172;
   letter–writing: xi, 99, 103, 134, 138
Dorchester, 124

East India Company, 149, 217 n.3
Elizabeth I, 46, 217 n.3
Elizabeth, Princess (1770–1840), 20,
   121, 126, 184–5, 199 n.24, 223 n.26;
   with FB: 36–7, 45, 54, 101, 103, 147,
   172–3, 175, 179–82, 184–7; *see also*
   Princesses
etiquette at court, 22–3, 26–8, 42,
   46–50, 56–7, 67–8, 100, 103
Exeter, 128

Fauconberg Lodge, 91–2, 101, 208 n.2,
   210 n.44

Fiennes, Celia, 49
Finch, Charlotte, Lady, 33, 53, 119,
   203 n.12
de la Fite, Marie-Élizabeth, 42, 65–8,
   70, 79
Fitzherbert, Mrs Maria, 21, 152, 199
   n.29
Fox, Charles, 150–2, 156, 158–60, 163
Fox–Strangways, Lady Susan, 122,
   172, 221 n.37
Francis, Clement, husband of
   Charlotte Burney, 142–3, 150
Francis, Clement, son of the above,
   180
Francis, Philip, 149–50, 217 n.5
French Revolution, 53, 123–4, 126,
   158, 164–7, 177, 203 n.12
Frogmore House, 181

Garrick, David, 69–70, 100
Garrick, Mrs, 76
de Genlis, Stéphanie Félicité, 68, 205
   n.9
George I, 27
George III (1738–1820), appearance
   and manner: 20, 23–6, 47, 93, 127;
   abstinence and frugality: 34–5, 54,
   60–1; courage: 42–4; curiosity: 19,
   24–5; criticised: ix–x, 19, 35, 53, 61,
   75; interests: astronomy: 70–1, card-
   games: 54, farming: 19, hunting: 19,
   60–1, theatre: 68–70, 93, 100, 205
   n.14; opinion of Shakespeare: 25–6;
   relationship with Queen: 19–20, 54,
   113, 118, 212 n.36, with Princes: 21,
   57, 73–4, 101, 107, 121, 211 n.14,
   with Princesses: 21, 25–6, 55, 104,
   119, 172–3, with FB: 23–6, 30, 36,
   41, 52, 81–2, 95, 101–2, 106, 117–19,
   146–7, 159–60, 163, 170–2, 220
   n.25, with Mrs Delany: 14, 16–18,
   80–2, with Digby: 95–6, 102, 110–11,
   137, 212 n.33; illness: 91, 105–13,
   116–21, 178, 185, 189, 211 nn.11,
   20, 212 n.37; visits to Oxford: 44–7,

Cheltenham: 91–3, 96–7, 101–4;
Weymouth: 123–8, 133, Exeter: 128,
Plymouth: 128–31; trial of Warren
Hastings: 150, 159–60; and *passim*
Gillray, James, 35, 75
Gilpin, William, 34
Gloucester, 93, 100, 116
Gloucester, William Frederick Duke
of, husband of Princess Mary, 184
Gloucester, William Henry Duke of,
King's brother, 124
Gloucester Lodge, 124–6, 213 n.12
Goethe, 65
Goldsworthy, Martha, 33, 52, 59, 87,
108, 110, 119, 168, 207 n.26
Goldsworthy, Colonel Philip, 59–61,
63, 72–3, 79, 82–3, 85, 87–8, 107–8,
132–4, 146, 157, 168, 189, 208
n.34
Goter, 92, 115–16, 146
Great Bookham, 167
Greville, Colonel the Honourable
Robert Fulke, 59, 84, 94, 111, 116,
118, 169, 182, 207 n.16, 212 n.37
Grey, Honourable Charles, 151, 163
de Guiffardière, Reverend Charles, 51,
58–9, 64, 84, 189
Gunning, Charlotte, later Digby, 98,
111, 115, 122, 135–7, 172, 210 n.28,
215 nn.6, 12
Gunning, Sir Robert, 98, 134, 136, 210
n.27
Gwynn, Colonel Francis Edward, 59,
75, 98–9, 102, 135, 146, 157, 169
Gwynn, Mary, 75, 126–7, 169

Hagedorn, Mrs Johanna, 30, 62, 75
Handel, George Frederick, 10, 35, 54,
102, 138
Harcourt, George Simon, Lord, 44–5,
94, 169, 202 n.7
Harcourt, Elizabeth, Lady, 20, 44–6,
48, 94, 113, 169, 171
Harcourt, Mrs Elizabeth, 50, 109, 202
n.28, 212 nn.33, 36

Harcourt, General William, 50, 202
n.28
Hastings, Marian, 61–2, 150, 160, 169
Hastings, Warren, 61–2, 148–61, 217
nn.4, 11, 218 nn.16, 28, 31, 219 n.40
Hemlow, Joyce, xiii, 192, 207 n.19,
208, n.34
Henry VIII, 18, 47 (portrait), 58
Herschel, Caroline, 71, 206 n.29
Herschel, William, x, 70–2, 206 nn.27,
31
Hesse–Homburg, Duke of, 184, 223
n.29
Holcroft, Thomas, 69, 205 n.15
Holdernesse, Mary, Lady, 53, 203 n.12
Howard, John, 100, 210 n.34
Hutton, James, 206 n.34

von Imhoff, Baron, 150
Inchbald, Elizabeth, 69, 205 n.15
India, 148–61

Jacobi, Miss, 163
Johnson, Dr Samuel, ix, 2, 5–7, 13, 65,
67, 69, 141, 153, 193, 196 n.23
Jordan, Dora, 100, 210 n.32
Juniper Hall, 164–5, 219 n.7

Kemble, John Philip, 168
Kent, Edward Duke of, 4th son of
George III, 21, 223 n.36
Kew, Gardens: 16, 70, 117; Palace,
18, 114; the White House: 18, 33, 55,
85, 105, 112, 146, 185, 198 n.14
King's Lynn, 3
Knight, Charles, 18–19, 29

de Laclos, Choderlos, 165
de Lafayette, Marquis, 166
Larrey, Baron, 178
Llanover, Augusta, Lady, 35, 57, 81, 83,
88–90
Lock, Augusta and Amelia, 39
Lock, Mrs Frederica, 'Fredy'
(1750–1832), 13–14, 36, 39, 62, 157,

164, 166–7, 171, 186, 220 n.26, 222
n.9; visits to FB at court: 34, 68, 73,
75, 84–5, 121, 138, 143; recipient of
journals: 14, 32, 37, 52, 85, 138, 155
Lock, William, 13–14, 34, 68, 84, 121,
138, 164, 166, 175, 177–8
Locke, William, 84–5, 171, 179
Longleat, 15
Louis XVI, 124, 164–5
Louis XVIII, 178, 180, 187
Louis–Philippe, King of France, 184
Lower Lodge, Windsor, 18, 146
de Luc, André, 54, 64, 72, 75–6, 144–5
de Luc, Mrs, 144, 168
Lunardi, Vicenzo, 192, 224 n.8

Macaulay, Thomas Babington, 160,
219 n.41
Manners, Colonel Robert, 72, 82–3,
85, 87, 146, 182
Mary, Princess (1776–1857), 20; with
FB: 54, 145–6, 184–5, 187, 223 n.36;
see also Princesses
Mickleham, 14, 167
Milbanke, Judith, 208 n.5, 215 n.6
Montagu, Mrs Elizabeth, 9, 76, 188
More, Hannah, 76
Mount Edgcumbe, George, Lord,
130–1, 214 n.38
Mount Edgcumbe, Emma, Lady,
130–1, 214 n.42

Napoleon Bonaparte, 177–8, 180
Narbonne, Louis comte de, 165, 167
Newton, Sir Isaac, 5
Nicholson, Margaret, 42–4, 67, 201
n.3, 205 n.6
Norbury Park, 14, 73, 85, 114, 175,
179
Nuneham Courtney, 44–6, 50, 54, 202,
nn.9, 10
Ogle, Dr Newton, and daughter
Esther, 100
Omai of Otaheite, 5–6, 196 n.15
Ord, Mrs Anna, 31, 76–7, 136, 141,

162–3, 179, 188, 220 n.17
Orléans, Philippe duc de, 53, 68, 205
n.9
Otway, Thomas, 69
Oxford, 44, 46–50, 91, 202 n.20

Pacchierotti, Gasparo, 131, 214
n.42
Papendiek, Mrs Charlotte, 39–40, 65,
119
Paris, 4, 124, 126, 165, 178, 203 n.12
Pembroke, Elizabeth, Lady, 48, 113
Pepys, Sir Lucas, 109, 116, 169
Phillips, Fanny, 73, 78
Phillips, Molesworth, 11, 66, 167, 175,
177, 205 n.5, 221 n.46
Phillips, Norbury, 73, 175
Phillips, Susanna, *see* Burney
'Pindar, Peter' (John Wolcot), ix–x,
61, 183–4
Piozzi, Gabriel, 13
Piozzi, Hester, see Thrale
Pitt, William, x, 82, 148–9, 217 n.11
Planta, Margaret (1754–1834), 21, 62,
101, 168, 209 n.10; companion to
FB: 45–6, 49, 67, 75–6, 92–3, 95, 100,
111, 119, 129, 131, 146, 189–90;
curiosity about Digby: 96–7, 107,
116, 132–3, 135; letters to FB: 167,
179
Plymouth, 128–30, 181
Pope, Alexander, 15
Port, Georgina Mary Anne,
'Marianne', later Waddington
(1771–1850), 18, 20, 23, 31, 73,
80–9, 93, 100, 104, 157, 208 n.34
Portland, Margaret Dowager Duchess
of, 16–17, 21, 80, 89, 198 nn.4, 9
Price, Major William, 33, 46, 48, 59,
83, 169, 200 n.19
Princesses, 20, 29, 40, 44–6, 54, 57, 70,
91, 107, 111, 123, 127–8, 130–1, 135,
151, 163, 171–3, 180, 189, and see
entries under individuals
Prussia, Frederick III King of, 180

Queen's House London, 18, 57, 160, 174
Queen's Lodge Windsor, 18–19, 21, 31–2, 49, 54, 69, 73, 109–11, 113, 138, 141, 170, 172

Reynolds, Sir Joshua, 2, 5, 76, 95, 128, 153, 191–2, 196 n.15, 224 n.4
Robinson, Mary, 192, 224 n.7
von la Roche, Sophie, 65–7, 70, 150, 205 n.6
Rowe, Nicholas, 69
Rowlandson, Thomas, 64, 75

St James's Palace, 10, 18, 33, 56–8, 68, 75, 146, 175
St Katharine at Tower, 103, 210 n.43
St Martin's Street (Burney home), 5
Salisbury, 124, 162
Saltram House, 128, 132–3, 136, 215 n.45
Sandsfoot Castle, 127
Schwellenberg, Elizabeth Juliana (c.1728–97), x, 30, 34; relationship with royal family: x, 44, 61–2, 116, 118, 124, 141, 144–6; with FB: 33, 35, 40–1, 44, 61–4, 75–6, 79, 84, 104, 112, 116, 136, 139, 143, 146, 164, 167–8, 171–2, 204 n.38; with household: 61–4, 75, 83; with Mrs Hastings: 62, 150
Shakespeare, 25–6, 69, 126
Sheridan, Richard Brinsley, theatre manager: 9, 168; plays: 69–70; politician: 148, 151–2, 157, 160; private life: 100
Sherborne Castle, 94, 126, 213 n.24
Siddons, Sarah, 52, 69, 126, 157, 168, 220 n.22
Skillicorne, Henry, 93
Smelt, Leonard, 29–30, 32, 68, 74, 113–14, 116, 122, 169, 200 n.2
Sophia, Princess (1777–1848), 20, 106, 201 n.28, 223 n.26; with FB: 54, 146, 163, 171, 187; *see also* Princesses

de Staël, Germaine, 165, 219 n.10
Stanhope, Edwyn Francis, 144–6
Streatham Park, ix, 7, 9
Stuart, Dorothy, 185, 223 n.26
Swift, Dean Jonathan, 15, 17, 27, 80, 199 n.39

Tewkesbury, 93, 96, 100
Thielcke, Anne, 34, 37, 201 n.35
Thrale, Henry, ix, 7, 12–13
Thrale, Hester, later Piozzi (1741–1821), friend of Dr Burney: 2, 5, 7; relationship with FB: 7–13, 19, 31, 36, 40–1, 52, 163, 168–9, 179, 185–6, 188–9; interest in fashion: 10, 197 nn.35, 37; Baretti's attack: 90
Thrale, Hester, 'Queeney', 7, 13, 169
Torrington, John Byng, Viscount, 124 (quoted), 213 n.13
Troide, Lars E., xiii, 6
Twining, Reverend Thomas, 140
Twiss, Richard, 6

Vanbrugh, Sir John, 69
Vernon, the Misses, 45, 50
Victoria, Queen, 61, 223 n.36
Voltaire, 167

Waddington, Benjamin, 88
Wales, George Prince of, later Prince Regent then George IV (1762–1830), 75, 94, 163; relations with King and Queen: x, 21, 57, 73–4, 107, 110, 112–14, 121, 199 n.29, 204 nn.25, 26; with Princesses: 20–1, 173, 184; observed by FB: 21, 74, 113–14
Walpole, Horace, 52–3, 76–7, 140, 188–9
Waterloo, Battle of, 178, 181
Weymouth, 123–5, 133, 181, 213 nn.14, 16
Williams, Anna, 2

Willis, Dr Francis, 113, 117–18, 193,
　211 n.20
Willis, Dr John, 113, 117–18
Willis, Reverend Thomas, 113, 189
Wilton House, 49
Windham, Honourable William, 141–2,
　151, 153–60, 169, 218 nn.16, 36
Windsor Castle: 18, 120; South
　Terrace: 29–30, 32, 54–5, 73–4,
　171–2; Castle Hill: 29–31;
Windsor town: 18–19, 119, 133; St
　Alban's Street: 17–18, 31, 91

Windsor uniform, 29, 35, 102, 127
Wollstonecraft, Mary, 30
Woodforde, James, 127
Worcester, 100, 102
Wordsworth, Dorothy, 19, 29, 200 n.3
Würtemberg, Prince Frederick of, 173,
　221 n.41
Wycherley, William, 100

York, Frederick Duke of (1763–1827),
　21, 73–4, 101, 113, 121, 171
York, Frederica Duchess of, 168